COST OF CAPITAL, Q MODEL OF INVESTMENT
AND CAPITAL ACCUMULATION

For my parents

Cost of Capital, Q Model of Investment and Capital Accumulation

Tax reform, cost of capital and capital accumulation

JUN YOUNG KIM
Department of Economics
Sung Kyun Kwan University

Ashgate

Aldershot • Brookfield USA • Singapore • Sydney

© Jun Young Kim 1998

Published by
Ashgate Publishing Ltd
Gower House
Croft Road
Aldershot
Hants GU11 3HR
England

Ashgate Publishing Company
Old Post Road
Brookfield
Vermont 05036
USA

British Library Cataloguing in Publication Data
Kim, Jun Young
   Cost of Capital, Q model of investment and capital
   accumulation
   1. Capital - Korea 2. Korea - Economic policy 3. Korea -
   Economic conditions - 1945 -
   I. Title
   339.4'3'09519

Library of Congress Catalog Card Number: 97-78428

ISBN 1 85972 581 3

Printed in Great Britain by The Ipswich Book Company, Suffolk.

Contents

Figures and Tables

Preface

Scholars choose the topics they study based on more than the topic's importance. To a large extent, they choose topics based on their ability to say something novel. It is for this reason that the field of the cost of capital and the capital accumulation became dormant and then reawoke.

The purpose of this books is to present the cost of capital approach to capital accumulation and economic growth in Korea, whose economic growth has been oriented to rapid capital accumulation. This book combines new results with expositions of the main research that appeared from the 1960s through the 1990s. The discussion stresses the empirical implications of the theories and the relation of some hypothesis to data and evidence. This is a combination of theory and the ongoing resurgence of work on the cost of capital, capital accumulation, and economic growth.

The analytic approach adopted in this work differs from previous works. First, by using the cost of capital approach, we condense the extensive economic variables (tax system confronting corporations and individuals, types of assets, financial sources, inflation, interest rates, tax incentives, depreciation rate) that affect capital formation into estimating the cost of capital and the effective tax rate. However, the traditional investment analysis considered the subset of the extensive variables, which has limitations in investigating actual fluctuations in investment, since capital formation is based on the complex behavior of entrepreneurs and investors. Second, by measuring the marginal q value, capital formation in this work is analyzed by the integrated theories between the neoclassical theory of investment and the neo-Keynesian theory of investment. This marginal q model of investment differs from an average q model taken up in most of the other studies on the investment, because this approach to investment incorporates both marginal cost of capital and marginal profit of capital into a marginal q value. Third, the tax-adjusted marginal q and the cost of capital are estimated to be significant in determining capital formation and capital stock in Korea. These results are evidence of the usefulness of the neoclassical and neo-Keynesian theories of investment. Such estimated results are important, since in most previous works an average q turned out to be insignificant in explaining capital formation.

Our research will be presented in the following eight steps in analyzing how tax policy has been historically related to capital formation in Korea since 1966, when the first economic development plan ended. With this introduction we briefly trace Korea's macroeconomic policy in economic growth, and structural changes in the process of economic growth in Chapter 2 and Chapter 3 respectively. In Chapter 4 we investigate historically how the tax structure and tax system as well as the tax policy and tax reform have changed for the past three decades in order to increase investment. In Chapter 5 we estimate the cost of capital, the tax wedge, and the effective tax rate according to industries classified into 26 categories, sources of finance, and types of assets in order to link tax policies to capital formation. The cost of capital approach is very useful in formulating the complex tax incentives applied in the process of economic development in Korea into a compact form. Through these estimates we analyze how tax policies have generated distortions across different industries in the industrial policy aspect, and have contributed to lowering the cost of capital and the tax wedge in the macroeconomic aspect. In Chapter 6 we reexamine the international perspective of Korean tax policy and the cost of capital, and make an international comparison of tax reform, the cost of capital, and the effective tax rate. It is extended to cover all the OECD countries. This international comparison is meaningful because the Korean economy has been heavily dependent on foreign economies, and the tax policy specified in the tax reform has been also closely connected to international tax reforms. In Chapter 7 estimates of capital stock (physical capital stock, inventory stock, and human capital stock) are presented, and capital stock is classified into 37 industries and three assets. Although several attempts have been made to estimate capital stock in Korea, they could not generate confident outputs. In a sense, this is the first estimate of capital stock by using the polynomial benchmark year method. In particular, the estimate of capital stock in this work is distinctive in the sense that capital stock is based on estimating the realistic depreciation rates and retirement rates. The gross capital stock and the net capital stock during 1968-1989 are to be reported. In Chapter 8 we make a theoretical combination of the cost of capital and a Tobin q model of investment, and then estimate the q value derived as the ratio of the marginal profit to the cost of capital. This q value is a tax-adjusted marginal q because it reflects the extensive tax policies. By regressing an investment function on the tax-adjusted q value and a capital function on the cost of capital, we see how tax policy has been related to capital formation. According to our results, the neoclassical investment theory and the q model of investment are worthwhile to use in analyzing Korea's investment supporting rapid economic growth. Finally, our conclusions are to be summarized in Chapter 9. Human capital as well as physical capital turn out to be key sources of the economic growth.

When researching and writing this book, I benefited from the input of many scholars and colleagues. I am grateful to Professor Dale W. Jorgenson at Harvard, who provided thoughtful comments on my manuscript, and Professor James M. Poterba at MIT for his encouragement of my research. Professor Eiji Tajika at Hitotsubashi University gave me a sharp insight of the analytic model. It is also a pleasure to express my gratitude to all the faculties at the School of Economics, Sung Kyun Kwan University, and the editorial staff at Ashgate. My research assistant, Yong H. Kim, did an excellent job of turning the manuscript into a finished product.

Finally, I would like to thank my parents, my wife Myung H. Yoo, my daughter Yun Soo and my son Jong Hyun for providing pleasant externalities.

Jun Young Kim

Myung Ryun Dong, Seoul

January 1998

1 Introduction

A continuous increase in economic growth and living standard in the long run is dependent on a high level of capital formation. During the last decade a small but growing group of academics, policy-makers, and business men has argued that the differential behavior of capital formation in many countries is a rational response to disparities in their economic environments and cultural factors.

The main purpose of this work is to examine how tax reforms have affected the cost of capital and capital formation in the process of economic growth. This is an extensive study, and its contents include investigating the Korean tax system and tax policies to estimating capital stock and capital formation in 37 industries. Further, in this work, given the importance of the cost of capital in corporate investment decisions, we compare the estimated cost of capital in different nations, OECD countries, and Korea, and trace the underlying economic and institutional factors that may contribute to the cost of capital disparities. This study is useful not only in searching for the sources of different levels of capital formation in economic growth but also in projecting the international competitiveness of each country in the future.

Under the shortage of domestic capital stock at the beginning of economic development in 1960s, the Korean government played a leading role in allocating national resources. Since investment and exports were identified as the major components of demand growth, the government's role was concentrated in promoting investment and exports. There were two types of government policies in Korea: macroeconomic development plans; and microeconomic industrial policy. Because of political and social instability after the Korean War (1950−53), the Korean government could not pursue economic development policies until 1960. In the 1960s and 1970s the economic development plans had a socialistic flavor because they put more emphasis on rationing resources, but from the mid-1980s there was a shift to indicative plans that emphasized the market mechanism. The industrial policy targeted industries on the basis of their importance to Korea's overall economic activity, and developed them into export industries. These government policies were implemented through fiscal and financial policies: fiscal and financial policies for capital formation and to key industries, favorable allocation of foreign exchange, and subsidized loans.

According to Rostow's definition of the take-off stage of economic development, and to Kuznets' definition of the modern economic growth, Korea entered a phase of modern economic growth in 1963, when there was a tendency for growth to accelerate and for structural change to become rapid. Since then, the Korean economy grew rapidly at an average rate of 10 percent a year between 1962, when the first five-year economic development plan began, and 1991 with the end of the seventh five-year development plan. This rapid economic growth has been driven by exports and investment on the demand side and accumulation of capital on the supply side. The estimated result of the capital stock during 1968–1989 reveals that the annual growth rate of capital stock exceeded that of economic growth. Such rapid capital accumulation and capital formation was not due to the pure market oriented mechanism, but rather to public policies. In particular, fiscal policy based on extensive tax incentives has been directed to capital formation and supporting key industries. Hence, the key points of this work are focused on analyzing interdependence among tax policies, cost of capital, and capital formation during the last three decades (1960–1990). In particular, this interdependence is analyzed according to three types of assets (buildings and structures, machinery and equipment, transportation equipment), three sources of finance (debt, new shares, retained earnings), and industries (in 26 or 37 classifications) as well as an aggregate economy. Such a disaggregated analytic approach is very important because tax policies in Korea have been implemented for industry-specific and assetspecific objectives.

Through a series of tax reforms, the government introduced extensive tax incentives in the process of economic development. Major tax reforms were carried out in 1974, 1976, 1982, and 1986. Beginning with the introduction of tax holidays in 1949, special depreciation in 1961, and the investment tax credit in 1967, Korean tax policy incorporated a series of tax preferences for specific forms of capital income. They could stimulate capital formation by reducing the cost of capital. However, these tax incentives also heightened the discrepancies among tax burdens born by different types of capital. Such tax induced distortions led to the tax reforms of 1982 and 1986 and a sharp change in the direction of Korean policy for taxation of income from capital.

Statutory tax rates were lowered in 1983, but the tax base was broadened by a gradual elimination of tax preferences for corporations. For example, the 1982 tax reform repealed tax holidays and lowered the investment tax credit to 6 percent, and further the 1986 tax reform abolished special treatments for key industries.

In the 1980s, Korean tax reforms were carried out in close connection with international tax reform. Especially the U.K. budget for 1984 and the U.S. Tax Reform Act of 1986 halted the erosion of income tax base by curtailing investment incentives and broadening the base for income taxes. This international new approach to tax reform by lowering tax rates and broadening the tax base was pervasive in many OECD countries from the mid1980s: for example, Australia in 1988, Canada in 1986, France in 1985, Germany in 1986, Japan in 1988, and Sweden in 1985. Hence, in this work Korean tax reform is investigated from both the international and the domestic aspects of capital formation.

As for the Korean tax system, direct and indirect tax ratios have been closer recently, although the tax revenue was traditionally heavily dependent on direct taxes, and the proportion of local taxes will be higher in the future as the local autonomous government has been in effect since 1990. Compared with OECD countries, Korea has imposed a high corporate tax rate (inclusive of surcharges): 45 percent in the 1960s, 53 percent in the 1970s, and 43.8 percent in the 1980s. While the personal income tax on dividends and investments has stayed at low rates of 10—25 percent. Personal and corporation income taxes are not integrated, and in 1990 the new tax system related to landownership was put into effect.

The tax incentives introduced by tax reforms, in particular tax holidays, the investment tax credit, and special depreciation, were found to lower the cost of capital, but resulted in increasing tax wedges among different assets, sources of finance, and industries. In types of assets the cost of capital and the effective tax rate of machinery and equipment were in general lower than those of other assets. In sources of finance, the cost of capital and the effective tax rate from debt were lower than those of other sources of finance, while retained earnings lowered the cost of capital and effective tax rates more than new share issues did. Out of 26 industries, the construction industry had a low effective tax rate as well as a low cost of capital in the 1980s, whereas for the mining industry the reverse was true. In our analysis of tax wedges, the tax wedge of transportation equipment is greater than those of other assets. Through our work we have found that the personal tax wedges and therefore the effective personal tax rates of all three assets were negative. These results were different from those of all OECD

countries. They were due to high interest rates under excess demand in the
capital market, the dual structure of the capital market, and low personal
income tax rates to stimulate saving. In this context there were severe distortions in taxation between the corporate income and the personal income
originating in the corporate sector. However, the 1982 and 1986 tax reforms
were of significance for the cost of capital and the tax wedge. Because these
tax reforms curtailed tax incentives for capital formation and broadened the
base for income tax, the cost of capital and the tax wedge were noticeably
reduced, and the gap in the cost of capital and the effective tax rate between the highest and the lowest industries was narrowed. The reduction of
the tax wedge through the tax reforms improved economic efficiency in resource allocation between saving and investment, resulting in excess saving
to domestic capital formation and capital exports in 1986–89 with trade
surplus.

The international comparison of the cost of capital and the effective tax
rate, were substantially different among OECD countries and Korea. Although trying to find some common underlying cause for either high or low
average effective marginal tax rates across countries is not easy, differences
in them are analyzed to depend on the considerable heterogeneity of the
tax system, sources of finance, inflation, the interest rate, and the tax treatment to types of assets and depreciation. In the overall average effective tax
rate in 1989 or 1990, Canada, Turkey, Sweden, Denmark, the Netherlands,
Finland, and Spain showed high effective tax rates, while Greece and Belgium had very low rates. Because Korea in recent years has suffered from
inflation, a high corporate tax rate, and a relatively high interest rate, its
overall effective tax rate belongs to the middle group of OECD countries'
effective tax rates. In the category of average effective tax rates according to
sources of finance, debt was the most efficient form of finance in the majority
of countries. The deduction from tax on nominal interest payments significantly reduced the marginal tax rate on investment through debt. Australia,
Finland, New Zealand, and Turkey have the full integration system between
personal and corporation income tax rates and so had almost identical effective tax rates between retained earnings and new shares. In particular,
Norway was typical in that the effective tax rate on retained earnings was
much higher than on debt and new equity, due to higher capital gains tax
rates on shares (40 percent). Looking at the asset-specific effective tax rates,
in most countries, except for Ireland, Spain, and Turkey, the effective tax
rate on machinery was lowest among three assets :building and structures,
machinery and equipment, and inventories.

In order to analyze the effect of tax policies on capital formation, we estimate capital stock in 37 industries for Korea based on the polynomial benchmark-year method. The primary emphasis of our study is estimating a more realistic value of the retirement rate and the depreciation rate. According to the above estimates, the gross capital stock and the net capital stock expanded by an average rate of 12.9 percent and 13.1 percent respectively, between 1968 and 1989. This verifies the nature of a fastgrowing economy. Among the industries, capacity expansion (as measured by the gross of real assets) was faster in the manufacturing industry and the construction industry, but was slower in the service sectors and the mining industry. Both the aggregate capitaloutput ratio and the net capital-output ratio for the total economy amounted to 1.77−3.72 and 0.86−1.89, for the period 1968−89 respectively, exhibiting a slightly increasing trend. The aggregate capital-output ratio was higher in the electricity, gas and water, transport, storage and communication, and manufacturing industries, but was lower in the construction industry, the wholesale and retail trade, and the restaurant and hotel industry. According to the analysis of the real net capital stock-the real gross capital stock ratio, the deterioration of buildings and structures has improved, but the deterioration of machinery and equipment, and transportation equipment has rather deepened. Hence, changes in the structure of capital stock over the past two decades reflect some characteristics of a fast-growing economy experiencing structural adjustments.

Finally, this work incorporates the cost of capital into the marginal q model of investment. The model developed above features joint movements of the tax-adjusted marginal q and investment in which firms' profits and the cost of capital have an important role. In the model, firms maximize the present value of net profit, and we introduce the extensive tax policies in deriving marginal q. The tax-adjusted marginal q is derived as the ratio of the marginal profit to the cost of capital. In this context, this marginal q approach is distinct from the average q approaches used in other works. In Korea the marginal q values were very different among industries because of different costs of capital and tax incentives. Marginal q in the majority of industries had been less than one under the extensive tax incentives to investment, while the construction industry showed the highest marginal q values greater than one. In this paper we find evidence that the tax-adjusted marginal q is a significant variable in determining investment, and the cost of capital is also an important indicator in making a decision about capital stock. In this context, these results are contrasted with ones induced from an accelerator model of investment.

Hence, through an expenditure-based tax system in the 1960s and 1970s, and a sharp change in the direction of Korean tax policy resembling the

international new approach to tax reforms, the cost of capital and the tax
wedge have been lowered, and the accumulation of capital stock and capital
formation has increased rapidly. Such rapid capital formation has accelerated economic growth in Korea.

The analytic approach adopted in this work differs from previous works
in three ways. First, by using the cost of capital approach, we condense
the extensive economic variables (tax system confronting corporations and
individuals, types of assets, financial sources, inflation, interest rates, tax
incentives, depreciation rate) that affect capital formation into estimating
the cost of capital and the effective tax rate. However, the traditional investment analysis considered the subset of the extensive variables, which
has limitations in investigating actual fluctuations in investment, since capital formation is based on complex behavior of entrepreneurs and investors.
Second, by measuring the marginal q value, capital formation in this work
is analyzed by the integrated theories between the neoclassical theory of
investment and the neo-Keynesian theory of investment. This marginal q
model of investment differs from an average q model taken up in most other
studies on investment, because this approach to investment incorporates
both marginal cost of capital and marginal profit of capital into a marginal
q value. Third, the tax-adjusted marginal q and the cost of capital are
estimated to be significant in determining, respectively, capital formation
and capital stock in Korea. These results are evidence of the usefulness of
the neoclassical and neo-Keynesian theories of investment. Such estimated
results are important, since in most previous works an average q turned out
to be insignificant in explaining capital formation.

Our research will be presented in the following eight steps in analyzing
how tax policy has been historically related to capital formation in Korea
since 1966, when the first economic development plan ended. With this introduction we briefly trace Korea's macroeconomic policy in economic growth,
and structural changes in the process of economic growth in Chapter 2 and
Chapter 3 respectively. In Chapter 4 we investigate historically how the
tax structure and tax system as well as the tax policy and tax reform have
changed over the past three decades in order to increase investment. In
Chapter 5 we estimate the cost of capital, the tax wedge, and the effective tax rate according to industries classified into 26 groups, sources of
finance, and types of assets in order to link tax policies to capital formation. The cost of capital approach is very useful in formulating the complex
tax incentives applied in the process of economic development in Korea
into a compact form. Through these estimates we analyze how tax policies
have generated distortions across different industries in the industrial pol-

icy aspect, and have contributed to lowering the cost of capital and the tax wedge in the macroeconomic aspect. In Chapter 6 we reexamine the international perspective of Korean tax policy and the cost of capital, and make an international comparison of tax reform, the cost of capital, and the effective tax rate. It is extended to cover all the OECD countries. This international comparison is meaningful because the Korean economy has been heavily dependent on foreign economies, and the tax policy specified in the tax reform has been also closely connected to international tax reforms. In Chapter 7 estimates of capital stock (physical capital stock, inventory stock, and human capital stock) are presented, and capital stock is classified into 37 industries and three assets. Although several attempts have been made to estimate capital stock in Korea, they could not generate confident outputs. In a sense, this is a first estimate of capital stock by using the polynomial benchmark year method. In particular, the estimate of capital stock in this work is distinctive in the sense that capital stock is based on estimating the realistic depreciation rates and retirement rates. The gross capital stock and the net capital stock during 1968−1989 are reported. In Chapter 8 we make a theoretical combination of the cost of capital and a Tobin q model of investment, and then estimate the q value derived as the ratio of the marginal profit to the cost of capital. This q value is a tax-adjusted marginal q because it reflects the extensive tax policies. By regressing an investment function on the tax-adjusted q value and a capital function on the cost of capital, we see how tax policy has been related to capital formation. According to our results, the neoclassical investment theory and the q model of investment are worthwhile to use in analyzing Korea's investment supporting rapid economic growth. Finally, our conclusions are to be summarized in Chapter 9. Human capital as well as physical capital turn out to be key sources of the economic growth.

2 Macroeconomic policy

During the last three decades, the Korean economy has achieved a miraculous economic performance. Since the First Five Year Economic Plan was launched in 1962, the Korean GNP grew at an average annual rate of 8.5 percent. Exports grew at a breakneck rate of 30 percent from 1970–90. The structure of the economy also underwent rapid transformation from a largely agricultural subsistence economy into a newly industrialized one. The growth experience and development process of Korea provide a sharp contrast to the lackluster growth experienced by many other developing economies.

The economy was literally in ruin at the end of Korean War (1950–53). Fixed investment was less than 9 percent of GNP, and exports, consisting mainly of primary goods, accounted for only 2 percent of GNP. Imports were 2.3 times as large as exports. In the 1950s Korea attempted an economic development on the basis of an import substitution strategy, encouraging domestic production of nondurable consumer goods. Quotas and strict licensing were imposed on imports in order to promote domestic production. After devaluation of the currency in 1953, the exchange rate remained overvalued in order to reduce inflation and imports, but it also deterred exports throughout the period. In the 1950s exports contributed less than 10 percent of GNP growth.

Since the military government took power in 1961, it adopted a new economic development strategy of export-oriented industrialization. The strategy was to align the prices of Korean products with international prices in order to exploit the country's comparative advantage and maintain the competitiveness of its exports. To stimulate exports, the government initially introduced various incentives: preferential export credits, a generous waste allowance on imported inputs, import-export links, reduction in direct and indirect taxes, tariff exemptions on imports of capital goods, rationing of long- and medium-term loans for export-related investment, and prefer-

ential rates for electricity and rail transport. Among these incentives, two
of them played key roles in promoting exports: granting unrestricted and
tariff-free access to imported intermediate inputs used in export production;
and granting automatic access to bank loans for the working capital needed
for all export activity. In order to maintain the price competitiveness of
Korean products in world markets, the government controlled wages, re-
stricted union activities, and adjusted the exchange rate frequently in 1961,
1964, 1965, 1968, and 1969.

In the 1970s oil prices aggravated the world recession and worsened the internal and external environments. Despite suffering from stagflation due to
oil shocks, the Korean economy continued to grow through export-promotion
strategies with reductions in import production, lowering tariffs, and the
liberalization of import restrictions. In particular, owing to the sales of construction services to the Middle East, its exports reached a peak of $51.6
billion in 1976 compared to $13.9 billion in 1975. The rapid increase in
exports improved its credit in world capital markets, inducing a growing
inflow of foreign capital and accelerating the economic growth. However,
from 1979 to 1980 under stagflation, the economy suffered serious damage,
with a growth rate of only 2.4 percent in 1979 and a growth rate of minus
6.2 percent in 1980. This abrupt downturn of economic growth was due to
complex social and political factors: political disruption in 1979, a poor
harvest, the exchange rate overvaluation, and the recession in developed
countries. Korea's economic problems during the late 1970s could be traced
from the change in industrial strategy to promote the so-called heavy and
chemical industries. This shift made a trade strategy reversal from export
promotion to import substitution. The heavy and chemical industries policy
was pursued through a broad range of policy instruments, import controls,
including tariff protection for selected goods, fiscal preferences, and credit
allocation at controlled low interest rates. The allocation of credit by so-
called policy loans reduced the availability of export loans, damaging the
export industries. This heavy and chemical industries policy resulted in the
creation of excess capacities in some unprofitable industries and the distortion of investment funds. Further, the high rate of investment in these
industries was supported by, in part, an increase in money supply, and, in
part, foreign borrowings. In this context, the heavy and chemical industries policy implemented in the late 1970s accelerated inflation, increased
the external debt, and reduced economic growth.

After experiencing a severe setback in 1980, the economy made remarkable
progress with high economic growth and low inflation, and improved external balances during the period of 1983–89, when the average growth rate

was 10.6 percent, inflation was held under 7 percent, and exports grew at an average annual rate of 16.7 percent. There were many factors that generated such achievements. Among the external factors were low oil prices, interest rate, favorable exchange rates, and economic growth in developed countries. Internally, the government followed tight fiscal and monetary policies to decrease domestic sources of inflation and decelerated wage growth rate. For example, a major devaluation of 24 percent in 1980 and small devaluations up to the mid-1980s, a deceleration of nominal wage growth rate of 20.2 percent in 1980 to 11 percent in 1987, and a decreased money (M_2) growth rate from 21 percent to 13 percent were important macroeconomic policy instruments. The most notable economic performance in the post-1980s was the emergence of a surplus in the current account, the first ever in its modern economic history. At its peak in 1988, during the Seoul Olympic Games, the trade and the current account surplus amounted to some \$11.4 billion and \$14.2 billion, respectively, and the foreign exchange reserves rose to \$12.4 billion at the end of 1988, which is almost double that of \$6.5 billion in 1980. However, this large trade surplus has become a principal source of economic friction between Korea and the U.S.. Korea was under pressure from the U.S. to open its domestic markets further and to revalue its currency, both of which were done. Most of the domestic markets, including banking, insurance, tourism, technology, and transportation were opened, and the effective protection of intellectual property rights was settled in 1989. From 1985 to 1987 its currency appreciated by 9 percent, and by the end of 1989 had risen more than 23 percent against the U.S. dollar. The appreciation of the Won as well as trade liberalization caused many traditional export industries to lose their international competitiveness. Further, labor disputes had made the economic environments even worse. After more than two decades of military dictatorship, as the country entered a new epoch of democracy, labor disputes of strike and work stoppages were common place in the late 1980s and continued into the early 1990s. Labor demanded not only wage increases and improvement of working conditions, but also social reforms and participation of unions in management and political activity. Labor disputes increased uncertainties and risks in the business world. Domestic investments in manufacturing sectors thus remained stagnant. Since 1990, the government tried to have an influence on wage settlements in the private sector, especially big firms, by setting low growth in public sector wage rates. This type of wage guideline has not had a realistic influence on the private sector's wage settlements because of a high inflation rate and a rapid increase in the price of housing. In addition, due to presidential and national assembly elections, a recessed security market, slowdown in exports, and the slackening of GNP growth since 1988, the monetary policy was expanded, where money supply (M_2) increased from 13 percent in 1983–85 to near 21 percent in the late 1980s. The budget deficits have also widened in spite of increasing tax revenues. This expansion of monetary and fiscal policies in the late 1980s generated inflationary expectations, and boosted land speculation. In short, Korea through monetary and fiscal actions was unable to neutralize the full effects of the export boom (1986-89), which in turn led to high wage demands and a resumption of inflation.

In the early 1990s, facing these situations at home and abroad, Korea's exporting industry had serious difficulties in recovering price competitiveness and developing new technology. The new civilian government, from February 1993, followed a stable monetary policy, with moves toward small government. In addition, the government pursued social, political, and economic reforms, with the intention of eliminating institutional irrationality and corruption. In particular, the new government introduced the real-name financial transaction system in August 1993, when will be explained more in Chapter 4. Since the recovery of the Korean economy in the second half of 1993, when the economic growth rate in 1993 was stagnant at 5.8 percent, GNP has grown at 8.4 percent in 1994 and 8.7 percent in 1995. However, the Korean economy moved toward recession in 1996, having reached the peak in the fourth quarter of 1995. This recession was due to the cyclical factors in the short run, and the structural problems defined as high cost and low efficiency. On the other hand, the Korean economy has actively participated in the globalization of the world economy and international economic cooperation, and became a member of OECD on December 12, 1996.

Finally, let me point out some characteristics of the financial and fiscal policies implemented in the pursuit of economic growth. First, budgetary discipline was maintained by concentrating authority over total spending to the relatively powerful Economic Planning Board, while a rapid growth in revenue was made possible by a rapidly growing economy. Second, fiscal policy tended to damp down fluctuations in national income. A stabilization of fiscal policy arises partly from the structure of expenditure and taxation, and partly from the priority policy-makers accord to stabilizing the growth of income. This is unusual among developing countries, where fiscal policy tends to be pro-cyclical and is often a major source of macroeconomic disturbance. Third, during the last three decades, the most noteworthy pattern to Korea's financial and monetary policy is a long policy cycle from financial liberalization in the 1960s, to an aggressive use of credit for industrial policy purposes in the 1970s, back to a second wave of more substantial financial liberalization in the 1980s. The financial liberalization included the privatization of the commercial bank, lowering barriers to entry, gradually moving toward freer interest rates, gradually opening the financial sector to foreign investment and greater participation by foreign banks. As the financial liberalization proceeded, the role of the Bank of Korea shifted from direct credit allocation to the broad monetary aggregates, and from asset management to liability management. Fourth, the government did not rely heavily on seigniorage as a source of revenue. Although seigniorage amounted to 2–3 percent of GDP in 1970s, much of this seigniorage, rather than being taken into government revenues, was dissipated in the form of low interest loans by the Bank of Korea to commercial banks, and through them to the favored sectors of the economy, especially export promotion and, after 1973, the heavy and chemical industries. Thus the government gave to favored sectors more financial support, indirectly, than showed up in budget expenditures, in amounts that exceeded 1 percent of GDP during the 1970s, but gradually declined to less than 0.5 percent in the late 1980s. Both tax policy and industrial policy will be explained in detail in Chapter 4.

3 Structural change

3.1 Introduction

Historically, Korea's sovereignty was restored in 1945, and the Republic of Korea was formed on August 15, 1948. Liberation from Japanese control in 1945 brought the beginning of Korean control of their own affairs, though in two nations rather than one. American military government in South Korea was replaced by an elected Korean government in August 1948. Unfortunately soon after Korea tried to resume the independent formulation of economic policies, the Korean peninsula suffered the Korean War from 1950–53. After the cease-fire agreement was signed in 1953, it took at least several years for Korea to reconstruct the social capital destroyed during the war. In this sense, the Korean government could not pursue economic development policies until 1960, because of political and social instability after the Korean War; thus the year 1960 is the benchmark for the modern economic history of Korea.

Since Korea lacks oil, iron, and many other important raw materials, as well as domestic capital stock, the Korean government played a leading role in the early period of economic development. How important was this governmental role in orchestrating economic growth and economic development? Investment and exports were identified as the major components of demand growth, so the government's role was concentrated in promoting investment and exports, while actively introducing foreign capital. There were two types of government policies in Korea: macroeconomic development plans; and microeconomic industrial policy.

Economic development plans were begun in 1962 and continued to the present day, with the plans being renewed every five years. In the 1960s and 1970s the plans had a socialistic flavor, putting as they did more emphasis on rationing social resources, but from the mid-1980s there was a shift to indicative plans that emphasized the market mechanism. The Economic Planning

Board, which both created and led the economic development plans, usually announced five-year plans and set targets for the growth rate of the GNP and for its demand components. However, those economic plans were more forecasts than directives. The EPB was given authority to allocate funds and raw materials in cooperation with the Ministry of Finance and the Ministry of International Trade and Industry. During most of the period proceeding the economic development plans, actual growth outpaced each of the EPB's plans except for some periods (e.g., the first and second oil shocks, the political crisis in 1980, the economic recession in 1992), and an initial five-year plan was usually revised in the first two or three years. In the mid-1980s the characteristics of the economic development plans changed from the industry development plans to the economic and social (welfare) development plans, as the public demanded comprehensive social welfare programs. Moreover, the economic development plans in the 1960s and the 1970s were engineered by the government's direct measures based on fiscal and financial policies (e.g., extensive tax incentives, subsidies under low interest rates), but they were gradually shifted to indicative plans to signal the private sector investment projects and sales projections from the mid-1980s. For example, it is often the case that investment in structures and equipment in a particular industry will not occur unless sales projections are favorable. Uncertainty might make investors pessimistic and keep the economy in a low-demand equilibrium. If an announcement by the government provides credible information on output projections for various industries and government expenditures, it stimulates investment decisions in the private sector. When the private sector believes the plan and behaves as a main body, the plan becomes self-fulfilling. Indicative planning can thus help to select a particular equilibrium among many possible equilibria. Hence, at this point, some 30 years since the start of modern economic growth in Korea, it is desirable that government planning is limited to solving the coordination failure that occurs under incomplete information in macroeconomic models in the Keynesian tradition.

The other type of government policies in the process of economic development is industrial policy. This policy assigned targeted industries mainly on the basis of their importance for Korea's overall economic activity. Those industries received favorable allocations of foreign exchange, preferential tax treatments and subsidized loans through government agencies during the 1960s and the 1970s. For example, the prior allocation of foreign reserves for the purchase of capital equipment and raw materials, the extensive tax incentives, and policy finances through treasury funds and national investment funds were given to machinery and equipment investment, and key industries (textile, steel, shipbuilding, chemical, electronics). The industrial policy was targeted to develop the export industry, and it was successful in bringing about a rapid increase in exports from the late 1960s. Given a greater demand for the product created by export subsidies and import restrictions, a targeted industry could increase its capacity quickly, so that its average cost would drop. Thus, it could become cost-competitive by itself and grow into a large-sized industry. In general, the industrial policies were effective in the 1960s and 1970s. In the 1980s, government policies based on fiscal policy and industrial policy were gradually thinned out. Instead, the private sector demanded a more market-oriented economy with social and political democratization. The role of market mechanisms in resource allocation become more emphasized and liberalization in foreign trade, international investment, and financial markets was sought after in the 1980s. In the late 1980s and the early 1990s the macroeconomic policy for fast economic growth was critically re-examined, and the aim became instead stability of the economy. For example, the economic growth rate of·1993 was 5.8 percent, and the new government, which came to power February 1993, was more concerned with improving the fairness of society and income distribution. Even administrative guidance had an impact on the behavior of the private sector. The final evaluation of industrial policy is mixed, however. It is true that some targeted industries blossomed and contributed to exports and Korea's economic growth, but these policies resulted in the concentration of economic power and wealth in the targeted industrial group, while the small- and medium-sized companies lagged behind.

3.2 Economic growth

3.2.1 Historical background of economic growth before 1960

Let's trace out the economic growth during the period 1945–1960 before investigating the modern economic growth. The South Korean economy during 1945–48 was much weaker and less viable than might have been expected from its early history. Under the division of the country, the breakdown of trade with both the northern half of Korea and with Japan in 1945 cut off the sources of supply in the manufacturing industry. The separation from the complementary coal, electricity, fertilizer and heavy industry of the North was another blow. Inflation was also a major disrupting force during this time, and agriculture in South Korea suffered even more than industry from the division of country, due to the lack of fertilizer, which was produced in the North.

The period from August 1948 to June 1950 was one of generally improving economic conditions and the semblance of increasing political and social order under an autocratic, conservative regime. By early 1950 much of Japanese investment had been either rehabilitated or replaced, and South Korea seemed to be on the point of establishing more normal economic and social conditions. Then on June 25 invasion by North Korea completely disrupted the economy, generated much physical damage, and brought extensive social changes. The physical damage to property in South Korea from the Korean War had been estimated as equal to Korea's annual GNP in 1953, or more than ten times the annual rate of fixed capital investment. About 40 percent of this loss was in housing, with one-fifth or more of the total destroyed or suffering major damage. Private industry suffered about 20 percent of the total physical damage. Together with damage to public enterprises, such as transportation and utilities, this amounted to a heavy loss of industrial capacity and output. There was also a drastic decline in population, which was not recovered for ten years, and rapid inflation from 1950 to 1956 that weakened confidence in the government.

The basic problem after the Korean War was to provide for immediate emergency consumption needs and to rebuild the badly damaged economy. Rapid wartime inflation (which caused more than a 20-fold increase in prices between 1950 and 1953) was slowed to a 20 to 30 percent annual rate of increase during 1953–56, except for a sharper rise in 1955, by increasing inflow of aid goods and domestic production. The period of relatively rapid postwar reconstruction and growth extended from 1953 through 1958. During this period, the GNP growth averaged 5.5 percent annually. Agricultural growth averaged 3.9 percent annually between 1954 and 1958, while value added in manufacturing grew about 18 percent annually through 1956, then averaged 10 percent in the next two years. Much of the growth of manufacturing was in consumption goods and depended upon imported materials.

In particular, 1957 (5 years after the Korean War) was a remarkable year in which per capita income levels returned to, or exceeded, their pre-Korean War levels. Production of coal and electricity were then above any level achieved since 1945, and the scars of wartime physical damage were becoming much less extensive. The year 1957 was also the beginning of Korea's first significant period of postwar price stability. A stabilization program was instituted to increase the mobilization of domestic resources and control the budget deficit, and also the increase in money supply was limited to 20 percent. The exchange tax (later exchange auction) was introduced to encourage exports and curb imports. These economic policies and a record rice harvest resulted in a significant decline in food and grain prices in 1958, and a small decline in the overall price index. Real GNP grew by 9 percent in 1957 and 5.5 percent in 1958, with agricultural production increasing at about the same rates.

This economic growth was, however, rapidly reduced in the slow growth period of 1958–62, during which GNP rose about 3.6 percent yearly. This reflected economic factors in the first half of the period, and political and economic uncertainty in the second half. During 1958–59 economic growth slowed due to a drop in agricultural production and a slowing of industrial output as the overvaluation of the Won was reduced. During 1960–61 political and social instability under the new civilian government and the military coup resulted in an uncertain climate for investment.

3.2.2 Modern economic growth after 1960

The real GNP growth rate of Korea averaged more than 10 percent per year between 1960 and 1990, during which modern economic growth was pursued. As a result, the Korean economy in 1990 was 12 times its 1960 size in real GNP terms, while during the same 30 years the United States and the Japanese economies grew 2.65 times and 9 times, respectively. Under higher GNP and per-capita GNP, demand for social capital, infrastructure, residential housing stock, parks, highways, and electricity has been excessive and ever increasing.

In many cases there has been a tendency for growth to accelerate and for structural change to become rapid when an economy has reached some critical point in its development. This point is called the 'takeoff' by Rostow (1960) and the 'start of modern economic growth' by Kuznets (1959).

Rostow (p.39) defines the takeoff by three conditions: (1) The ratio of productive investment to GNP rises from 5 percent or below to 10 percent or above. (2) At least one strong manufacturing industry grows at a high rate. (3) The political, social, and institutional framework exists to take advantage of economic externalities for expansion in the modern sector.

Kuznets (Lecture 1) lists the characteristics of modern economic growth as the following: (1) the application of modern scientific thought and technology; (2) a sustained and rapid increase in real product per capita, usually (but not always) accompanied by a high rate of population growth; (3) a rapid transformation of the industrial structure (changing sectoral output, labor force, and capital stock distribution); and (4) an expansion of international contracts.

Under this definition we date the start of modern economic growth in Korea to the period 1963–1966, during which time there was a sudden

Table 3.1: Annual growth rate in Korea (%)

Year	real GNP	GNP deflator	capital stock	population
1961	4.17	12.56	2.66	3.00
1962	3.08	13.94	3.23	2.90
1963	8.97	28.67	3.46	2.80
1964	8.56	32.07	4.21	2.60
1965	6.08	8.23	6.30	2.60
1966	12.39	14.26	7.17	2.50
1967	7.78	13.98	8.97	2.30
1968	12.63	11.82	10.84	2.31
1969	15.01	13.19	13.83	2.30
1970	7.86	15.34	11.58	2.20
1971	8.63	12.50	11.03	1.99
1972	5.07	16.67	11.57	1.89
1973	13.22	13.61	15.57	1.78
1974	8.15	30.54	14.02	1.73
1975	6.42	25.23	12.06	1.70
1976	13.08	21.25	13.49	1.61
1977	9.84	16.62	12.20	1.57
1978	9.78	22.80	20.63	1.53
1979	7.19	19.62	22.36	1.53
1980	-3.74	23.99	17.04	1.57
1981	5.92	16.93	10.46	1.57
1982	7.17	7.06	10.20	1.56
1983	12.61	5.00	10.36	1.49
1984	9.28	3.90	10.40	0.99
1985	6.96	4.17	9.49	0.93
1986	12.91	2.80	11.24	0.95
1987	12.97	3.50	11.42	0.96
1988	12.42	5.92	9.48	0.97
1989	6.78	5.24	11.75	0.97
1990	9.31	10.62	12.16	0.93

Source: *Economic Statistics Yearbook*, The Bank of Korea

Table 3.2: Average growth rates of real GNP (%)

five-year economic plan	period	average growth rate
–	1953–1958	5.50
–	1958–1962	3.60
1	1962–1966	7.78
2	1967–1971	10.39
3	1972–1976	9.19
4	1977–1981	5.80
5	1982–1986	9.79
6	1987–1991	10.30

increase in the speed of economic growth. From a review of the studies cited above it is fair to conclude that Korea entered a phase of modern economic growth from 1963.

Since then, the most remarkable aspect of the Korean economy is its rapid economic growth as shown in Table 3.1 and 3.2. Between 1962, the beginning of the first five-year economic development plan, and 1991 which saw the end of the seventh economic development plan, the economy grew at an average rate of 10 percent a year. The secret of this rapid economic growth, or high-speed growth, has attracted many researchers. Figure 3.1 concisely illustrates the history of economic growth in Korea. With the logarithm of real GNP measured on the vertical axis, the slope of the solid line shows the rate of economic growth. This steep line shows rapid and steady growth.

It is important to look into the major constraints on growth rather than only the major driving forces. It can be pointed out that in the 1960s and the 1970s Korea's foreign exchange reserves set a ceiling on growth. Since economic growth in Korea increased Korea's imports of raw materials and intermediate goods, while its exports were determined by the growth of foreign countries' demand, too, a high growth rate in Korea meant a deterioration of Korea's foreign exchange reserves under the fixed exchange-rate regime. When foreign reserves declined, policy measures were taken to slow down the growth of aggregate demand. The constraint of foreign exchange reserves was partially mitigated by foreign borrowings. In contrast, after the 1970s the constraint become effective on the aggregate supply side. The growth in technological progress as well as in capital and labor inputs defined the ceiling of growth after the 1980.

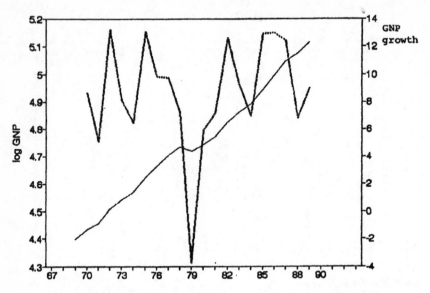

Figure 3.1: History of Korean economic growth

3.3   Sources of economic growth

Economic growth can be viewed from the demand side and the supply side.
Balanced growth can be achieved only if both demand and supply grow
without disruption, since output in the long run should be equal to aggregate demand. On the demand side, a small country must rely on exports
in order to grow substantially. Therefore, developing international competitiveness is crucial to ensuring demand growth. In addition, consumption,
investment, and government expenditure are important factors affecting aggregate demand. On the supply side, the accumulation of capital in the
form of modern factories and machines is important for increasing productive capacity. Using the source approach to analyze economic growth, the
output can be expressed as a production function on inputs of capital, labor,
and the technological level. Thus, growth can occur through capital accumulation, through increases in working hours and employment, or through
technological progress that enhances the productivity of existing capital and
labor.

Korea had a high (absolute) contribution to its growth rate from both
factors of labor and capital. The spirit of "hard working", working even

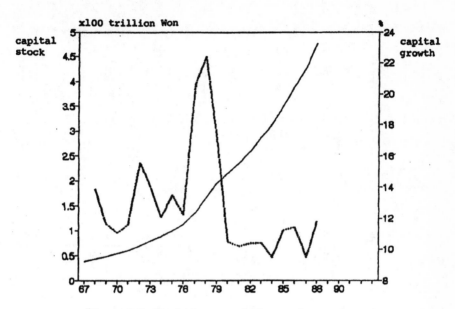

Figure 3.2: Capital accumulation and growth

on weekends, and the rapid increase in capital accumulation, whose rate exceeded, on average, the economic growth rate, were the major elements for the high growth of Korea. In particular, capital accumulation was more important than any other factor when working hours and employment were constrained as the economy developed, as shown in Figure 3.2[1].

As Korea's productive capacity expanded sharply, expenditures on the output necessarily increased. Among the components of aggregate demand, investment and exports both played key roles in the rapid expansion of expenditures. The ratio of private fixed investment to GNP remained very high from 1968 to 1989. Figure 3.3 shows the ratio of private fixed investment to GNP and that of exports to GNP in real terms. In this Figure, it is clear that the ratio of investment to GNP was higher than 20 percent, and the ratio of exports to GNP had been increasing. Thus, in real terms,

---

[1]The production function in Korea during 1970–1988 was estimated in the form of Cobb-Douglas with the labor coefficient of 0.432 and the capital coefficient of 0.665, where the labor input was measured by the quarterly working hours:

$$\log Y_t = -4.265 + 0.432 \log L_t + 0.665 \log K_t$$

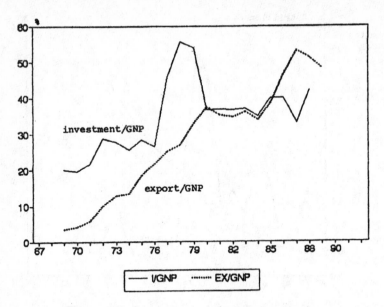

Figure 3.3: Investment and exports growth

investment and exports had contributed to absorption of output. This analysis of the demand side suggests that Korea experienced investment-led and exports-led growth for the past three decades.

3.4   Structural change

It has always been the case that an economy experiences a significant change in industrial structure during a period of rapid economic growth. Production and employment shift from agriculture to the manufacturing sector and the service sector. Korea was no exception. Table 3.3 shows the shares of income and employment accounted for agriculture, forestry, and fishing (column I), mining & manufacturing (column II), and service industries (column III) for selected years. A shift of population from agriculture to manufacturing occurred without causing the severe shortage in the food supply, except for the early period of economic development during 1962–1970: this was made possible by increases in land productivity and diversification of food consumption.

Agriculture played important roles in the development of the Korean economy. Agricultural production grew to fill the domestic need for food, so that

Table 3.3: Industrial structure

year	employment ratio			national income ratio		
	I	II	III	I	II	III
1963	63.1	8.7	28.2	47.74	11.74	40.53
1965	61.7	10.9	32.7	47.05	12.95	40.00
1970	50.4	14.3	35.2	34.25	19.26	46.49
1975	45.7	19.1	35.2	27.25	26.24	46.51
1980	34.0	22.5	43.5	16.33	32.42	51.25
1985	24.9	24.4	50.6	14.18	34.68	51.25
1990	18.3	27.3	54.4	8.42	36.98	54.60

not much foreign exchange was spent on agricultural imports. Agricultural imports remained low, and the domestic price of agricultural goods relative to industrial goods stayed stable. The agricultural policy was especially meaningful from the political side, since rice shortages often caused riots and social instability. In this context, although the agricultural sector has been shrinking in employment and production, it still remains as a basic sector in sustaining Korea's economic growth

Korea therefore developed from a primarily agricultural state to a light-manufacturing (including textile) industrial state before 1980, first by import substitution and then by export substitution. Korea repeated the same process for heavy manufacturing industries after 1980. The process of Korea's economic development is distinctive from other countries in the sense that the mining and manufacturing sector (II) has expanded more rapidly than the service sector (III) in employment and production since the early 1960s. For example, both employment and production of the mining and manufacturing sector in 1990 was more than three times their 1963 sizes. This rapid structural change from the agricultural state to the manufacturing industrial state was accelerated through the fiscal and financial policies.

Through this brief investigation of the economic growth and development in Korea, it is clear that capital accumulation and investment have been major factors: Such rapid capital accumulation and investment have not been made under the pure market-oriented mechanism, but led by public policies. In particular, fiscal policy based on extensive tax incentives has been directed to capital formation and supporting key industries. Although they resulted in distortions in efficiency and equity, extensive tax incentives played effective roles in aiding the economic development objectives imposed by the government. The tax policy has been specifically incorporated into the economic development plans in macroeconomic aspects and the industrial policy in microeconomic aspects, as pointed out. Hence, in the following chapter we will investigate how the tax structure and tax system as well as the tax policy and tax reform have changed over the past three decades.

4 Tax reform and tax policy

4.1 Tax structure and tax system

4.1.1 Tax structure

Early in the history of the Republic of Korea, tariffs, income taxes, and excise taxes were the major sources of government revenue. The ratio of direct taxes to internal taxes was higher than that of indirect taxes to internal taxes until the mid-1970s. However, these ratios were reversed in 1977 immediately after the value added tax system was introduced. Since the late 1980s the proportion of direct taxes and indirect taxes for internal tax revenue has been closer. During 1977–1989, 60 percent of total tax revenue, both national and local, was, on average, from indirect taxes. In particular, the value added tax has been a major source of revenue since its introduction in 1976. The most notable change in the tax structure resulting from the introduction of the value added tax system was that the Korean indirect tax system became more reliant on the general consumption tax than on selective excise taxes.

The importance of the direct taxes has also grown since 1980. Of all the direct taxes, the role of the personal income tax and the corporation tax has become more significant in raising revenue. About 40 percent of total tax is collected from individual income taxation and corporate income taxation.

Compared to other countries, less than 2.5 percent of GNP was collected as personal income tax, while in most Western countries the level is around 10 percent. The reasons why personal income tax revenue was so low were: (i) the general level of income tax compliance and administration was very poor; (ii) capital gains from financial asset transactions were completely untaxed; and (iii) capital gains from real asset transactions were undertaxed. From 1960 to the mid-1980s the corporation tax was less than 10 percent of total revenue (less than 15 percent of internal revenue), because tax policy

27

Table 4.1: Direct and indirect tax in internal taxes (%)

	1975	1977	1980	1985	1990	1995
1. Direct taxes	57.2	48.6	32.1	35.6	43.6	51.1
(1) Income tax	19.6	21.1	18.0	19.8	24.7	29.1
(2) Corporation tax	12.9	14.0	13.2	15.0	16.9	19.2
(3) Inheritance tax	1.1	1.0	0.3	0.6	1.5	2.4
(4) Others	23.6	12.5	0.6	0.2	0.5	0.4
2. Indirect taxes	36.6	49.0	65.4	60.8	54.3	47.3
(1) Value added tax	–	14.4	40.0	38.7	36.4	34.0
(2) Special comm tax	–	5.9	15.8	13.1	10.0	6.4
(3) Liquor tax	8.0	7.4	8.1	6.1	5.3	4.0
(4) Telephone tax	1.0	1.2	1.3	2.2	1.4	1.2
(5) Security tax	–	–	0.2	0.1	1.2	1.7
(6) Others	27.6	20.1	–	–	–	–
3. Other internal tax (stamp revenue & others)	6.2	2.4	2.5	3.6	2.1	1.6

Source: Economic Planning Board, Korean Statistical Yearbook
Note: Other direct taxes include excess profit tax, excess increased value of land tax, and revaluation tax. Other indirect taxes include excise and turnover taxes

had reduced the effective corporate tax by introducing extensive incentives, such as tax holidays, investment tax credits, accelerated depreciation, and so on. As these incentives were almost eliminated in the 1986 tax reform, the proportion of the corporation tax in total revenue has recently been closer to 15 percent (20 percent of internal revenue). As a proportion in national tax revenue customs duties represented more than 10 percent, but this level was reduced to less than 10 percent after liberalization policy in the 1980s. Surcharges on income and other major taxes-defense tax, education tax-totaled about 15 percent in the 1980s. The education tax disappeared from national taxes in 1991.

In addition to national taxes, the Korean tax system has local tax bases. As the tax system had been centralized by the national government by the 1980s, it collects almost 90 percent of total revenue. There was little overlap in the tax bases for national and local taxes. The major revenue source for the central government was consumption and income taxes, while that of

Table 4.2: The tax revenue structure (%)

	1975	1980	1985	1990
Central Government	89.8	88.3	87.8	84.0
1. National taxes	81.0	80.6	81.6	84.0
(1) Internal taxes	65.3	55.9	55.4	59.8
(2) Customs duties	11.7	11.7	11.6	8.7
(3) Defence surtax	4.0	13.0	12.3	13.3
(4) Educational surtax	–	–	2.3	1.6
2. Monopoly profit	8.8	7.7	6.2	–
Local Government	10.2	11.7	12.2	16.0
Local taxes	10.2	11.7	12.2	16.0
(1) Ordinary taxes	8.7	9.8	11.1	14.6
(2) Earmarked taxes	1.5	1.9	1.1	1.4
Total	100.0	100.0	100.0	100.0

Source: Economic Planning Board, Major Statistics for Korean Economy

the local government was property-related taxes. However, as local autonomy has been pursued since 1990, the local government has been granted the power to levy its own kinds of taxes and to change tax rates in response to the needs of local residents. The basic requirement for guaranteeing local autonomy is to secure financial self-reliance. Unfortunately, with only a few exceptions, most local governments in Korea are in a weak position financially. The shortfall in tax revenues needed to meet their expenditures are in general financed by transfers and subsidies from the central government. Hence, the adjustment of the tax structure between national and local taxes will be a key issue in the immediate future. Currently, local taxes represent about 20 percent of the total tax revenue, a ratio that will increase in the future, and will include acquisition tax, registration tax, license tax, inhabitant tax, property tax, excess land-holding tax, tobacco tax, city planning tax, and so on.

The overall ex post elasticity of national revenue with respect to GDP between 1977 and 1987 was 1.12, implying that revenues grew about 12 percent more rapidly than nominal GDP. A somewhat surprising feature of the Korean tax system is that revenues do not seem to be especially responsive to downturns in economic activity, such as that which occurred

in 1980, or to slowdowns such as in 1985. In 1980 revenue rose 4 percent
more rapidly than nominal GDP, about the same elasticity as the 3 percent
average for the decade. In many economies, tax revenues typically grow less
rapidly than GDP in a weak year, due to a downturn in corporate profits, a
rise in unemployment, and a decline in consumption of highly taxed goods.

By comparison with all OECD countries and many developing countries,
Korea has a relatively low level of governmental activity, as measured by
government expenditures, of less than 20 percent of GNP. Within this total,
Korea has had a larger than average share of military expenditures, between
4 to 6 percent of GNP. Military expenditures relative to GNP have fallen
slowly over the past decade, while non-military expenditures have grown,
for a slow net increase in the size of the government sector.

4.1.2   Tax system

Income taxes

Individual income tax in Korea is almost comprehensive in the sense that
almost all income is included in the global income. The global income com-
prises wage and salary income, business income, real estate income, dividend
income, and interest income. It is taxed by a highly progressive rate scheme,
ranging from 5 to 50 percent, as shown in Table 4.3, exclusive of surcharges.
However, interest incomes and most of dividend income has been taxed separately at 10 percent plus surcharges, including 5 percent education tax.
Retirement income, capital gains from sales of real assets, and timber income are also taxed under a separate schedule. Capital gains from financial
asset transactions are not taxed. As liberal deductions and exemptions are
allowed in the income tax law, about 60 percent of workers and 65 percent
of proprietors lie in the zero bracket.

The corporate income tax applies to all corporate profits net of depreciation, interest payments, and other expenses, whether those profits are
retained or distributed. The payment of dividends does not affect the corporate tax as it does in the United States. Basic corporate income tax rates
range from 20 to 32 percent as shown in Table 4.4, which with the defense
and other surcharges brings the maximum corporate tax rates to 43 percent.
Somewhat lower rates are applicable to corporations that list their shares
and are traded publicly. Before 1966, the local tax of 5 to 10 percent was
added as a surtax to corporate tax, and the corporate tax raised by 10 percent during 1967–70 while the surtax was eliminated. The resident tax of
7.5 percent was introduced as a local tax in 1973. The defense tax of 20 to

Table 4.3: Personal income tax rate (1993)

Income	Marginal tax rate(%)
10 Thousand Won	–
below 400	5
400-800	10
800-1600	20
1600-3200	30
3200-6400	40
above 6400	50

Source: The Income Tax Law

25 percent enacted in 1975 has been surcharged on corporation tax. Capital gains from real property sales are separately treated. They are taxed as nominal corporate income, and then an additional tax of 25 to 35 percent is also charged. This is to make corporate capital gains taxes consistent with the high tax rate on capital gains of individuals. Related to corporate income tax, it should be pointed out that various incentive measures to capital formation were introduced in Korea. For example, extensive preferential tax treatments, such as tax holidays, investment tax credits, accelerated depreciation, and tax-free reserves for investment, were applied to key industries until the mid-1980s. However, since such a tax policy generated economic distortions and an imbalance of industrial structure, those tax incentives were removed in the 1986 tax reform, except for research and development investment, investment in small and medium industries, and relocation of industries away from large metropolitan areas.

Tax incentives

As we already pointed out Korea has applied extensive tax incentives to investment. Among these the most important tax incentives are tax holidays, the investment tax credit, and special depreciation. There are two methods used in calculating depreciation: assets are allowed to be depreciated by a fixed amount, or at a fixed rate annually. Here we consider the depreciation system based on a fixed rate (declining balance), because this system of caculation has been accepted as the preferable one for the corporate side in Korea. The depreciation rate has been applied to 90 percent of the purchasing price of assets.

Table 4.4: Structures of corporate tax rate

	unlisted profit corporation				listed profit corporation			
	below		above		below		above	
	100	500	5000	5000	100	500	5000	5000
1962	20	20	20	20	10	10	10	10
1963	20	25	25	25	10	12.5	12.5	12.5
1964	25	30	30	30	12.5	15	15	15
1966	20	30	35	35	10	15	17.5	17.5
1968	25	35	45	45	20	30	35	35
1969	25	35	45	45	15	20	25	25
1972	20	30	40	40	16	20	27	27
1975	20	30	40	40	20	20	27	27
1976	20	30	40	40	20	20	27	27
1977	20	30	40	40	20	20	27	27
1979	20	30	40	40	20	20	27	27
1981	25	25	25	40	25	25	25	33
1982	22	22	22	38	22	22	22	33
1983	20	20	20	30	20	20	20	30
1984	20	20	20	33	20	20	20	30
1988	20	20	20	33	20	20	20	30
	below 8000		above 8000		below 8000		above 8000	
1989	20		33		20		30	
1990	20		33		20		30	
	below 10000		above 10000		below 10000		above 10000	
1995	18		32		18		32	

Source: The corporate tax law,   Income unit: 10,000 Won

In addition to the general depreciation system a special depreciation system was introduced in the 1962 corporate tax law, which allowed the special depreciation rate of 20 percent for machinery and equipment in manufacturing industries to be operated for more than 16 hours daily. The special depreciation rate was extended to heavy equipment in construction industries in 1969. During 1975-82 a special depreciation rate of 80 percent was allowed for mining, fishery, manufacturing and construction industries, while a special depreciation rate of 40 percent was applied to the other industries. During 1983-85 the special depreciation rate was reduced to 20 percent for machinery and equipment in the mining, manufacturing, electricity and water and gas industries, and heavy equipment in construction industries.

Since 1986 the special depreciation system in the corporate tax has allowed different rates for machinery and equipment in the mining and manufacturing industries according to the operating hours per day. For example, a special depreciation rate of 20 percent, 30 percent, and 50 percent has been respectively applied to those firms operating for 12-15 hours, 15-18 hours, and more than 18 hours a day. From 1993 this special depreciation system has been extended to include the computer industry.

Tax holidays introduced in 1949 exempted all corporate tax for the first industrial group (consisting of petroleum refining, shipbuilding, iron and steel refining, copper refining, cement manufacturing, and chemical fertilizer industry) during the first 5 years of normal operation of those businesses, and for the second industrial group (consisting of mining and plate glass industry) during the first 3 years. In 1954 the tax exemption given to the first industrial group was reduced from 5 years to 3 years, while the tax exemption to the second industrial group was reduced from 3 years to 1 year. In addition, for the next two years the corporate had an exemption of 2/3 and 1/3, respectively. In 1963 the mining industry moved from the second industrial group to the first industrial group, and the corporate tax was exempted for the first industrial group for 4 years. Petroleum refining and the chemical industry were excluded from tax holidays in 1966.

The investment tax credit substituted tax holidays in 1967, since the latter had distorted firms' investment pattern in the sense that it was not applied to investment for improving industrial facilities and for the expansion of production facilities. Investment tax credit allowed a 6 percent tax credit for shipbuilding, iron and steel, chemical fertilizer, synthetic fiber, automobile, machinery, pulp, foods-processing, petroleum chemical products, electrical and electronics, mining and construction industry. In 1974 investment tax credit was absorbed into the special tax treatment for strategic industries.

After the oil shock, tax holidays, investment tax credit and special depreciation were integrated into the special tax treatment for strategic industries in 1974. Each firm in a strategic industry was allowed to choose only one type of special tax treatment among tax holidays, investment tax credit, and special depreciation.

Tax holidays exempted 100 percent of corporate tax for the first three years, and 50 percent for the next two years. Investment tax credit allowed an 8 percent tax credit for machinery and buildings (10 percent tax credit for Korean-made machinery and buildings). The special depreciation system allowed a 100 percent depreciation rate. Petroleum chemicals, shipbuilding, machinery, electronics, iron and steel, mining, iron manufacture, electricity, water, and gas and chemical fertilizer comprised the strategic industries.

By the revision of tax law in 1982, tax holidays were abolished completely, while the investment tax credit was limitedly applied to the machinery and electronics industries and was reduced from 8 to 6 percent. Petroleum chemicals, iron and steel, chemical fertilizer, and electricity, water and gas were excluded from investment tax credit.

In 1982 temporarily, 5 percent of tax-free reserves for investment was given with a 100 percent special depreciation. In this context, special depreciation remained consistently the most important preferential tax system. But special depreciation disappeared in 1986 from the special treatment, and at the time all special tax treatments for strategic industries in the Tax Exemption and Reduction Law were also eliminated. Following the elimination of special tax treatments for strategic industries in 1986, the special depreciation system was substantially scaled back in the corporation tax law, but the 10 percent investment tax credit was allowed in establishing facilities for saving energy, reducing pollution, improving safety, improving transportation systems, and for machinery in small and medium industries.

Consumption Taxes

The current structure of the consumption tax system settled down in 1977 after the value added tax system was introduced. The value added tax is the major consumption tax in Korea. Other consumption taxes are the special excise tax, liquor tax, telephone tax, stamp tax, and tobacco sales tax. In raising revenue, tobacco sales tax, special excise tax, and liquor tax are important. The Korean value added tax system is a typical EC type, with a flat rate of 10 percent and 0 rating. For small firms with difficulty in book-keeping, the special taxation system is applied, where eligible firms are taxed on a turnover basis. Because too many are taxed under this special taxation system, the merits of the value added tax are not fully exploited.

Currently more than 70 percent of the value added tax payers are taxed under this system.

The special excise tax was first introduced to mitigate the regressivity of the single rated value added tax. At present 36 items classified as single commodities, groups of similar commodities, or services are taxed at rates ranging from 10 to 100 percent. Incidence of this tax is estimated to be less regressive when compared with the value added tax, but it is not really improving income distribution. Liquor taxes are ad valorem and the tax rates range from 10 to 300 percent.

Tobacco production and sales had been monopolized by the government until very recently when the business unit was changed to a public corporation. Previously, the profit from tobacco business was included as indirect tax revenue of the central government, but currently similar revenue is generated by local government taxation of tobacco consumption.

Property-related taxes

Tax on capital gains from real property transactions, the inheritance and gift tax are categorized as taxes on property transfers. Taxes on capital gains were originally created to control real estate in the mid-1960s, but are now incorporated in the income tax law and the corporation tax law as discussed above. Recently, a new tax, the tax on excess profit from land, has been introduced. This tax is a selective capital gains tax levied on an accrual basis. The inheritance tax in Korea is not really an inheritance-type tax, but an estate-type tax. Gifts or *inter vivos* transfers are taxed separately unless such transfers take place within three years before the death of the donor. In such cases, the gift amount is added to the estate tax base. The gift tax base is calculated by accumulating the *inter vivos* transfers from a donor for three consecutive years.

Both taxes are highly progressive, ranging 5 to 55 percent in the case of the inheritance tax and 5 to 60 percent for the gift tax. In addition, a 20 percent tax is surcharged on both taxes. Exemption levels are not very high. However, these taxes have generated insignificant revenue in spite of such high tax rates. This supports the fact that they have not contributed significantly to redistributing wealth. Such poor performance has been due to the unrealistically low assessment of assets.

Local governments tax property holdings, acquisition, and registration. They have been important revenue sources for local governments.

As the public concept of land ownership gained the support of populas opinion from the late 1980s, a new tax system related to land was enacted in

1990, consisting of the global land holding tax, the excessive land profit tax, and the system to retake development profits. We will discuss these taxes in some detail in the following section.

4.2   Tax reform and tax policy

Historically, a set of tax laws were first enacted in 1948 when the Republic of Korea was formed. The tax law introduced income tax, corporation tax, commodity tax, liquor tax, inheritance tax, and other minor taxes. Under this tax system the major target of income tax changed from the rural landlord class to the urban capitalist class, due to the collapse of the landlord class after implementing the land reform.

During the Korean War (1950–53) the tax system was replaced by the wartime emergency tax system, and then tax reform was carried out in 1954 and 1956. In this tax reform, tax rates were lowered in general, resulting in increasing dependence of tax revenue on indirect taxes. Around the end of the 1950s, as the government put more weight on industrialization and economic growth, fiscal policy introduced tax incentives to promote capital formation and exports (e.g., tax holidays, the special tax treatment on the acquisition of foreign currencies).

In the 1960s when the Korean government pursued export-oriented rapid economic growth, tax policy was focused on encouraging saving, investment, and foreign exchange earnings. In the 1961 tax reform, capital taxation was drastically reduced, interest income was almost untaxed allowing financial transactions without personal identification, income from foreign exchange earnings was taxed at a preferential rate (50 percent of the nominal rate), and tax holidays were expanded to strategic industries. Special depreciation was introduced in 1962. In the 1967 tax reform, the global income tax system with progressive rates was partially introduced, and the corporation tax system introduced the discriminative tax rates between open corporations and closed corporations in order to encourage the opening of corporations and to foster the domestic capital market. Further, the 50 percent capital gains tax was imposed on real estate transactions to hold down speculation in land, and investment tax credit was introduced in 1967, which temporarily replaced tax holidays.

In the 1970s the Korean government used tax policy to make an adjustment of industrial structure toward the heavy and chemical industries, while attempting to reform the tax structure and system. Tax policy during this period resulted in inefficient and excessive use of tax incentives to channel resources to the heavy and chemical industries. In the 1970s there were three tax reforms (1971, 1974, 1976) and two emergency measures (1972, 1974). In the 1971 tax reform, tax rates on wages, salaries and business income were lowered with an increase in the basic exemption level, while interest income was brought under taxation at a rate of 5 percent. Due to the unfavorable situation for business, the corporate tax rate was also reduced and investment incentives expanded. Under two emergency measures taken to revive the economy from slump and the first oil shock, the 1972 emergency measure, which lasted until 1974, extended generous investment incentives, including accelerated depreciation allowances and investment tax credit, and incentives for research and development to select firms in the heavy and chemical industries. The 1974 emergency measure gave income tax relief for low-income workers suffering from inflation. In addition, two important tax reforms were carried out in the mid-1970s in order to improve economic efficiency and equity as well as administrative efficiency. In the 1974 major tax reform, an almost global personal income tax was introduced, replacing the dual structure of the personal income tax structure. Further, all major incentives divided among complex tax laws were unified and rearranged under the article of "special tax treatment for key industries" in the Tax Exemption and Reduction Control Law. This special treatment allowed select firms in the heavy and chemical industries to choose one of three tax incentives, namely tax holidays, investment tax credit and special depreciation. Another tax reform in 1976 introduced the value added tax and special excise taxes, replacing the business tax and other indirect taxes. To compensate for the anticipated side effects of the newly introduced value added tax, this tax reform allowed additional tax relief for the low and middle income class, and mitigated taxes on land sales and inheritance.

In the 1980s Korea faced rapid changes in the economic and political environments. The role of market mechanism in resource allocation became more emphasized and liberalization in foreign trade, international trade, international investment and financial markets was sought after. Both tax revisions and tax reforms made in the 1980s tried to accommodate these trends in economic development. The tax revision in 1981 increased the personal income deductions, lowered income tax rates, cut 30 percent off the special excise tax rate imposed on certain consumer durables, and introduced the education tax. The 1982 tax reform, the most significant tax reform introduced in the early 1980s, had as its guiding principle low taxes and low exemption. It streamlined the industrial tax incentive system as well as lowered the personal and corporate income tax rates. In particular, the tax incentives for key industries were almost removed. For example,

tax holidays were completely abolished, and the investment tax credit was
lowered to 6 percent for a limited number of industries. On the other hand,
incentives for research and development and investment in small and medium
firms were reinforced. Tax-free reserves for investments was temporarily introduced for 1982 only. Finally, in 1986 the special treatment for key industries in the Tax Exemption and Reduction Control Law was abolished. Under the changing political and social environment, the government adopted a
functional or indirect approach, in contrast to the previous industry-specific
direct approach in providing industrial incentives.

The period from the late 1980s to the early 1990s may be considered to be
one of the most important turning points in Korea's modern history. During this period the economy of the country was doing well with double digit
economic growth rates, large trade surpluses (1986–89) and price stability.
The Korean public, having waited to be compensated for economic growth,
was ready to demand for more social welfare and social and political democratization. The ensuing social and political changes had enormous influence
both on the policy-making process and future policy objectives. Specifically,
the 1988 tax reform was the first one carried out in response to the proposals of the tax reform committee established in 1985. The major features of
the reform were an increase in the personal exemption level of income tax,
a reduction in the number of brackets and the marginal tax rates of the
income tax and the inheritance tax, and a downward adjustment in many
excise tax rates.

Another tax reform in Korea has been related to how to use tax measures to control land speculation. Speculation on land has been a serious
economic and social problem in Korea since the beginning of industrialization. Although several kinds of taxes to control land speculation were
enacted from the mid-1960s to the early 1980s, the vicious cycle over land
speculation has not yet improved, raising serious social conflicts in wealth
distribution, concentrating the distribution of real assets, and causing a severe shortage of land for housing and business. Hence, a new system on
land holding and the public concept of the ownership of land was enacted
in 1990. Proposals claiming public control over land holding and utilization
seemed to gain public support. As a result, a full-fledged global land-holding
tax and other rather extreme measures to control speculative land holding
were introduced in the new system. This new system can be summarized
as consisting of the global land-holding tax system, the excessive land profit
tax system, and the system to retake development profits.

The global land-holding tax (the aggregate land tax) system classified all
land owned by individuals and corporations into three groups: (i) properties

representing added up nationwide landholding of an individual or a corporation to be taxed at progressive rates ranging from 0.2 percent to 5 percent under the main global scheme; (ii) properties mainly comprising land for commercial use to be taxed at the 2 percent maximum rate under the secondary global income; (iii) properties to be taxed at low flat rates of 0.1 to 0.3 percent and at the high flat rate of 5 percent regardless of the amount of land owned by an individual or a corporation. This tax is administered as a local tax, which will likely result in administrative difficulties in the future, since each local government collects its proportional share from a single taxpayer who owns land under multiple jurisdictions. After the introduction of this system in 1990, the traditional property tax now only applies to buildings and structures, mining lots, aircrafts, and vessels.

The other tax measure enacted in 1990 dealing with land speculation was the excessive land profit tax system. This is a tax on excessive gains accrued to land holdings. Accrued net capital gains (net of capital expenditure on the land) in excess of normal gains (national average rate of land price increase) are taxed at 50 percent every three years. This system critically depends on the accuracy and fairness of the assessment of all land prices as well as on the judgement of the tax authority with regard to the utilization status of each piece of land.

The new 1990 tax system enacted the return of development profits to the state, reflecting the strong view of the public concept of land ownership. This system requires that the developer of a land project pays 50 percent of the assessed profit from the project to the government. In addition, the new system introduced a ceiling on the holding of residential land in city areas in 1990. Under this system a household unit holding residential land in excess of 660 square meters in any of six major city areas must pay 7 to 11 percent of the value of the excess land annually.

Finally, the real-name financial transaction system was introduced on August 12, 1993 by announcing the presidential decree to ban the use of pseudonyms in all financial deals, and the government gave account holders two months to either identify themselves or face partial appropriation of assets. About 96 percent of accounts (2.74 trillion Won) under false names have been converted to real-name accounts by the October 12 deadline for voluntary conversion. In addition, 2.92 trillion Won in borrowed-name accounts has been put under the names of actual account holders. The banks and short-term financial institutions, if found to have made irregularities, will be dealt severe punitive measures, including the dismissal of related excutives or partial suspension of business.

However, the introduction of the real-name system has significantly weakened a fund intermediation function of non-banking financial institutions in the short run, resulting in the drop in velocity. The central bank (The Bank of Korea) increased the money supply to make up for the market liquidity shortage in particular to small- to medium-size industries. The growth rate of M_2, which had remained below the 17 percent mark (its original M_2 target) during the first half of the year, soared to 19 to 22 percent during the second half of the year. Accordingly, there were growing concerns about inflationary expectations in the face of the ever-increasing money supply.

Along with the real-name financial transaction system, liberalization of bank interest was carried out on November 1, 1993, and money market interest rates have remained comparatively stable. Most bank interest imposed on loans was liberalized, and the program to boost savings was developed. Further, the added tax revenues to be gained from transparent commercial operations would induce the promising tax reform to reduce tax rates and broaden the tax base. For example, the tax reform would lead to lightening the tax burden of small- to medium-size industries, lowering tax rates for wage earners and enterprises, and a preferential tax treatment to the incomes of pensioners and retirees in the absence of an adequate social security system.

5 Effective tax rate

5.1 Introduction

A continuous increase in living standards in the long run is dependent on a
high level of investment. As the period of sustained economic growth enjoyed
in the 1950s and 1960s has retreated, there has been increasing concern over
capital formation. Many countries have experienced a decline in the rate
of capital formation with a reduction in the stock market's valuation of
corporate assets. This decline in investment and the market's valuation has
occurred in conjunction with substantial changes in the cost of capital and
the effective taxation of capital income. Under these circumstances there
emerged a gradual consensus in favor of some sort of tax incentives for
capital formation in the 1970s, and governments in many countries have
shown increasing interest in policies designed to stimulate investments and
productivity. For example, OECD countries and some countries outside the
OECD have applied various kind of tax incentives for capital formation.
In particular Korea was a typical country to implement comprehensive tax
policies for forming capital stock and supporting key industries in the 1960s
and 1970s for the purpose of sustaining high economic growth. The Korean
government introduced extensive tax incentives during the period through
a series of tax reforms. Beginning with the introduction of tax holidays in
1949, the special depreciation in 1961, and the investment tax credit in 1967,
Korean tax policy incorporated a series of tax preferences for specific forms
of capital income. They could stimulate capital formations by reducing cost
of capital. However, these tax incentives also heightened the discrepancies
among tax burdens born by different types of capital. These discrepancies
gave rise to concerns about the impact of tax-induced distortions on the
efficiency of capital allocation.

Hence, as we already investigated in the previous chapter, the tax reforms
in 1982 and 1986 represented a sharp change in the direction of Korean

policy for taxation of income from capital. Statutory tax rates were lowered
in 1983, but the tax base was broadened by a gradual elimination of tax
preferences for corporations. This led to sharp cutbacks in tax incentives
for investment. The 1982 tax reform repealed tax holidays, and lowered the
investment tax credit to 6 percent. While the 1986 tax reform abolished
special treatments for key industries.

In this chapter the main interests are in analyzing how Korean tax policy
and tax reforms affected the cost of capital, the tax wedges, and the effective
tax rate. The cost of capital, the tax wedges, and the effective tax rate are
estimated according to types of asset, sources of finance and industries. In
the next section we will summarize the foundations of the cost of capital
and the effective tax rate. After explaining the analytic model in section 3,
estimating results of the cost of capital, the tax wedges, and the effective tax
rate will be investigated in relationship with tax reforms in section 4. The
stimulation effects of inflation and the corporate income tax on the effective
tax rate will be dealt with in sections 5 and 6, respectively. Finally, we
summarize the main results of this chapter in section 7.

5.2   Foundations of cost of capital and effective tax rate

Ever since the neoclassical theory of capital opened new horizons on the
microfoundations of capital formation, the approach based on the cost of
capital and the effective tax rate has been a useful analytic method in investigating investment behavior. This framework had its origins in two con-
cepts introduced in the 1960s: the effective tax rate pioneered by Harberger
(1962); and the cost of capital originated by Jorgenson (1963). The cost of
capital and the effective tax rate were combined in the marginal effective
tax rate introduced by Auerbach and Jorgenson (1980). They used marginal
effective tax rates to expose differences in the tax treatment of income from
different types of capital in the 1981 U.S. Tax Act. Marginal effective tax
rates under the 1981 U.S. Tax Act were measured for all types of assets and
all industries by Jorgenson and Sullivan (1981). Subsequently, these effective tax rates were used by Jorgenson and Yun (1991) to frame the debate
over alternative proposals that led to the U.S. Tax Reform Act of 1986, and
were presented for international comparisons by King and Fullerton (1984).
Recently, the effective tax rates in OECD countries were compared by using cross sectional data in 1991. Tajika and Yui (1988) compared the cost
of capital and effective tax rate between U.S. and Japanese manufacturing

industries, and their analytic model is modified in this work.

Many important issues in analyzing the marginal effective tax rates and the cost of capital have been debated for nearly a quarter of century. The first issue is the incorporation of inflation in asset prices into the cost of capital. This involved making empirical simulations of the effect of inflation on the cost of capital and investment expenditure. A second empirical issue related to the effective tax rate as the measurement of economic depreciation. Although there were diversified debates over measuring economic depreciation, the stability of patterns of decline in efficiency in the face of changes in tax policy and shocks, such as the sharp rise in energy prices during 1970s, has been carefully documented in Hulten, Wykoff and Robertson (1989). A third issue is to reflect investment incentives, such as the accelerated depreciation and the investment tax credit, into the cost of capital model. The modelling of investment incentives for new assets was originated by Hall and Jorgenson (1967, 1969, 1971). A fourth empirical issue relates to the treatment of debt and equity in the corporate tax structure. Jorgenson and Yun (1990) assumed that the debt–capital ratios are the same for all assets within the corporate sector, while Bosworth (1985), and Gordon, Hines and Summers (1987) have argued that different types of asset should be associated with the different debt–equity ratios. These two approaches are summarized as the so-called "traditional view" and the "new view". In the traditional view the marginal source of equity finance is new issue, whereas in the new view it is retained earnings. This issue has an important implication in the sense that investment expenditures of the firm are independent of the rate of taxation on dividends at the individual level in one case, and not in the other. A fifth issue in realizing the cost of capital and the effective tax rate is the inclusion of taxes at the individual level on corporate distributions to holders of equity. Since nominal interest expenses are deductible at the corporate level, while nominal interest payments are taxable at the individual level, an important issue is the impact of inflation on nominal interest rate. Additionally, this issue is useful for investigating the double taxation problem. Feldstein and Summers (1979), and King and Fullerton (1984) have studies on this issue. A sixth issue in the impact of inflation on the cost of capital is the relationship between accrual and realization of capital gains. In most countries capital gains are taxed when they are realized and not when they are accrued. However, capital consumption allowances for used assets reflect the price at which the asset is acquired. The optimal strategies for churning related to the capital consumption allowances are analyzed by Gordon, Hines, and Summers (1987), Gravelle (1987), and Sunley (1987). A final set of issues in corporate finance relates to more detailed description of the tax structure for capital income. These issues revolve around multi-period tax rules. For example, firms experiencing losses may be unable to avail themselves of the tax benefits of deductions for interest, depreciation, and so on. However, some of benefits may be carried forward to a period in which the firms make profits. A general approach to this problem has been developed by Auerbach (1986) and implemented empirically for data on individual firms by Auerbach and Poterba (1987). Further, Ballentine (1987), and Fullerton, Gillette, and Mackie (1987) have argued for the importance of these provisions.

5.3   The analytic model

Since the framework to present the cost of capital approach to the analysis of tax policy for capital income was developed by Jorgenson in 1963, there has been widespread use of the cost of capital approach integrated into the marginal effective tax rate. This methodology has been pervasively used for the evaluation of domestic tax policy related to tax reform and the international comparison of corporate and personal tax policy. The first successful international comparison of the taxation of income from capital was compiled by King and Fullerton (1984).

The analytic model in this work is connected with their models, and some characteristics of this model can be pointed out as follows.

For the first characteristic of our model here we introduce personal tax on capital income into the process of deriving the formulas for cost of capital. Since the income raised by corporations is distributed to individuals in one way or another, and corporations have to satisfy their shareholders with paying at least a minimum rate of return they require, it is quite natural to investigate how the taxation on the personal side affects the cost of capital. Further, the personal tax system has important effects on dividend payout decisions. As we will see later, Korea's tax system has been characteristically engineered to enhance capital accumulation from the personal as much as from the corporate side.

The second characteristic of our analysis is to introduce how investment is financed according to three types of assets: buildings and structures; machinery and equipment; and transportation equipment. Here we consider the cost of capital as financed by borrowing, new share issuance, and retained earnings.

The third characteristic of our analysis has to do with tax incentives to investment. As we already explained, in Korea, tax holidays, the depreciation system, and investment tax credit were the most influential tax incentives for investment. So we would like to show how the cost of capital has been affected by these preferential tax systems and to present a formulation which allows us to quantify the effects of these tax policies.

5.3.1 Cost of capital according to sources of finance

We will first derive the formulas of cost of capital and effective tax rate which take into account taxes on personal capital income. We assume that investors expect a minimum rate of return (ρ^*) to their investment. The investors receive from the firm the dividend income D and the capital gains. Dividend and capital gains are assumed to be taxed at the rates θ and c, respectively. New shares amounting to V^N are assumed to be issued or repurchased, and the capital gains received by the investors are equal to $\dot{V} - V^N$, where $\dot{V}$ is the derivative of the value of the firm (V) w.r.t. time t.

Investor's portfolio choice will yield the following equation :

$$\rho V = (\dot{V} - V^N) + (1 - \theta)D \tag{5.1}$$

Solving this first-order differential equation of V,

$$V = (1 - \theta) \int_0^\infty e^{-\rho^* t}(D - \frac{1}{1 - \theta}V^N)dt \tag{5.2}$$

The economic value of capital stock K is to depreciate at the rate δ. Hence, net capital increase at time t is given by

$$\dot{K} = I - \delta K \tag{5.3}$$

where I is the gross investment.

The dividend distributed by the firm at t, D is expressed by

$$D_t = (1 - \tau)\Pi(K_t) - \left(1 - k_t - \tau \int_0^\infty \hat{\delta}e^{-\hat{\delta}(s-t)}e^{-\rho^*(s-t)}ds\right) P_t I_t$$
$$+ \left(1 - e^{-\rho^* t} - i(1 - \tau) \int_t^{t+\iota} e^{-\rho^*(s-t)}ds\right) B_t + V_t^N \tag{5.4}$$

where ρ^* : the rate of return to investment after tax,
$\Pi(K)$: the corporate income before tax,

k : the rate of investment tax credit,
$\hat{\delta}$: the rate of depreciation in tax law,
P : the price of investment goods,
B : the funds raised by issuing bonds,
ι : the maturity of bond,
i : the rate of interest paid by the firm.

As for the sources of financing investment, the fractions of investment, α_1 and α_2 are financed by issuing bonds and new shares, respectively. So the fraction, $\alpha_3 = 1 - \alpha_1 - \alpha_2$ is financed by retained earnings (R_t).
    That is,

$$B_t = \alpha_1 P_t I_t$$
$$V_t^N = \alpha_2 P_t I_t$$

The problem of optimization at the time of corporate establishment is to maximize the value of the firm,

$$
\begin{aligned}
V \;=\;& (1-\theta) \int_0^\infty e^{-\rho^* t}((1-\tau)\Pi(K_t) - (1 - k - \tau z - s\alpha_1 \\
& + \frac{\theta}{1-\theta}\alpha_2)P_t I_t)dt
\end{aligned}
\tag{5.5}
$$

subject to $\dot{K} = I - \delta K$,
where

$$z = \int_0^\infty \hat{\delta} e^{-(\rho^* + \hat{\delta})t} dt = \frac{\hat{\delta}}{\rho^* + \hat{\delta}}$$

$$s = 1 - e^{-\rho^* \iota} - \frac{i(1-\tau)(1 - e^{-\rho^* \iota})}{\rho^*}$$

In this optimization the tax bill saving due to depreciations on existing capital installed before time 0 is ignored, as it will be irrelevant for investment decisions from time 0 onward. The Hamiltonian for this problem is

$$
\begin{aligned}
H_t \;=\;& e^{-\rho^* t}[1 - \theta\left((1-\tau)\Pi(K_t) - (1 - k - \tau z - s\alpha_1 + \frac{\theta}{1-\theta}\alpha_2)P_t I_t\right) \\
& + q_t^*(I_t - \delta K_t)]
\end{aligned}
$$

where q_t^* is the shadow price of installed capital. This dynamic optimization problem can be solved using the Pontryagin maximum principle. Solving the first order conditions $\partial H_t/\partial I_t = 0$, where $P_t I_t = B_t + V_t^N + R_t$ and $\partial H_t/\partial K_t = q_t^*$, the formula of *the cost of capital* for each asset in an industry can be derived as

$$C = \alpha_1 C^B + \alpha_2 C^N + \alpha_3 C^R \qquad (5.6)$$

where

$$C^B = \frac{1 - s - k - \tau z}{1 - \tau}(\rho^* + \hat{\delta} - \frac{\dot{P}}{P})$$

$$C^N = \frac{1 + \frac{\theta}{1-\theta} - k - \tau z}{1 - \tau}(\rho^* + \hat{\delta} - \frac{\dot{P}}{P})$$

$$C^R = \frac{1 - k - \tau z}{1 - \tau}(\rho^* + \hat{\delta} - \frac{\dot{P}}{P})$$

C^B, C^N and C^R are each capital cost financed by borrowing, new shares and retained earnings, respectively. Equation (5.6) implies that the cost of capital for each asset in an industry is the weighted average of each cost of capital under the three modes of finances, with weights being the fractions of investment financed by the corresponding financial sources. By the way, in this work we will use the cost of capital net of depreciation by subtracting the depreciation rate from the cost of capital derived above, that is $C - \hat{\delta}$. This concept was already used as the social rate of return by Jorgenson and the pretax rate of return net of depreciation by King and Fullerton.

The solution to the optimization problem must also satisfy the transversality condition

$$\lim_{t \to \infty} q_t^* e^{-\rho^* t} = 0$$

One of important variables affecting the cost of capital is the discount rate(ρ^*) shown in the above equations, representing the rate of return to investment. With perfect certainty and no tax, the discount rate would be equal to the market interest rate. Under distortionary taxes, however, the discount rate will differ from the market interest rate and in general will depend upon the source of finance. For debt finance, since nominal interest

income is taxed and nominal interest payments are tax deductible, the rate
at which firms will discount after-tax cash flow is the net of tax interest rate.
In other words, for the case of debt finance

$$\rho^* = i(1 - \tau)$$

where i is the weighted average interest rate of the short-term interest rate,
the long-term interest rate, and the interest rate in the private loan market.

For the two other sources of finance, the discount rate depends on both
the personal tax system and the corporate tax system, affecting the dividend
payout decision. In the corporate tax system King and Fullerton introduce
the tax discrimination variable between retention and distribution. The variable is defined as the opportunity cost of retained earnings in terms of gross
dividends foregone. Under a classical system of corporate tax (such as that
in Korea), no additional corporate tax is collected or refunded when dividends are paid out, so the value of the tax discrimination variable is unity.
For new share issues the net of tax dividend yield, $(1-\theta)\rho^*$, must be equal
to the investor's opportunity cost rate of return, $(1-m)i$, where m is the
marginal personal tax rate on interest income. Hence the discount rate for
new share issues is given by

$$\rho^* = i\left(\frac{1-m}{1-\theta}\right)$$

Similarly, for financing through retained earnings the net retained earnings
yield, $(1-c)\rho^*$, must be equal to the investor's opportunity cost rate of
return, $(1-m)i$. Then the discount rate for retained earnings is

$$\rho^* = i\left(\frac{1-m}{1-c}\right)$$

To aggregate the cost of capital net of depreciation over different types of
asset, sources of finance, or industries, we make a weighted average of each
cost of capital. In particular, the average cost of capital resulting from all
the possible combinations of assets and sources of finance in this work is
derived from King and Fullerton's definition, which is a weighted average of
the cost of capital net of depreciation for the individual projects:

$$\bar{C} = \sum_{i=1}^{n} \tilde{C}_i \alpha_i$$

where $\tilde{C}$ is the cost of capital net of depreciation $(C_i - \hat{\delta})$ on the ith project
and α_i is the share of the ith project.

Here, let's discuss the effects of taxation of personal capital income on the cost of capital. The capital gains tax, c, will raise the after-tax rate of return (ρ^*) required by investors, increasing the cost of capital under various financial sources. The dividend income tax rate, θ, affects the cost of capital when investment is financed by new shares marginally. Since in practice the rate of tax on dividend income may be considered to be higher than that of capital gains tax, the increase of the dividend income tax will raise the cost of capital.

5.3.2 Cost of capital and tax incentives

Now we explore the theoretical model reflecting tax incentives of a depreciation system, tax holidays, tax-free reserves, and surtax on corporate tax as applied in Korea.

Depreciation system

As we pointed out previously, let's consider the depreciation system based on a fixed rate, where the depreciation rate has been applied to 90 percent of the purchasing price of assets in Korea. This feature of depreciation system in the corporate tax law has led us the following relationship:

$$\hat{\delta} = -\log 0.1/T$$

So the present value of depreciation for a unit of investment is

$$z = \int_t^{t+T} \hat{\delta} e^{-(\rho^*+\hat{\delta})(s-t)} ds = \frac{\hat{\delta}}{\rho^*+\hat{\delta}}(1 - e^{-(\rho^*+\hat{\delta})T}) \tag{5.7}$$

Here it is assumed that the expected return to investment is defined as the discounted rate after tax, because the corporate tax is imposed on the marginal rate of return to capital, not imposed on capital gains in Korea.

Further, the present value of depreciation reflecting special depreciation system is

$$z' = \frac{\hat{\delta}(1+r)}{\rho^*+\hat{\delta}(1+r)}(1 - e^{-(\rho^*+\hat{\delta}(1+r))T}) \tag{5.8}$$

where r is the special depreciation rate.

Tax holidays

Under tax holidays the special tax rate τ_1, τ_2 and the normal tax rate τ are assumed to be applied for the first period of h_1, the next period of h_2 and the remaining period of h_3, respectively. Since tax holidays allowed different tax rates according to the period, an average tax rate for the period of tax holidays is convenient to our analysis without loss of generality. The average tax rate can be measured from dividing the present value of the actual tax payments by the present value of returns before tax to a unit investment.

The present value (VR) of returns before tax to a unit investment is

$$VR = \frac{R}{\rho^* + \hat{\delta}}$$

where R is the flow of returns before tax to investment.

The present value (VT) of the tax payment under tax holidays is

$$
\begin{aligned}
VT &= \int_t^{t+h_1} \tau_1 R e^{-(\rho^*+\hat{\delta})(s-t)} ds + \int_{t+h_1}^{t+h_1+h_2} \tau_2 R e^{-(\rho^*+\hat{\delta})(s-t)} ds \\
&+ \int_{t+h_1+h_2}^{\infty} \tau R e^{-(\rho^*+\hat{\delta})(s-t)} ds \\
&= \frac{R}{\rho^* + \hat{\delta}} \left(\tau_1 + (\tau_2 - \tau_1) e^{-(\rho^*+\hat{\delta})h_1} + (\tau - \tau_2) e^{-(\rho^*+\hat{\delta})(h_1+h_2)} \right)
\end{aligned}
$$

Hence, the average tax rate (u) is

$$\mathbf{u} = \frac{VT}{VR} = \tau_1 + (\tau_2 - \tau_1) e^{-(\rho^*+\hat{\delta})h_1} + (\tau - \tau_2) e^{-(\rho^*+\hat{\delta})(h_1+h_2)} \quad (5.9)$$

Further, the rate of depreciation, $(\tau z)^*$ under tax holidays is

$$
\begin{aligned}
(\tau z)^* &= \int_t^{t+h_1} e^{-\rho^*(s-t)} \tau_1 \hat{\delta}(1+r) e^{-\hat{\delta}(1+r)(s-t)} ds \\
&+ \int_{t+h_1}^{t+h_1+h_2} e^{-\rho^*(s-t)} \tau_2 \hat{\delta}(1+r) e^{-\hat{\delta}(1+r)(s-t)} ds \\
&+ \int_{t+h_1+h_2}^{t+T} e^{-\rho^*(s-t)} \tau \hat{\delta}(1+r) e^{-\hat{\delta}(1+r)(s-t)} ds \\
&= \frac{\hat{\delta}(1+r)}{\rho^* + \hat{\delta}(1+r)} (\tau_1 + (\tau_2 - \tau_1) e^{-(\rho^*+\hat{\delta}(1+r))h_1} \\
&+ (\tau - \tau_2) e^{-(\rho^*+\hat{\delta}(1+r))(h_1+h_2)} - \tau e^{-(\rho^*+\hat{\delta}(1+r))T}) \quad (5.10)
\end{aligned}
$$

where $T > h_1 + h_2$,

$$(\tau z)^* = \frac{\hat{\delta}(1+r)}{\rho^* + \hat{\delta}(1+r)}\left(\tau_1 + \tau_1 e^{-(\rho^* + \hat{\delta}(1+r))T}\right) = \tau_1 z'$$

where $h_1 < T < h_1 + h_2$, and

$$(\tau z)^* = \frac{\hat{\delta}(1+r)}{\rho^* + \hat{\delta}(1+r)}\left(\tau_1 + (\tau_2 - \tau_1)e^{-(\rho^* + \hat{\delta}(1+r))h_1} - \tau_2 e^{-(\rho^* + \hat{\delta}(1+r))T}\right)$$

where $h_1 > T$.

If the rate of depreciation $(\hat{\delta})$ in tax law is equal to the rate of depreciation (δ) in economic sense,

$$z = z' = \frac{\delta}{\rho^* + \delta}$$

and

$$(\tau z)^* = uz' = uz = \frac{u\delta}{\rho^* + \delta}$$

Tax-free reserves for investment

Tax-free reserves for investment were temporarily applied to machinery and equipment in 1982. It allowed 5 percent of an accounting price on investment to machinery and equipment for tax-free reserves, treating as a loss of the year. And then tax-free reserves would be taken into account as return to investments by equal amounts of 3 years only after 4 years since tax-free reserves were made. So the feature of tax-free reserves (B_{IR}) to machinery and equipment had led us to the following relationship

$$B_{IR} = \int_0^\infty \frac{0.05\mu\tau}{\rho^{**}}\left(1 - \frac{e^{-4\rho^{**}} + e^{-5\rho^{**}} + e^{-6\rho^{**}}}{3}\right)ds$$

where $\rho^{**} = \rho^* + \hat{\delta}(1+r)$, and μ is the proportion of investment to machinery and equipment.

Surtax on corporate tax

There have been several kinds of surtax on the corporate income tax in Korea. Until 1966 surtax of 5 percent to 10 percent had been imposed as a local tax. In 1967 the special tax law substituted a 10 percent increase in

the corporate tax for the 5 percent to 10 percent of surtax. As the special
tax was abolished in 1970, resident tax as a local tax of 7.5 percent was
imposed on the corporate tax in 1973. And in 1975 the defense tax of 20
percent to 25 percent of corporate income, including tax-deduction, was
introduced, while the defense tax rate for corporate tax deduction increased
by 50 percent from 1980. Hence, the tax payment under surtax and tax
holidays for a unit of corporate income is

$$\mathbf{u}^* = u + ul + uf + (\tau - u)f' \tag{5.11}$$

where l is local tax rate, f defense tax rate, and f' the increased defense tax
rate in 1980, i.e., $f' = f$ for $t < 1980$ and $f' = 1.5f$ for $t > 1980$.

Tax-free reserves for export

The purpose of this system is to substitute the 50 percent tax deduction for
foreign exchange earnings which was applied before 1973, and introduced
both tax-free reserves for developing new export markets and tax-free reserves for loss from exports. Each tax-free reserve system allows its upper
limit for reserves within 1 percent of exports, and thereby the maximum
tax-free reserves for export are 2 percent of exports. The tax-free reserves
for export would be taken into accounts as return to investments by equal
amounts for 3 years only after 2 years since tax-free reserves were made. So
the tax benefit (B_{XR}) through the tax-free reserves for export is

$$\mathbf{B_{XR}} = \int_0^\infty 0.02\tau\varepsilon P_Q(1-\nu)\frac{\partial Q}{\partial K}Me^{\rho^{**}(s-t)}ds \tag{5.12}$$

where $M = 1 - \frac{1}{3}(e^{-2\rho^{**}} + e^{-3\rho^{**}} + e^{-4\rho^{**}})$, ε is the ratio of export to
output, P_Q the export price, ν the average indirect tax rate, and $\partial Q/\partial K$
the marginal product of capital.

Therefore, the cost of capital net of depreciation ($\tilde{C}$) reflecting the above
fiscal incentives to investment can be reconstructed as

$$\hat{C} = \alpha_1 C^{\mathbf{B}} + \alpha_2 C^{\mathbf{N}} + \alpha_3 C^{\mathbf{R}} - \hat{\delta} \tag{5.13}$$

where

$$\tilde{C}^{\mathbf{B}} = \frac{1 - s - (k + (\tau z)^*)(1-f') - uzf'}{(1-u^*) + (B_{XR} + B_{IR})(1-f')}\left(\rho^* + \hat{\delta} - \frac{\dot{P}}{P}\right) - \hat{\delta}$$

$$\tilde{C}^N = \frac{1 - \frac{\theta}{1-\theta} - (k + (\tau z)^*)(1 - f') - uzf'}{(1 - u^*) + (B_{XR} + B_{IR})(1 - f')}\left(\rho^* + \hat{\delta} - \frac{\dot{P}}{P}\right) - \hat{\delta}$$

$$\tilde{C}^R = \frac{1 - (k + (\tau z)^*)(1 - f') - uzf'}{(1 - u^*) + (B_{XR} + B_{IR})(1 - f')}\left(\rho^* + \hat{\delta} - \frac{\dot{P}}{P}\right) - \hat{\delta}$$

$$z = \int_o^\infty \hat{\delta} e^{-(\rho^* + \hat{\delta})t} dt = \frac{\hat{\delta}}{\rho^* + \hat{\delta}}$$

$$s = 1 - e^{-\rho^* \iota} - i(1 - \tau^*)(1 - e^{-\rho^* \iota})/\rho^*$$

5.3.3 Tax wedges

The tax wedge is the difference between the pretax real rate of return on a marginal investment, net of depreciation $(\tilde{C})$ and the post-tax real rate of return on the savings used to finance the investment $(\tilde{S})$:

$$W = \tilde{C} - \tilde{S} \tag{5.14}$$

The former is the cost of capital net of depreciation $(\tilde{C})$ we derived, and the latter $(\tilde{S})$ is given by

$$\tilde{S} = i(1 - m) - \dot{P}/P \tag{5.15}$$

where i is the weighted average of the nominal interest rate and m is the personal tax rate on interest income. In our analysis we assume that arbitrage leads to an outcome in which all projects offer the same rate of return to savers before personal tax.

The *tax wedge* consists of the corporate tax wedge (W_c) and the personal tax wedge (W_p), which is associated with corporate and personal taxes:

$$W = W_c + W_p \tag{5.16}$$

The *corporate tax wedge* is defined as the difference between the before tax rate of return and the after corporate, before personal tax rate of return:

$$\mathbf{W_c} = \tilde{C} - \rho^* \tag{5.17}$$

Similarly, the *personal tax wedge* is defined as the difference between the after corporate, before personal tax rate of return and the after tax rate of return to saving:

$$\mathbf{W_p} = \rho^* - \tilde{S} \tag{5.18}$$

And the *average tax wedge* ($\bar{W}$), the average corporate tax wedge ($\bar{W}_c$), and the average personal tax wedge ($\bar{W}_p$) are a weighted average of tax wedges for the individual projects, a weighted average of corporate tax wedges, and a weighted average of personal tax wedges, respectively:

$$\mathbf{\bar{W}} = \sum_{i=1}^{n}(\tilde{C}_i - \tilde{S}_i)\alpha_i = \bar{C} - \bar{S} = \sum_{i=1}^{n} W_i\alpha_i \tag{5.19}$$

$$\mathbf{\bar{W}_c} = \sum_{i=1}^{n}(\bar{C}_i - \rho_i^*)\alpha_i = \bar{C} - \bar{\rho}^* = \sum_{i=1}^{n} W_c^i\alpha_i \tag{5.20}$$

$$\mathbf{\bar{W}_p} = \sum_{i=1}^{n}(\rho_i^* - \tilde{S}_i)\alpha_i = \bar{\rho}^* - \bar{S} = \sum_{i=1}^{n} W_p^i\alpha_i \tag{5.21}$$

5.3.4 Effective tax rate

The statutory rate of corporate income tax does not represent the real tax burden, for various special treatments like the investment tax credit, special depreciation, tax holidays, and tax-free reserves reduce tax liabilities. On the other hand, the idea of an effective tax rate is essentially to seek such a rate of corporate income tax that would realize by itself the cost of capital which prevails under the existing tax system. In this sense, the effective tax rate is the condensed rate of corporate income tax.

To be specific, let's consider the cost of capital under all preferential taxes mentioned above and the rate of economic depreciation.

Then the effective tax rate (τ^E) is the marginal rate of corporate income tax to bring about the marginal cost of capital that emerges under all preferential taxes and the rate of economic depreciation:

$$\frac{(1 - \tau^E z^E)\tilde{S}}{1 - \tau^E} = \tilde{C} \tag{5.22}$$

where z^E is the present value of the stream of economic depreciation of a unit-value worth of investment, and $\tilde{C}$ on the right-hand side is the cost of capital net of depreciation.

Thus, the *effective tax rate* is

$$\tau^E = \frac{\tilde{C} - \tilde{S}}{\tilde{C}} = 1 - \frac{\tilde{S}}{\tilde{C}} \tag{5.23}$$

which is defined to be the tax wedge divided by the before tax rate of return, net of depreciation.

Similarly, the *effective corporate tax rate* (τ_c^E) and the *effective personal tax rate* (τ_p^E) are defined as the ratio of the corporate tax wedge to the before tax rate of return and the ratio of the personal tax wedge to the after corporate, before personal tax rate of return, respectively:

$$\tau_c^E = \frac{W_c}{\tilde{C}} = \frac{\tilde{C} - \rho^*}{\tilde{C}} \tag{5.24}$$

$$\tau_p^E = \frac{W_c}{\rho^*} = \frac{\rho^* - \tilde{S}}{\rho^*} \tag{5.25}$$

And the *average marginal effective tax rate* $(\bar{\tau}^E)$ is defined as the ratio of the average tax wedge $(\bar{W})$ to the average rate of return before taxes $(\tilde{C})$:

$$\bar{\tau}^E = \frac{\sum_{i=1}^n (\tilde{C}_i - \tilde{S}_i)\alpha_i}{\sum_{i=1}^n \tilde{C}_i \alpha_i} = \frac{\bar{W}}{\tilde{C}} \tag{5.26}$$

The *average marginal effective corporation tax rate* $(\bar{\tau}_c^E)$ and the *average marginal effective personal tax rate* $(\bar{\tau}_p^E)$ are defined as follows:

$$\bar{\tau}_c^E = \frac{\bar{W}_c}{\tilde{C}} \tag{5.27}$$

$$\bar{\tau}_p^E = \frac{\bar{W}_p}{\bar{\rho}^*} \tag{5.28}$$

5.4   Analytic results on tax reform, cost of capital, and effective tax rate

We classify Korean industries into 26 industries (9 aggregate industries, 18 sub-manufacturing industries): (Appendix A), and investigate the cost of capital and the effective tax rate corresponding to types of asset and sources of finance since 1966. Large-scale corporation covers all firms with corporate income more than 50 million Won in the tax law. The corporate tax rate (τ) of unlisted and large-scale firms is used in this analysis, since they occupy the major group of the industry. The nominal corporate tax rate surtaxed by resident tax and defense tax is actually paid, shown in Table 5.1.

The tax rate (θ) of dividend income was about 25 percent. The capital-gains tax (c) is neglected in the analysis, for the tax law did not specify it in Korea. Tax holidays, investment tax credit, special depreciation and tax-free reserves for investment are applied in the analysis. The rate of depreciation in economic sense (δ) has come essentially from Hulten and Wykoff's estimates (Appendix B): their estimates of δ of 33 assets have been based on given weights which are equal to the shares of investment of each type of assets. We already calculate the minimum rate of return (ρ^*) required by investors. Here i is derived by the weighted average of the interest rates of private borrowings, time savings, firm's bond, and industrial financing bonds, for they are widely distributed. As for the price, GNP deflator is used, and the expected price is projected on past prices. The fraction of investments, α_1, α_2 and α_3, financed by issuing bonds, new shares, and retained earnings are regressed through two stages. Firstly, $\alpha_1, \alpha_2,$ and α_3 are annually calculated in each industry, and compute the cost of capital under fiscal incentives to investment on the basis of the calculated values of $\alpha_1, \alpha_2,$ and α_3. Secondly, regress $\tilde{C}$ on $\tilde{C}^B, \tilde{C}^N$, and $\tilde{C}^R$ in equation (14), and estimate each industry's α_1, α_2 and α_3 under the restriction of $\alpha_1 + \alpha_2 + \alpha_3 = 1$. In Appendix C the estimated results of α_1, α_2 and α_3 are summarized in each industry according to three types of assets, buildings and structures (B), and machinery and equipment (M), and transportation equipment (T). Appendix C shows that in most industries the fraction of borrowing (α_1) occupies a larger portion, while the fraction of retained earnings (α_3) occupies a smaller portion. Because they have the limitation in financing their investments through their own earnings, and the fiscal incentives to investments have been in favor of borrowing especially in the inflationary period.

We estimate the cost of capital and the effective tax rate of the Korean economy consisting of 26 industries. The cost of capital is the pretax real return an investment project must earn to be profitable. The cost of capi-

Table 5.1: Nominal corporate tax rate

'66	'67	'68	'69	'70
0.385	0.35	0.45	0.45	0.45
'71	'72	'73	'74	'75
0.45	0.40	0.43	0.43	0.53
'76	'77	'78	'79	'80
0.53	0.53	0.53	0.53	0.53
'81	'82	'83	'84	'85
0.53	0.5035	0.43725	0.43725	0.43725
'86	'87	'88	'89	'90
0.43725	0.43725	0.43725	0.43725	0.43725*

(* corporate tax rate (33%) + defense tax rate
(8.25%) + resident tax rate (2.475%) = 43.725%)
Source: The corporate tax law

tal therefore directly affects the optimal investment policy of corporations. While the cost of capital is simple in concept it is quite complex in practice, as we derived. The cost of capital depends upon the required returns investors demand, on the tax treatment of investment, on the depreciation of investment assets, and on inflation. The effective tax rate was already defined as the tax wedge between the social and private rates of return, divided by the social rate of return, net of inflation. In this sense, the effective tax rate introduced by Auerbach and Jorgenson (1980) represents the complex provisions of tax law in terms of a single ad valorem tax. Here it is analyzed how Korean tax reforms have affected the cost of capital and the effective tax rate.

5.4.1 Cost of capital

Let's investigate the cost of capital according to industrial sectors, types of assets, and sources of finance.

First, the cost of capital in the corporate sector was high in the late 1960s, declined in the early 1970s, reaching bottom in 1974 after the 1972 emergency measure and the 1974 major tax reform. It then increased from the mid-1970s to the peak in 1980 due to stagflation and oil shock, and was on a downward trend from the early 1980s (see Figure 5.1). The cost

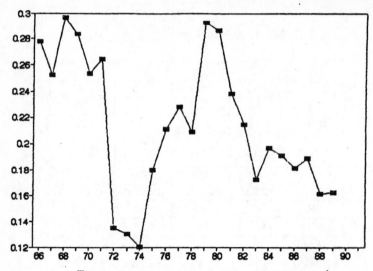

Figure 5.1: Cost of capital (overall average)

of capital in each industry reflected the trend in the corporate sector as a whole. In particular, we can discover that the tax reforms in 1982 and 1986 undertook a sharp change in the direction of Korean policy for taxation of income from capital and contributed to lowering the cost of capital in 1980s. These tax reforms were characterized as lowering personal and corporate tax rates with gradual elimination of tax preferences for corporations. For example, the corporate tax rate (inclusive of surcharges) was lowered from 53 percent to 43.8 percent in 1983, and tax incentives, e.g., tax holidays and investment tax credit, were almost eliminated in the late 1980s. Hence, the decline of the cost of capital in 1980s through tax reform was due to mitigating tax-induced distortions on the efficiency of capital allocation. This can be further supported by the fact that the tax wedge was narrower in 1980s. The overall average cost of capital in the corporate sector was 27.8 percent in 1966, 25.4 percent in 1970, 17.9 percent in 1975, 28.7 percent in 1980, 19.1 percent in 1985, and 15.9 percent in 1990, as in Table 5.2.

Second, according to the cost of capital in types of asset in the corporate sector, the cost of machinery and equipment had been in general lower than those of any other assets, while the cost of transportation equipment had been higher, as in Table 5.2. Such a trend in the cost of capital in three types of asset is noticeable in the manufacturing industry, the construction industry, and the wholesale & retail industry.

Tax reform had given more favorable incentives to the investment of machinery and equipment in key industries. However, in other industries

Table 5.2: Cost of capital by types of asset

	1966	1970	1975	1980	1985	1989	1990
Buildings	27.4	25.0	17.0	26.9	18.9	15.3	15.2
Machinery	26.5	22.7	17.4	26.0	17.7	15.0	15.1
Transportation	26.3	26.4	19.3	31.4	20.2	17.6	17.5
overall average	27.8	25.4	18.0	28.7	19.1	16.2	15.9

under weak tax incentives, the cost of buildings and structures had been
lower than that of machinery and equipment. For example, the mining industry, utilities, the finance sector, and the service sector belong to this
category. The cost of capital in types of asset was on average reduced by
11.9 percent from 1966 to 1990. And the cost of buildings and structures
was almost same as that of machinery and equipment in 1990.

Third, the interesting point is that there had been structural changes in
the cost of capital among industries. The cost reversals can be found between the construction industry and the mining industry. The construction
industry had stayed in the high group for the cost of capital until 1980, but
became part of the low group in the 1980s. However, the mining industry
had done the opposite. The typical changes in the cost of capital in the
two industries were due to the industrial competitiveness adjusted through
tax reform implemented in the 1980s. However, the cost of capital in the
service sectors had remained at high level. In 1966, the service sector had
the highest cost of capital at 37.0 percent, while the utility sector had the
lowest at 21.8 percent, so that the gap between costs of capital for two sectors was 15.2 percent. In 1990 the mining industry had the highest at 28.3
percent, and the construction industry had the lowest at 15.9 percent. The
gap between the top and bottom was narrowed from 15.2 percent in 1966
to 6.8 percent in 1990.

Table 5.3: Cost of capital by industries

industry	1966	1970	1975	1980	1985	1989	1990
1	35.6	29.8	25.9	37.3	21.3	17.9	17.7
2	27.2	31.2	17.8	28.3	24.1	21.1	22.3
3	30.0	27.8	19.0	31.1	21.0	17.8	17.6
4	21.8	26.0	13.6	22.7	20.2	17.1	17.0
5	33.5	25.3	26.1	37.6	19.8	15.7	15.9
6	22.3	15.7	9.2	19.2	10.3	6.9	7.0
7	28.6	23.7	20.0	29.5	18.3	15.7	15.5
8	35.4	30.5	17.0	35.3	23.1	20.4	20.5
9	37.0	32.2	26.6	37.8	23.7	20.6	19.9
average	27.8	25.4	18.0	28.7	19.1	16.2	17.0

Fourth, another primary factor to affect the cost of capital is corporate financing decisions. The cost of capital in our model was derived as depending on three sources of financing investment. Typically, the tax system tends to favor debt finance, because corporate interest payments are deductible from the corporate tax base, and because effective tax rates on interest are low. Further capital gains on share transactions were not taxed in Korea, while dividends were taxed at 25 percent. In this context, there had been the problem of financial distortions, which is one of the major issues in capital income tax reforms. Seen from the Korean perspective, it may seem obvious that the tax system discriminates heavily against new shares. The cost of capital according to sources of finance in each asset reflected the financial distortions. As in Table 5.4, in all assets, the cost of debt was lowest, while the cost of new shares was higher than that of retained earnings. The discrepancies of the cost of capital among sources of finance have been reduced since 1966 so that financial distortions decreased. And the tax reforms in the 1980s induced the larger reduction of costs of capital from new shares and retained earnings than that from debt in 1990.

Fifth, share repurchases and acquisitions had constituted an important aspect of Korean corporate behavior. In the process of economic development small independent firms were acquired by the group of the largest firms. And in a few industries (e.g., the construction industry, the commerce sector) corporate share repurchases exceeded ordinary dividend payments. Buying shares is a cheaper way of acquiring real assets than buying

Table 5.4: Cost of capital by sources of finance

asset.	finance	1966	1970	1975	1980	1985	1989	1990
buildings & structures	debt	11.3	6.6	-1.2	4.0	8.1	6.5	6.1
	n.s	69.6	67.1	58.0	78.7	44.8	37.3	37.0
	retained earnings	33.4	30.0	24.8	36.7	22.1	17.7	17.5
machinery & equipment	debt	8.2	3.0	-2.4	3.0	5.3	5.0	5.0
	n.s	74.1	69.0	63.1	82.0	47.8	41.3	41.1
	retained earnings	33.2	28.2	24.8	35.0	20.8	17.3	17.0
trans-portation equipment	debt	6.0	3.2	-2.3	4.6	5.6	5.6	5.8
	n.s	77.4	78.0	71.8	92.5	55.6	48.6	48.4
	retained earnings	34.0	32.1	29.3	41.0	23.9	20.0	19.8
overall average	debt	8.6	3.8	-2.1	3.4	6.1	5.4	5.6
	n.s	73.5	69.6	62.7	82.2	47.6	41.0	42.2
	retained earnings	33.3	29.1	25.2	35.9	21.4	17.6	18.1

(n.s: new shares)

investment goods.

It is also a method of distributing dividends that circumvents personal income tax if retained earnings finance, and, if debt finance, is a convenient way of enjoying the tax advantages of a higher degree of corporate leverage. Our analytic model includes the issues of share purchases in the equation (2), in which the negative value of V^N implies share repurchases. From the estimate of the ratio of new shares to investment cost (α_2), we discover share repurchases in some industries. This corporate behavior could be supported from the fact that α_2 was negative in them. Textiles and clothes, wood and wood products, paper and paper products, petroleum refining, other coal and petroleum products, and construction industries belong to this category.

The overall average cost of capital in share repurchases industries had been decreasing from 34.1 percent in 1966 to 15.9 percent in 1990, which was lower than the overall average cost of capital in the corporate sector.

Table 5.5: Tax wedge by types of asset

	1966	1970	1975	1980	1985	1989	1990
Buildings	13.5	15.1	10.5	15.9	9.7	8.2	8.1
Machinery	13.2	13.4	11.1	15.8	8.8	8.4	8.2
Transportation	13.6	17.2	15.3	21.5	11.8	11.3	11.2
overall average	13.3	14.2	11.4	16.4	9.2	8.6	9.2

5.4.2   Tax wedges

The tax wedge is the difference between the rate of return on investment and the rate of return on the savings used to finance the investment. The former is the pretax real rate of return net of depreciation (the cost of capital), which is the return society earns on a particular investment of one extra unit. The latter is the post-tax real rate of return to the saver who supplied the finance for the investment, which is to be treated as fixed. The tax wedge is an important indicator to measure the distortion (welfare cost) between saving and investment in a closed economy, and the capital flow (capital imports or capital exports) in an open economy.

The tax wedge on corporate source income can be divided between the corporate tax wedge and the personal tax wedge. The corporate tax wedge is defined as the difference between the pretax rate of return and the after corporate, before personal tax rate of return. Similarly, the personal tax wedge is defined as the difference between the after corporate, before personal tax rate of return and the post-tax rate of return. The sum of components associated with provisions of corporate and personal tax wedges is the tax wedge. Here, we analyze how changes in these tax wedges had been related to tax reforms.

First, the tax wedge on corporate source income was on average 13.3 percent in 1966, 14.2 percent in 1970, 16.4 percent in 1980, and 9.2 percent in 1990, as in Table 5.5. According to the tax wedge among three types of asset, the tax wedge of transportation equipment had been higher than those of other assets, and the tax wedge of machinery .and equipment had been on average almost the same as that of buildings and structures.

It is noticeable that the overall average tax wedge was reduced to less than 10 percent in 1980s from 16.4 percent in 1980. This rapid decrease in the tax wedge would be the result of the tax reforms in 1982 and 1986, and the sharp change in the direction of Korean policy for taxation of income from

Table 5.6: Personal tax wedge by types of asset

	1966	1970	1975	1980	1985	1989	1990
Buildings	-0.2	-1.2	-3.1	-3.1	-0.9	-0.7	-0.7
Machinery	-0.01	-1.2	-3.0	-3.5	-0.8	-0.7	-0.6
Transportation	-0.2	-0.08	-2.7	-2.0	-0.7	-0.5	-0.5
overall average	-0.07	-1.1	-3.0	-3.5	-0.8	-0.7	-0.6

capital. That is, the tax wedge was lowered in the 1980s by a continuous decrease in the cost of capital as we already analyzed.

Second, the personal tax wedge according to three types of asset had been negative, as in Table 5.6, although it was negligible. The high interest rate due to excess demand in the capital market and low personal capital income tax rate are inferred to result in the negative personal tax wedge. The personal tax wedge was narrowed in 1980s to the negligible amounts of -0.5 to -0.9 percent. This implies that the economic inefficiency personal income tax was relatively reduced in the 1980s, when the tax reforms in 1982 and 1986 induced remarkable changes in tax policy. In addition, the personal tax wedge has shown quite different discrepancies among sources of finance. The personal tax wedge of debt had been negative, since the personal income tax rate on interest income was less than the corporate tax rate. However, the personal tax wedge of new shares and retained earnings had been positive. The indicators of these results accord with the theoretical analysis of our model. The personal tax wedge of new shares had been in absolute values higher than those of other sources of finance, because the personal income tax rate on dividends had been higher than that on interest and the capital gains tax rate under the classical system. It is, however, noted that the overall average personal tax wedge had been negative, as in Table 5.6, since the ratio of debt to investment cost (α_1) was on average strictly greater than the ratio of new shares (α_2) and the ratio of retained earnings (α_3) to investment cost in three types of asset.

On the other hand, the corporate tax wedge had been slightly greater than the total tax wedge on corporate source income, but was rapidly reduced in the 1980s, see Table 5.7, by the tax reforms passed in 1982 and 1986. Hence, both the personal tax wedge and corporate tax wedge in the 1980s were lowered with to a noticeable margin in comparison with in the 1960s and 1970s. The abrupt change in tax wedge in the 1980s that resulted from tax reforms can be surmised to have feedback effects on domestic saving,

Table 5.7: Corporate tax wedge by types of asset

	1966	1970	1975	1980	1985	1989	1990
Buildings	13.7	16.3	13.6	19.5	10.6	8.9	8.7
Machinery	13.2	14.6	14.1	19.3	9.6	9.1	9.0
Transportation	13.8	17.3	18.0	24.5	12.5	11.8	11.6
overall average	13.4	15.3	14.4	19.9	10.0	9.3	9.8

investment, capital flow, and trade balance. Such interdependences are to be discussed in the following section.

5.4.3 Investment, saving, and capital flow

We already discovered that both the personal tax wedge and corporate tax wedge decreased in the 1980s along with the total tax wedge. In the theoretical point on the capital market of a small open economy facing a given international rate of interest, a rise of the corporate income tax rate will increase the corporate tax wedge, thereby reducing domestic investment and net capital imports. Korean tax reforms in the 1980s aimed to reduce the statutory corporate tax rate and eliminate tax preferences and so resulted in decreasing the corporate tax wedge. The role of the personal income tax rate merits particular attention also. An increase in the personal income tax on interest lowers the personal tax wedge in absolute values. And the personal income tax is also seen as a subsidy on real investment because it reduces the opportunity cost of funds retained in the firm, and increases the relative profitability of corporate investment financed by retained earnings, thereby reducing the corporate tax wedge. The higher the personal tax rate, the smaller is the investment tax wedge and the larger the firm's optimal level of investment. This particular interpretation of the personal income tax results in paradoxical changes in the allocation of the available aggregate capital stock. An increase in the personal income tax for owners of corporate shares induces a real allocation of the aggregate stock of capital from the noncorporate to the corporate sector, regardless of whether it is matched by a tax increase for the owners of noncorporate firms. In an open economy, one country's personal income tax rate would affect capital imports. The higher the personal income tax rate, the more profit would be retained by domestic companies for the purpose of internal investment and the less capital is available for reinvestment in the capital market. The shortage of funds boosts the domestic interest rate and attracts foreign capital. Via an appreciation of the domestic currency and the subsequent current account deficit, the foreign capital succeeds in entering the domestic economy and makes an increase in aggregate domestic investment possible.

A reduction of the corporate tax rate and a mild increase in the personal income tax on interest rate in the 1980s' tax reforms would be evaluated as decreasing both personal and corporate tax wedges, and thereby accelerated capital imports by the mid-1980s. The evidence for this analysis in Korea is supported from the statistics that a foreign debt was at a peak in the mid-1980s. However, the consistent reduction of the corporate tax wedge, the domestic interest rate being higher than the international rate of interest, and the rapid economic growth in the 1980s raised national savings in a steep rate in the late-1980s.

From 1986 the ratio of domestic savings to GDP exceeded the ratio of investment to GDP, and linked to current account surplus. The increase in demand for investment due to a reduction of the corporate tax wedge in the 1980s could be supplied by domestic savings. World Bank data show that Korea's national saving rose from just 8 percent of GDP in 1965 to 38 percent in 1988. Such an abrupt change in saving and investment at the turning point of the mid-1980s was influenced by tax reforms in the 1980s, which is shown in Figure 5.2. Before the mid-1980s capital imports were induced by the investment in excess of savings, but there was an excess of savings after the mid-1980s as savings and investment shifted upward $(S \to S', I \to I')$.

5.4.4 Effective tax rate

As we defined, the effective tax rate is the ratio of the tax wedge to the before tax of return (the cost of capital). On the basis of estimates of the tax wedge and the cost of capital, we analyze the structure of the effective tax rate according to industrial sectors, types of asset, and sources of finance. The effective tax rate is also divided into the effective personal tax rate and the effective corporate tax rate.

First, the effective tax rate in the corporate sector was high in the late 1960s and declined in the early 1970s, reaching bottom in 1973 after the 1972 emergency measure. It then increased from the mid-1970s to the early 1980s, dropped again in 1983, and was on a upward trend since the mid-1980s, as in Figure 5.3. The effective tax rate in each industry represented a similar trend to the corporate sector. The effective tax rate in the corporate sector was 32.7 percent in 1966, 45.4 percent in 1970, 38.0 percent in 1975, 41.0

rate of return

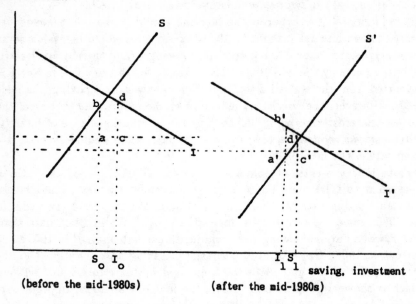

(before the mid-1980s)   (after the mid-1980s)

{ a b and a′ b′ : the personal tax wedges
{ c d and c′ d′ : the corporate tax wedges

Figure 5.2: Tax wedge, saving, and investment

percent in 1980, 39.2 percent in 1985, and 42.1 percent in 1990, as in Table
5.8. These effective tax rates in Korea had been lower than the nominal
corporate tax rate inclusive of surtaxes. When we trace out the trend of the
effective tax rate in all industries, an interesting discovery is the increasing
phase of it from the mid-1980s in spite of reductions in the cost of capital and
the tax wedge. We could find out the paradoxical changes of the effective tax
rate in relation to the cost of capital and the tax wedge. Here, the important
variable is how the after tax rate of return on savings responds to changes
in the cost of capital. In Korea after the mid-1980s the effective tax rate
increases under the reductions in the cost of capital and the tax wedge if,
and only if, the elasticity of the after tax rate of return on savings with
respect to the cost of capital is greater than one. In this context, the fact
that the after tax rate of return to saving was elastic, with respect to the
cost of capital, supported the upward trend of the effective tax rate since
the mid-1980s. The overall average effective tax rate increased by 10 percent
from 1966 to 1990.

Second, according to the effective tax rate in types of asset in the corporate sector, the effective tax rate of transportation equipment had been in
general higher than those of other assets, see Table 5.8. The effective tax
rate of machinery and equipment was lower than that of buildings and structures except for the period of 1975–78, 1980–82, and 1990. In particular, the
former has been uniformly lower than the latter in the manufacturing industry and the construction industry. However, in the agricultural, utilities,
and commerce sectors, the effective tax rate of buildings and structures has
been at its lowest. The effective tax rate of transportation equipment was
higher by 16 percent from 1966 to 1989, which exceeded the increase in the
overall average effective tax rate of 10 percent. In the 1980s both effective
tax rates of buildings and structures, and machinery and equipment were
very close to each other in relation to the cost of capital. And they had been
below the overall average effective tax rate since 1966.

Third, there have been structural changes in the effective tax rate among
industries. A contrasting case can be found between the mining industry and
the construction industry. The effective tax rate of the construction industry
even decreased from 42.6 percent in 1966 to 37.8 percent in 1990, becoming
part of the lowest group, while the mining industry had the low effective tax
rate of 29.3 percent in 1966, but showed up the highest effective tax rate at
54.2 percent in 1990. The utility sector was similar to the mining industry.
The agricultural sector and the service sector recorded a modest increase in
the effective tax rate. However, the manufacturing industry experienced a
large increase in the effective tax rate in the 1980s through the elimination

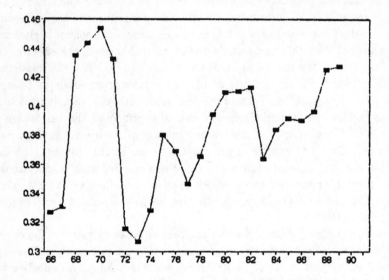

Figure 5.3: Effective tax rate (overall average)

Table 5.8: Effective tax rate by types of asset

	1966	1970	1975	1980	1985	1989	1990
Buildings	32.1	44.2	33.5	36.5	38.1	39.3	39.1
Machinery	31.3	40.9	37.9	38.1	36.4	40.2	40.1
Transportation	30.8	47.3	41.5	45.7	42.7	46.8	47.2
overall average	32.7	45.4	38.0	41.0	39.2	42.8	42.1

Table 5.9: Effective tax rate by industries

industry	1966	1970	1975	1980	1985	1989	1990
1	46.0	53.3	56.6	54.9	43.6	46.9	46.8
2	29.3	55.1	36.9	40.5	50.0	54.9	54.2
3	34.9	49.1	39.1	43.5	42.3	46.2	46.0
4	11.6	46.4	17.0	25.6	40.3	44.0	43.8
5	42.6	43.6	56.0	54.8	38.9	38.9	37.8
6	35.4	44.3	43.2	43.5	38.2	43.1	43.0
7	32.8	41.1	42.9	42.6	34.1	38.9	38.4
8	45.7	54.4	53.5	52.3	47.9	53.1	52.7
9	48.0	56.8	57.9	55.6	49.4	53.8	52.9
overall average	32.7	45.4	38.0	41.0	39.2	42.8	42.1

of tax incentives given to key manufacturing industries through tax reforms during the period. The gap between the lowest and the highest effective tax rates was reduced from 26.4 percent in 1966 to 16.4 percent in 1990. Hence, the tax reforms in the 1980s reduced the discrepancies of the effective tax rates among industries.

Fourth, since the tax system tends to favor debt finance, as pointed out in the cost of capital, the effective tax rate of debt had been negative, as in Table 5.10. And the effective tax rate on new shares was higher than that of retained earnings. As in the cost of capital, the discrepancies of the effective tax rates among sources of finance had been reduced from 1966 to 1989 through tax reforms in 1980s, when the negative effective tax rate of debt was lowered in absolute value.

Fifth, the effective tax rate can be reinterpreted by two components associated with provisions of corporate and personal taxes. The effective corporate tax rates provide the information for comparing incentives to investment in different types of asset and different industries. Differences among these tax rates indicate barriers to efficient allocation of capital among asset and industries. Similarly, the effective personal tax rates on income originating in the corporate sector are needed in order to compare incentives for saving through different financial instruments and different forms of ownership.

Differences among these tax rates indicate barriers to efficient allocation of capital among financial instruments and different forms of ownership. Due to the negative personal tax wedge shown in the previous section, the

Table 5.10: Effective tax rate by sources of finance

		1966	1970	1975	1980	1985	1989	1990
	debt	-26.3	-143.8	n/a	-181.0	-54.3	-52.9	-52.2
B	new sa.	69.9	76.0	77.5	75.6	72.1	73.4	73.1
	ret. ear.	37.5	46.4	47.9	47.6	43.4	43.8	43.5
	debt	-154.8	-236.3	n/a	-141.3	-135.8	-98.8	-96.5
M	new sa.	71.8	76.7	79.5	76.5	73.8	75.9	75.6
	ret. ear.	37.1	42.9	47.9	45.0	39.9	42.5	42.1
	debt	-248.2	-202.8	n/a	-118.3	-123.2	-77.5	-77.0
T	new sa.	73.0	79.4	82.0	79.2	77.5	79.5	79.4
	ret. ear.	38.6	49.9	55.9	53.1	47.7	50.3	50.0
	debt	-142.9	-173.4	n/a	-165.9	-104.9	-84.1	-75.2
A	new sa.	71.6	76.9	79.4	76.6	73.7	75.8	76.0
	ret. ear.	37.3	44.7	48.7	46.4	42.6	43.5	45.2

(B: buildings and structures; M: machinery and equipment;
T: transportation equipment; A: overall average)

Table 5.11: Effective corporate tax rate of assets

	1966	1970	1975	1980	1985	1989	1990
Buildings	50.0	65.2	80.0	72.5	56.1	58.2	58.8
Machinery	49.8	64.3	81.0	74.2	54.2	60.7	60.2
Transportation	52.5	65.5	93.3	78.0	61.9	67.0	67.3
overall average	48.2	60.2	80.0	69.3	52.4	52.8	62.1

Table 5.12: Effective personal tax rate of assets

	1966	1970	1975	1980	1985	1989	1990
Buildings	-35.8	-60.3	-232.5	-130.9	-41.0	-42.2	-42.0
Machinery	-36.9	-65.5	-226.8	-139.9	-38.9	-52.2	-52.4
Transportation	-45.9	-52.8	-273.1	-146.8	-50.4	-61.2	-61.5
overall average	-29.9	-37.2	-210.0	-92.2	-27.7	-21.2	-21.4

effective personal tax rate had been negative, while the effective corporate tax rate had been higher than the effective tax rate on corporate source income. The after tax rate of return to saving maintained high level due to the excess demand in the capital market and the dual interest structure between the formal financial market and the government policy to stimulate saving, resulting in the negative effective personal tax rate. Although the after tax rate of return to saving was on a downward trend in 1980s, it was still at a high rate. As in the effective tax rate, the effective corporate tax rate of transportation equipment had been also higher than those of other assets. The effective corporate tax rate showed on average a modest increase from 48.2 percent in 1966 to 62.1 percent in 1990, while the negative effective personal tax rate was, on average, reduced in the 1980s. Under the Korean tax policy of introducing tax preferences into the key industries and capital formation, there had been severe distortions in taxation between the corporate income and the personal income originating from the corporate sector by unsystematic tax treatment of income from capital.

5.5   Effect of inflation on effective tax rate

In the cost of capital and the effective tax rate the expected inflation rate is one of the important variables. In our estimate of them the expected inflation rate was projected on the past inflation rates.

Inflation has a complex series of effects on the cost of capital and the effective tax rate. First, a marginal investment has future depreciation allowances that are in general based on historical cost. Since inflation reduces the real value of these fixed nominal deductions, it tends to increase the effective tax rates. As inflation increases further, however, the real value of depreciation allowances falls at a reduced rate: only at an infinite rate of inflation does the real value of these deduction approach zero.

Table 5.13: Inflation and effective tax rate of asset

		1966	1970	1975	1980	1985	1989	1990
B	0(%)	21.8	35.0	27.2	30.7	34.8	35.9	36.0
	5(%)	25.5	38.8	29.8	33.1	38.9	39.6	39.7
M	0(%)	19.7	28.0	25.9	28.4	31.4	33.8	33.6
	5(%)	23.8	32.0	29.6	31.8	37.5	40.7	40.5
T	0(%)	18.7	33.8	28.5	35.0	37.2	39.7	39.8
	5(%)	22.9	37.9	32.4	38.6	43.9	47.4	47.5
A	0(%)	20.8	32.7	26.9	31.9	34.4	36.7	36.9
	5(%)	25.0	36.6	30.5	35.2	40.3	43.2	43.3

(B: building and structures; M: machinery and equipment;
T: transportation; inflation rate: 0%, 5%)

Second, inflation increases the nominal value of inventories. Under FIFO inventory accounting, taxable profits are measured by the difference between nominal sales price and nominal costs. Thus, for given real magnitudes, inflation tends to increase taxable profits and increase the effective tax rate.

Third, it is often the case that individuals are taxed on the nominal increase in the value of their shares when they realize them, and not their real value. Inflation will in this case require companies to provide a higher capital gain to shareholders, and it is modelled in this work by increasing the discount rate applied to retention finance. Hence, investment projects will need to earn a higher pretax return to be able to satisfy the ultimate financiers if capital gains are not indexed to inflation.

Fourth, inflation increases the nominal interest rate. Where nominal interest payments are deductible from the corporate income tax, inflation tends to increase these deductions and decrease the overall tax rate. Hence, inflation has mixed effects on the cost of capital and the effective tax rate. The inventory, capital allowance, and capital gains effects of inflation raise them, but the nominal interest deductibility effect lowers them. In order to simulate effects of inflation we estimate the overall cost of capital and the overall effective tax rate for inflation rates, varying from 0 to 5 percent. The simulation result is reduced to Table 5.13. The increase in inflation by 5 percent is simulated to raise the effective tax rate unambiguously by 5 to 7 percent. The variation of the effective tax rate due to higher inflation are different among assets. The effective tax rate of buildings and structures

Table 5.14: Inflation and effective tax rate in industries

		1966	1970	1975	1980	1985	1989	1990
1	0(%)	33.1	39.4	42.2	44.0	38.1	40.0	40.1
	5(%)	37.5	43.6	46.4	47.6	44.8	47.5	47.7
2	0(%)	15.5	40.4	24.4	30.5	44.3	47.6	48.5
	5(%)	20.4	44.9	28.5	34.1	51.3	55.4	56.7
3	0(%)	21.9	35.1	26.8	33.4	37.1	39.5	39.7
	5(%)	26.5	39.4	30.8	37.1	43.5	46.7	46.8
4	0(%)	8.8	33.9	11.8	19.1	35.3	37.6	37.8
	5(%)	13.6	37.9	14.8	22.0	41.4	44.5	44.6
5	0(%)	32.5	31.8	43.3	44.4	33.9	32.5	32.4
	5(%)	36.1	35.7	47.1	47.9	40.0	39.3	39.1
6	0(%)	21.7	31.4	32.4	35.2	33.4	37.2	37.1
	5(%)	26.4	35.5	36.0	38.3	39.2	43.6	43.5
7	0(%)	20.7	29.3	33.1	34.6	29.6	33.1	33.2
	5(%)	25.0	33.2	36.6	37.7	35.0	39.3	39.5
8	0(%)	30.8	40.0	40.0	42.6	42.6	46.6	46.7
	5(%)	35.8	44.4	44.4	45.9	49.1	53.6	53.8
9	0(%)	33.9	42.8	43.6	45.0	44.0	47.0	47.1
	5(%)	38.7	47.0	47.8	48.5	50.6	54.3	54.1

resulted in less increases than those of other assets, because the ratio of debt to investment cost in buildings and structures was on average higher than the ratio of new shares and the ratio of retained earnings.

Table 5.14 shows the effect of inflation on the overall effective tax rate in each industry. In all industries higher inflation is seen to increase the effective tax rate. It should be noted that the effective tax rate in any industry was more sensitive to inflation in the 1980s than the 1970s from the point when tax preferences were removed by tax reforms.

5.6   Effect of corporate tax on effective tax rate

The corporate tax rate has several direct effects on the effective tax rate. First, it affects the after tax profit, the debt-equity decision, the dividend payout decision, and the cash flow. Second, the corporate tax rate changes the deductibility of interest payments. Third, the tax savings from depreciation allowance is influenced by the corporate tax rate. In this context, changes in the corporate tax rate have pervasive and complex effects on the cost of capital and effective tax rate.

Table 5.15: Corporate tax reduction and effective tax rate in assets

	1966	1970	1975	1980	1985	1989	1990
Buildings	31.6	43.2	33.0	35.7	36.8	38.2	38.3
Machinery	30.5	39.5	36.5	36.9	34.9	38.8	38.9
Transportation	30.1	45.9	40.2	44.2	41.0	45.2	45.4
overall average	32.0	44.1	40.0	39.8	37.7	41.4	41.9

The results of a 5 percent reduction of the corporate tax rate (inclusive of surcharges) on the effective tax rate are summarized in Table 5.15 and Table 5.16. Comparing the effective tax rate under the actual corporate tax rate and a 5 percent reduction of it, we have a simulation result that the effective tax rate is unambiguously dropped by less than 2 percent in all assets. And the overall tax rate in each industry is also simulated to decrease by about 2 percent. Among all industries the construction industry shows the largest variation of the effective tax rate by a reduction of the corporate tax rate, which induces a more than 2 percent cut, while the effective tax rate in the service sector decreases by less than 1 percent, as in Table 5.16.

5.7   Concluding remarks

The purpose of this chapter is to discover the usefulness of the cost of capital approach in the relationship with tax reforms in Korea. As we pointed out Korea was a typical country to apply extensive tax preferences for capital formation and to key industries in the process of economic development. The tax incentives were received through a series of tax reforms. The major tax reforms were carried out in 1974, 1976, 1982, and 1986. The 1974 tax reform introduced an almost global personal income tax system, and major incentives divided among complex tax laws were unified under the article of "special tax treatment for key industries" in the Tax Exemption and Reduction Control Law. The tax reform in 1976 introduced the value added tax and the special excise taxes to settle down the current structure of consumption taxes. The 1982 tax reform under the principle of low taxes and low exemption streamlined the industrial tax incentive system as well

Table 5.16: Corporate tax reduction and effective tax rate in industries

industry	1966	1970	1975	1980	1985	1989	1990
1	44.7	51.8	54.5	52.9	41.8	45.3	45.4
2	29.3	53.7	36.8	40.2	48.4	53.4	53.6
3	34.3	47.7	38.1	42.4	40.7	44.6	43.7
4	11.8	44.7	16.9	25.3	38.3	42.1	42.3
5	40.6	41.1	53.4	52.1	36.4	36.3	36.7
6	34.6	43.5	41.3	41.9	36.8	42.0	42.1
7	31.5	39.7	40.5	40.4	32.2	37.2	37.5
8	45.1	53.8	52.1	51.1	46.7	52.2	51.8
9	47.1	55.9	56.2	54.0	48.1	52.6	51.9

as lowered the personal and corporate income tax rate. For example, tax holidays were completely repealed, and the investment tax credit was lowered to 6 percent for a limited number of industries. Finally, in 1986 the special treatment for key industries was abolished.

As for the Korean tax system, direct and indirect tax ratios have been closer recently, although tax revenue was traditionally heavily dependent on indirect taxes, and the proportion of local taxes will increase rapidly due to the greater local goverment autonomy granted in 1990.

The tax incentives introduced by tax reforms, in particular tax holidays, the investment tax credit, and special depreciation, were discovered to lower the cost of capital, but resulted in heightened discrepancies of tax burdens among different assets, sources of finance, and industries. In particular the emergency measure taken unexpectedly in 1972 had the strongest effects on the cost of capital and the effective tax rate, which were at their lowest for the last three decades in 1973–74.

In types of asset the cost of capital and the effective tax rate of machinery and equipment were in general lower than those of other assets. In source of finance the cost of capital and the effective tax rate from debt were much lower than those of other sources of finance, while retained earnings brought lower cost of capital and effective tax rate than new share issues. These discrepancies of tax burdens and the cost of capital were due to tax preferences for machinery and equipment, and debt. Among 9 aggregate industries the construction industry was in the low effective tax rate as well as low cost of capital in the 1980s, which was a drastic change compared to the 1960s, whereas the mining industry figures did the exact opposite.

In our analysis of tax wedges, the tax wedge of transportation equipment is greater than those of other assets. It is interesting to note that the personal tax wedges of all three assets were negative, although they were negligible. The negative personal tax wedge and thereby the negative effective personal tax rate were due to high a interest rate caused by excess demand in capital market and a low personal income tax rate intended to stimulate saving. In this context, there were severe distortions in taxation between the corporate income and the personal income originating from the corporate sector.

The tax reforms in 1982 and 1986 had special meanings in the cost of capital, the tax wedge, and the effective tax rate. Since the tax reforms were a sharp change in the direction of Korean policy for taxation of income from capital, the cost of capital and the tax wedge were noticeably reduced, and the gap in the cost of capital and effective tax rate between the highest industry and the lowest industry was narrowed in the 1980s. The reduction of the tax wedge through the tax reforms improved economic efficiency in the resource allocation between saving and investment, resulting in excess saving to domestic capital formation and capital exports in 1986–89 with a trade surplus.

6 International perspective

6.1 International new approach to tax reform

During the past decade the taxation of income from capital in industrialized countries has undergone a surprising series of reversals. The early 1980s saw a gradual shift from income to expenditure as the basis for taxation of capital income. At the corporate level the objective was to provide investment incentives, while at the personal level the goal was to stimulate saving. Earlier, several reports in industrialized countries (e.g., Sweden, the United States, the United Kingdom) proposed taking these developments to their logical conclusion by substituting expenditures for income as a basis of taxation at both corporate and personal levels. Tax incentives for investment were to accelerate capital consumption allowance and to offset tax liabilities by subsidies or grants for investment. In order to stimulate saving through tax policy, tax payers were permitted to establish tax-favored or tax-free accounts. The reversal in tax policies for capital income during the 1980s can be illustrated by the experience of the United States and the United Kingdom. The Tax Act of 1981 in the United States combined substantial reductions in statutory tax rates for individuals and corporations with sizable enhancements in investment incentives by adopting the Accelerated Cost Recovery System and the introduction of a 10 percent tax credit. The 1986 Tax Act substantially scaled up accelerated consumption allowances instead of eliminating tax preferences for both individuals and corporations, and repealing the investment credit. Similarly, the U.K. tax law in 1981 introduced immediate expensing of 75 percent of investment in industrial buildings with 100 percent expensing of manufacturing plant and machinery. The U.K. budget of 1984 phased out these tax incentives, and the corporate tax rate was continuously reduced from 52 percent in 1981 to 35 percent in 1986.

With the introduction of tax holidays in 1949, special depreciation in 1961, and the investment tax credit in 1967, Korean tax policy had incorporated a series of tax preferences for specific forms of capital income. These policy measures could stimulate capital formation by reducing the cost of capital. However, these tax incentives also heightened the discrepancies in tax burdens among different types of capital, and different sources of finance. These discrepancies gave rise to concerns about the impact of tax-induced distortions on the efficiency of capital allocation.

Therefore the tax reforms in 1980s were a sharp change in direction of the Korean policy of taxation of income from capital. Statutory tax rates were reduced in 1983, but the tax base was broadened by gradual elimination of tax preferences for corporations. This led to a sharp cutback in tax incentives for investment. The 1982 tax reform repealed tax holidays and cut the investment tax credit to 6 percent. Further, the 1986 tax reform abolished special treatments for key industries, while accelerated capital consumption allowances were substantially scaled back.

The Korean tax reform in 1986 as well as the U.K. budget for 1984 and the U.S. Tax Reform Act of 1986 halted the erosion of the income tax base by curtailing investment incentives and broadening the base for income taxes. This international new approach to tax reform of lowering tax rates and broadening the tax base was common to many OECD countries from the mid-1980s. For example, Australia in 1988, Canada in 1986, France in 1985, Germany in 1986, Japan in 1989, and Sweden in 1985. The additional revenues generated by broadening the base were used to reduce statutory tax rates at the corporate and personal levels. These rates were intended to reduce distortions in resource allocation.

In this work we will compare how such tax reform affects the recent effective tax rates in OECD countries as well as Korea, and analyze in detail the interactions between a series of tax reforms and the cost of capital in Korea. Since the cost of capital approach originates from Jorgenson (1963), the cost of capital and the effective tax rate were combined in the marginal effective tax rate by Auerbach and Jorgenson (1980), and the international comparison of the effective tax rates was followed by King and Fullerton (1984). On the basis of their analytic methodology our model is extended to investigating the tax reforms and tax policies in Korea and OECD countries. Since Korea introduced extensive tax incentives in the process of economic development and for sustaining economic growth, the analysis on the international perspective for the Korean tax reform and the cost of capital might generate valuable information transferable to other countries.

We have already investigated the Korean tax reform and tax system in the

Chapter 3, and the comparison of recent tax reforms and tax schemes among OECD countries and Korea is presented in Section 2 of this chapter. In Section 3 the analytic model is presented, and in Section 4 the international comparison of the cost of capital and the effective tax rate is shown. The analytic results on the cost of capital and the effective tax rate in Korea and OECD countries, and some implications of the international perspective on the Korean tax reform are abstracted in Section 5.

6.2 International comparison of tax reform and tax scheme

The tax reform on personal and corporation income has over recent years been a major preoccupation in many OECD countries. Personal and corporate tax systems have been criticized on the grounds of their alleged adverse effects on investment and savings, creating distortions in the international allocation of capital, complexity, and their lack of neutrality between corporate investment and activities of the unincorporated sector.

Here we have briefly outline how OECD countries have changed their tax schemes in the 1980s in order to mitigate these problems. As we already pointed out, the common characteristics of tax systems in most of OECD countries were to curtail investment incentives, to broaden the base for income taxes, and thereby to reduce statutory tax rates at the corporate and personal levels since the mid-1980s. Before summarizing each country's tax scheme, let's trace out some interesting points shared in those countries. First, among 24 OECD countries personal and corporation income taxes are integrated in 8 of them, partially integrated in 9, and not integrated in 7 countries. The majority of OECD countries are gradually moving toward the imputation system. Second, although both overall corporate tax rates and overall personal tax rates were lowered, the overall tax rates are widely different among the countries. For example, in the overall corporate tax rate, Germany and Norway is higher than 50 percent; in Canada, Finland, Greece, Iceland, Ireland, Japan, Italy, and Turkey it is 40–50 percent; The other countries are at 30–40 percent. In particular, Sweden has the lowest tax rate at 30 percent, and France, New Zealand, and the United Kingdom are all relatively low at less than 35 percent. Third, many countries have eliminated general investment allowance and general investment tax credit. However, some countries still maintain those tax incentives. For example, general investment credit is still available in Spain and Luxembourg; investment reserve is provided in Finland, Iceland, and Sweden; investment allowance is available in Austria, Belgium, Greece, Netherlands, and Turkey. Fourth, personal tax on interests and dividends in Ireland and Canada is imposed at a high rate, while Belgium, Iceland, and Turkey apply a low tax rate on them. Interest income is completely exempt in Iceland. Most of OECD countries except for Austria, Denmark, and Spain impose higher tax rate on dividends than interests. However, Australia, Germany, Portugal, Sweden, Switzerland, and Turkey are taxing at the same rate on both incomes. Fifth, some countries, Belgium, France, Germany, Greece, Luxembourg, Netherlands, New Zealand, and Switzerland, do not impose capital gains tax on shares, but Denmark, Finland, and Iceland tax it at a rate higher than 50 percent. On the other hand, corporate capital gains are taxed except for New Zealand. Although many OECD countries do not impose net wealth taxes on corporations and individuals, the tax rate is in general less than 1 percent. Sixth, machinery and buildings are depreciated by declining balance or straight-line method, and a switch over from the former to the latter is allowed only in some countries. In the methods of valuating cost of inventories many OECD countries prefer FIFO to LIFO. Finally, all OECD countries have deducted interest payments from corporate taxes.

Now we shall investigate tax reforms and tax schemes briefly in OECD countries.

Australia changed the way in which corporate source income was taxed in 1985 by replacing the previous classical tax arrangement with a system of full imputation. The company tax rate in Australia was reduced from 49 percent in 1985 to 39 percent in 1988, which is now well below the top marginal personal tax rate of 47 percent. The 1988 tax reform broadened the tax base by abolishing an accelerated (5/3) depreciation. However, a tax on capital gains was applied to real gains on realization from 1985, and the net capital gains are included in the taxpayer's taxable income and taxed at the nominal income tax rates. Gains on principal residence are excluded. Under the retirement measures announced in the 1989–90 budget, the Australian government is to introduce major changes for a better integrated system of social security and tax administration for age and service (veteran) pensioners. Under existing arrangements, by means of pensioner rebate that is progressively withdrawn above a threshold of income, full-rate pensioners are removed from income tax liability and the liability of part-rate pensioners is deducted. From 1995, this rebate will be increased for age and service pensioners so that part-rate pensioners in these categories will be removed from income tax liability and subject only to the 50 percent withdrawal rate on their income-tested pensions, with the rebate being withdrawn beyond the pension cut-out income level. Personal income taxes are scheduled from 0 percent to 47 percent.

In *Austria* personal and corporation income taxes are not fully integrated. However, distributed profits are taxed at half the progressive personal income tax rate. The overall tax rate of corporate income was reduced to 39 percent in 1990. Interest on loans economically connected with any type of taxable income or used for the purchase of business assets is deductible. Long-term debt is not deductible for the computation of the tax base for the business tax. Capital gains are now included in the taxable income, and depreciation is allowed by the straight-line method. Under certain conditions the gain on fixed assets can be charged against the sale of new assets in the same or the next three years, but the assets should be held at least seven years. An investment deduction of 20 percent is available on depreciable assets, and the eligible transport equipment rate is 10 percent. A special tax-free investment reserve of 10 percent of taxable profits less the investment deduction may be set up. Within 4 years this reserve must be used to purchase assets which qualify for the investment deduction. After 4 years the unused reserves plus 20 percent must be included in taxable profits. For each year the reserve is dissolved earlier the 20 percent surcharge is lowered by 5 percentage points. Individuals are subject to a tax on their net wealth of 1 percent a year. Personal tax rates are distributed between 10 percent and 50 percent.

Belgium does not integrate personal and corporate income taxes. However, the withholding tax on dividends is the final tax paid unless the taxpayer elects otherwise. The overall tax rate of corporate income is 39 percent, and the dividends are subject to the withholding tax of 25 percent. Capital gains realized within 5 years of the acquisition are taxed as ordinary income. The investment allowance can be taken in the year of investment or spread over the depreciation period. The base for the investment allowance depends on the inflation in the preceding year increased by 1 percent. Machinery and buildings are depreciated by straight line, and switch-over from declining balance to straight line is mandatory at the optimum point. Inventories are valued at cost price or replacement value, and the LIFO method is not permitted unless it approximates actual physical flows. Tax-free reserves can amount to 5 percent of the profits of the relevant year and may not exceed 7.5 percent of the highest profit made in the previous years.

During the 1970s and 1980s, *Canada* increased a degree of integration between corporate and personal income taxes through the dividend tax credit, and took a gradual shift from an annual income-based tax system to an expenditure-based tax system. For example, Canada introduced the tax-exempt saving through registered pension plan and registered saving plans, the 1,000 dollar investment income deduction, and the 3-year write off for expenditures on machinery and equipment in manufacturing and processing. Capital gains are included in taxable income at different rates according to the realization time, and depreciation is based on declining balance. The general investment tax credit was phased out from 1989 by the 1986 tax reform, while only regional investment tax credit and credits for R & D expenditures are retained at reduced rates. Trading stock in inventories valued at cost price, selling price or replacing value. Cost price can be determined by FIFO and the average cost method. The federal government levies a tax on the net wealth of the capital of deposit-taking institutions and life insurance companies at the rate of 1–1.25 percent. The overall tax rate is 35.74 percent for large corporations, and 20.24 percent for small corporations. Personal income is less progressively taxed from 17 percent to 29 percent. The joint federal-provincial marginal tax rates are on average 39.5 percent on interest income, 44.6 percent on dividends, and 10.5 percent on capital gains.

In *Denmark* personal and corporation income taxes are not fully integrated, and dividend income is subject to schedular tax at a lower rate than other kinds of income. The overall tax rate is 38 percent, and interest receipts are treated as ordinary income. Capital gains are exempted if held more than 3 years, while capital gains on real estate are exempt after 7 years. From 3 to 7 years the gains are taxed at a lower rate. Investment tax credit was phased out, and trading stock in inventories is valued at cost price by FIFO. Machinery is depreciated by a declining balance, and buildings by a straight-line method. Individuals are subject to a tax on net wealth of 1 percent. The weighted average marginal rates of personal income tax on dividends and interest are 37.6 percent and 51.1 percent respectively.

In *Finland* personal and corporation income taxes are integrated by a full imputation system. As a result distributed corporate income will be taxed according to the marginal tax rate of individual shareholders. The average overall tax rate of a company is 40.2 percent, and the overall tax rate in Helsinki is 39 percent. Capital gains are taxed as ordinary income, where capital gains on real estate and security are taxed differently. If security is owned for less than 5 years and real estate is owned for less than 10 years, the difference between 60 percent of the sale proceeds of such assets and the book value is added into taxable income and taxed at the normal income tax rates. Depreciation is based on declining balance, and investment tax credit is phased out. Trading stock is valued at acquisition price, cost price, or net selling price. Cost price can be determined by FIFO. Accelerated depreciation is allowed if economic life of asset is shorter. Finnish companies are entitled to several reserves, and the most important ones are operating reserves (maximum 30 percent of percent of wage and salary payment during the previous 12 months), reserve for future investments (20 percent of profits), and (maximum 25 percent of year-end inventory). Personal income tax is less progressive between 7 percent and 39 percent. The effective tax rates are 45.2 percent on dividends, 10 percent on interest income, and 5 percent on capital gains.

Unlike other countries *France* imposes income tax on a territorial basis, and only income sourced in France is subject to tax. From 1965 to 1985, the tax on corporate profits was levied at a rate of 50 percent, but it was steadily reduced to 37 percent in 1990. Personal and corporation income taxes are not fully integrated. However, distributed profits carry a tax credit to avoid double taxation. Capital gains for shorter term are taxed at 34 percent, capital gains for long term are taxed at 19 percent, and capital gains from the sale of bonds and on building sites are taxed at 25 percent. The standard type depreciation is the straight-line method, but accelerated depreciation on declining balance with a switch over to straight-line is allowed for equipment with a useful life of at least 3 years and for buildings having a useful life of under 15 years. Inventories are valued at the lower of historic cost or market value by FIFO. Interest income is treated as ordinary income. France had employed tax incentives to encourage investment. For example, a tax credit in 1975 applied to all assets to be depreciated on the basis of the declining balance, a tax deduction of 10 percent in 1981–82 for capital expenditure on equipment and some commercial buildings, and a new tax deduction in 1983–85 for capital expenditure on equipment were allowed. But the investment incentives were gradually limited to R & D from 1985. All R & D expenses other than depreciable assets are deductible in the year they occur, and a tax credit for research expenses is available. Reserve for investment abroad since 1988 and reserve for commodity market fluctuation are allowed. The net wealth tax is levied on wealth of other business assets from 0.5 percent. Personal income taxes are relatively progressively imposed between 5 percent to 56.8 percent. The average marginal tax rate on dividends is relatively high at 45 percent, while that on interest is very low at 5.6 percent. Capital gains on bonds are taxed at 16 percent if the total value of the sale is more than FF 307,600.

With the Law of Economic Stabilization and Growth in 1967, *Germany* introduced a special tax treatment to mitigate cyclical fluctuations of the economy. For example, during three recessions (1967, 1974–75, 1982–83) temporary reliefs for investment, especially tax-free investment grants, were applied. At the beginning of the 1970s, under the Investment Tax Law, tax-free investment grants were also introduced to speed up structural adjustment in a variety of areas such as energy saving, environmental protection, and regional policy. In the meantime some of these investment measures have been abolished or substituted by other policy tools. Regarding the general tax system, the main changes during the past 25 years were the reform of the corporate tax system with the introduction of full imputation in 1976, and a major income tax cut in 1975 and during the period 1986–1990. Hence personal and corporation income taxes are fully integrated. The most recent tax reform proceeded to lower tax rates and broaden the tax base, resulting in the biggest income tax cut. Compared to other countries, however, the income tax rate remains high, with the personal income tax rate reduced from 56 percent to 53 percent and the corporate tax rate from 56 percent to 50 percent. Further, the corporate tax rate for retained earnings is still the highest among OECD countries – reduced to about 45 percent in 1992. General depreciation allowances improved substantially in 1978 for equipment investment and in 1985 for business construction, and have remained unchanged. In addition, there are several investment incentives available for regional areas, Berlin, and border areas. Inventories are valued at cost price or market value, whichever is lower, by FIFO. The average marginal tax rate on interest and dividends in 1990 is 39.1 percent. Capital gains are exempt from tax, though there are a few exceptions: gains on the sale of land owned less than 2 years and other assets less than 6 months are taxed at the nominal income tax rates. Personal income tax rates are scheduled from 19 percent to 53 percent.

In *Greece* personal and corporation income taxes are fully integrated, and thereby dividends are fully deductible. The overall tax rate of corporation income tax is 46 percent. Capital gains from the sale of business assets are taxed as ordinary income, but capital gains from immovable property for business, the sale of machinery, and the sale of securities are exempted. Depreciation is based on straight-line, and accelerated depreciation up to 150 percent of the ordinary depreciation rates in some regions is applied to machinery. There are several investment tax credits for regional development amounting to 100 percent of the investment values. Mergers in the manufacturing, handicraft, mining, and quarrying enterprises, whose legal form is other than a limited company, are entitled to a partial exemption. Ten percent of the total net profits shown in the balance sheet are exempt from tax. Trading stock in inventories is valued at cost price or fair market value, whichever is lower. Cost price can be determined by FIFO, and the LIFO method is permitted. Individuals' interest income is included in their taxable income, but the interest received from government and bank deposits is exempted from income tax. Personal income taxes are distributed from 18 percent to 50 percent. Capital gains resulting from the sale of securities are tax-exempt.

According to *Iceland*'s tax law, personal and corporation income taxes are not fully integrated, where dividends received from corporations up to 15 percent of the total amount of shares owned by the individual and dividend payments of corporations up to 15 percent of total value of shares are deductible. The overall income tax rate is 45 percent. Interest receipts are treated as ordinary income, and capital gains on assets fall under the corporate income tax system, regardless of the year of acquisition. Depreciation of machinery and buildings is based on straight-line, and inventories are valued at cost price allowing for inflation by FIFO. Capital gains from the sale of securities and shares are subject to full taxation. Companies can allocate 10 percent of their net profits to an investment fund on the condition that 50 percent of the amount will be deposited in a special bank account within 5 months from the end of the accounting year. Iceland's personal income tax system has only one tax rate, i.e., the total marginal tax rate is 39.8 percent, made up of a 32.8 percent central government tax rate and a 7.0 percent local government tax rate. Personal interest income is fully exempt from taxation. The average marginal tax rate of dividends is estimated to be around 15.8 percent, and that of capital gains is approximately 20 percent. Capital gains from the sale of a residence held for a period of less than 5 years are fully taxable, and capital gains from the sale of other assets, including securities and shares, are subject to full taxation regardless of the period of ownership.

In *Ireland* personal and corporation income taxes are partially integrated, and the company tax rate was reduced from 43 percent in 1989 to 40 percent in 1991. Interest receipts are treated as investment income except where they are received in the course of a banking or similar trade, and companies are liable to corporate tax in respect of their capital gains. Depreciation of machinery is based on declining balance, but buildings are depreciated by the straight-line method. Although no investment credits are available, several investment incentives apply at different rates for present capital expenditure from the Industrial Development Authority. For example, for a company which is expanding its existing plant in Ireland, the maximum capital grant is 25 percent of the cost of eligible fixed assets, and if the project is new, the upper limit is 45 percent of the cost of eligible fixed assets. Trading stock of inventories is valued at cost price or market value whichever is lower. Cost price can be determined by FIFO. From 1990 the classification of personal income was simplified into three categories, with tax rates of 30, 48, and 53 percent, lowered to 29, 48, and 52 percent.

Italy has a full imputation system, and the rate of imputation is equal to the corporate tax rate. The major Italian tax reform in the post-war period occurred in 1973–74. A fully progressive personal income tax was introduced, and several indirect taxes were replaced by a single income tax on corporation. In the 1980s the tax system also changed to finance growing deficits under the growth of the public sector. Hence, the tax system to reduce the government's deficit broadened the base of many taxes and raised those taxes perceived as providing high yields. Tax revenue from the corporation tax was low during the late 1970s and the early 1980s, but has increased rapidly in recent years. Italy has introduced tax reliefs and investment grants in the Mezzogiorno (the Southern and relatively less developed part of Italy) and interest subsidies to industrial loans, although in coming years most of current incentives will probably be repealed in order to comply with EC directives. The overall tax rate is 47.83 percent, and interest receipts are treated as ordinary income. Capital gains are taxed at the corporation income tax rate, and a tax rate of 25 percent is levied on capital gains from the sale of shares. Machinery and buildings are depreciated by straight-line. Inventories are valued at cost price or market price by FIFO or LIFO. Personal income tax rates are scheduled from 10 percent to 50 percent. The average marginal tax rates on dividends, interest, and capital gains are 39.4 percent, 12.5 percent, and 25.0 percent respectively.

In *Japan* a comprehensive taxation of income was a principle in the period of the famous Shoup reform after World War II. However, the principle of comprehensive income taxation has been gradually eroded since then so that householders were able to choose between comprehensive income taxation and separate taxation on each source of income. Moreover, tax-free savings account within a certain limitation were allowed in order to promote higher savings. In 1989, the tax-free saving account was abolished, and a separate 20 percent withholding tax rate was introduced to tax the interest incomes. Personal and corporation income taxes are not fully integrated. A shareholder is allowed to deduct 10 percent of his dividends from the personal income tax, where the ordinary taxable income including dividends does not exceed 10 million Yen. The overall corporate tax rate is 49.98 percent, and a special capital gains tax is imposed on land and land rights. Capital gains are generated at the corporation income tax rates or at the normal income tax rates after a reduction of 500,000 Yen, and capital gains from the sale of certain stocks are subject to separate taxation at 20 percent through the filing of a final return. The taxpayer is allowed to switch over from the declining balance rate to the straight-line method in depreciation, where all assets can be depreciated up to 95 percent of the acquisition costs. The excess of the largest R & D expenses since 1967 can be credited against national corporate income tax for 20 percent with a maximum of 10 percent of that tax until March 31 1993. A small company (share capital less than 100 million Yen) can deduct from national corporate tax 6 percent of R & D instead of the 20 percent increment in R & D. The average marginal income tax rates on dividends and interest are 35 percent and 20 percent respectively.

Luxembourg does not have an integrated system of personal and corporation income taxes, and interest receipts are treated as ordinary income. The overall corporate income tax rate is 39.39 percent, and the withholding tax in dividends to shareholders is 15 percent. Capital gains are taxed at the standard corporation tax rate or at the normal income tax rate if real estate is sold within two years and gains on other property is sold within six months. If a shareholder sells more than 25 percent of his interest in a company, he is liable for half the income tax rate. The same rate applies to real estate sold after two years. The taxpayer has the option to switch over from the declining balance to the straight-line method of depreciation. Accelerated depreciation can be applied to machinery in the first year or in any of the following four years or may be spread over the first five years. An investment tax credit of 12 percent is accorded for additional investment in tangible depreciable assets other than buildings. The tax credit is calculated on the amount by which such an investment exceeds the previous five years' average. An additional tax credit between 2 to 6 percent is accorded on the purchase price of qualifying assets (tangible depreciable assets other than buildings) acquired over the year. Inventories are valued at cost price or selling value by FIFO. The average marginal taxes of personal income tax on dividends, interest, and capital gains are 24 percent.

In *Netherlands* personal and corporation income taxes are not integrated, and the overall corporation tax rate is 35 percent. Capital gains for the corporate sector are taxed at the corporation income tax rate, but capital gains for individuals are normally not taxed. Switch over from declining balance to straight-line and vice versa is allowed unless the only purpose of the switch over is obtaining a temporary fiscal benefit. Inventories are valued at cost price or any sound business practice by FIFO, LIFO, or the base-stock method. There is no investment tax credit. However, for certain small-scale investments, some percentage of the investment is deductible. The percentage varies from 2 percent to 18 percent, depending on the amount of investment. A wealth tax of 0.8 percent is levied on the net wealth of individuals. Taxable personal income after deduction of basic standard reliefs is classified by 3 categories, and taxed at 13 percent, 50 percent, and 60 percent. The average marginal tax rates of dividends and interest are relatively high at 49 percent and 42 percent respectively.

New Zealand introduced a new form of indirect taxation from October 1 1986, called Goods and Service Tax. This coincided with a lowering of the personal tax rate, and applied to most of the goods and services consumed in New Zealand. The basic rate of Goods and Service Tax is now 12.5 percent. The imputation system of personal and corporation income taxes came into effect on April 1 1988, and the overall corporate tax rate is 33 percent. Capital gains are not taxed with the exception of real estate property, and the taxpayer is allowed to switch from declining balance to straight-line but not vice versa. Trading stock in inventories is valued at cost price or replacement value by FIFO, average cost, standard cost, or retail inventory. Machinery and buildings are depreciated by the straight-line method, and the taxpayer is allowed to switch from declining balance to straight-line. R & D costs can be depreciated in the year they occur. The taxable income is classified by 2 categories, whose tax rates are 24 percent and 33 percent. The average marginal income tax rates on dividends and interest are 28.6 percent and 25.9 percent.

In *Norway* personal and corporation income taxes are fully integrated, except for the tax equalization fund when the shareholders are personal tax-payers. The overall corporate tax rate is 50.8 percent, and capital gains are taxed at the corporation income tax rate or are included in taxable income except for the gains on shares. Machinery and buildings are depreciated by a declining balance. Inventories are valued at cost price, selling value, or replacement value, not exceeding the lesser of cost or market value, and de-termined by FIFO. Investment tax credits were given in certain regions of Norway and for certain types of investment, such as environment-improving assets. However, they were abolished in 1991 as part of the tax reform in 1992. Norway applies tax-free reserves: resident companies can allocate 23 percent of net profits as calculated for the local income tax purposes to a consolidation reserve, and tax- free reserving may be created by mining en-terprises, enterprises recently engaging in a business, and for investment in northern Norway and areas of high unemployment.

Although *Portugal* does not integrate personal and corporation income taxes, distributed profits carry a tax credit to avoid double taxation. The overall corporate tax rate is 39.6 percent, and interest receipts are treated as ordinary income. Capital gains for the corporate are included in tax-able income, while capital gains from bonds, shares, and certificates are tax-exempt. Machinery and buildings are depreciated by the straight-line method, and inventories are valued at cost price determined by FIFO or LIFO. The personal income tax rates are imposed from 25 percent to 40 percent. The average marginal taxes on interest, dividends, and capital gains are 20–25 percent, 25 percent, and 10 percent respectively.

In *Spain* personal and corporation income taxes are not fully integrated, and the taxpayer can deduct 10 percent of dividends received from his personal income tax. The overall corporate tax rate is 35.34 percent, and the investment tax credit of 5 percent can be taken in the first year on the acquisition of a new asset. For certain assets and expenses used for export activities the tax credit is 15 percent. Capital gains for the corporate are taxed at the corporation income tax rates if not reinvested, while capital gains for individuals are divided by the number of year it is held or five years if the holding period is unknown. Machinery and buildings are generally depreciated by straight-line based on estimated lives of asset, and inventories are valued at cost price by FIFO. A tax credit of 15 percent for intangible and 30 percent for investment in fixed assets is available for expenditure in R & D. Plant and machinery used for R & D can be depreciated in five years. Buildings used in R & D can be depreciated in 7 years. Individuals are subject to a wealth tax from 0.2 percent to 2.0 percent. Personal income taxes are scheduled between 25 percent to 56 percent. The average marginal income tax rates on dividends and interest are 28.4 percent and 31.5 percent respectively.

In *Sweden* household taxes on dividends and interests were high, while the corporate tax system provided generous investment incentives to industries. The tax reform enacted in 1982 to be fully implemented by 1985 was designed to cut marginal income tax rates for the majority of full-time wage earners to a maximum of 50 percent, and to limit the value of interest deduction for earners in the higher marginal rate brackets to 50 percent. In this sense, the principle of combining cuts in tax rates with a broadening of the tax base was introduced through the 1982–85 tax reform in Sweden. This principle was further extended in 1990 to the corporate taxes. The tax reform in 1990 implemented in 1991 was designed to be revenue neutral and involved a substantial cut in statutory tax rates and a broadening of the tax base by eliminating or narrowing the extensive range of deductions and loopholes available to both householders and industries. It included a revocation of the time-honored scheme of stimulating investment, the investment fund system, and the possibility of undervaluing stock of inventories. Taxation on dividends, interest income, and capital gains replaced the regular individual income tax with a new proportional tax of 30 percent.

The value added tax was also broadened to include goods and services previously exempted or granted lower rates. The overall corporate tax rate is 30 percent, and machinery is depreciated at 30 percent by declining balance, whereas buildings are at 2–5 percent a year by straight-line. Cost price of inventories is determined by FIFO. Corporations may allocate funds to a tax equalization reserve, to be based on the corporations' equity capital, to a maximum of 30 percent. An alternative reserve option, normally preferable to corporations with a small equity, is a maximum of 15 percent of the corporations' gross payroll minus social costs. All kinds of capital incomes, including interest, dividends, and capital gains, are taxed separately from other income. A proportional flat rate of 30 percent is applied (no basic allowance), and therefore the average marginal taxes on these incomes are 30 percent.

In *Switzerland* personal and corporation income taxes are not integrated, and the overall income tax rate (Zurich) consisting of federal income tax, state income tax, local income tax and church income tax, ranges between 13.15 percent and 38.36 percent. Capital gains on immovable property are taxed by all cantons, whose tax rate depends on the holding period, but capital gains on movable assets are not taxed provided that they are not realized as a part of a business. In that case they are taxed at the normal income tax rate. Machinery and buildings are depreciated by the straight-line method or the declining balance rate. Inventories are valued at the purchase price, or if lower, the market price, and are determined by LIFO or FIFO. In particular, withholding taxes on interests and dividends are imposed at relatively high rate of 35 percent, and pension funds are tax-exempt. The average marginal tax rates on dividends and interest are both 30.8 percent.

In *Turkey* personal and corporation tax rates are integrated in the sense that no personal tax is charged on dividends distributed out of profit which have borne corporation tax. A withholding tax of 10 percent is applied to profits exempt from corporation tax. The overall corporate tax rate is 49.2 percent, and interest receipts are treated as ordinary income. Capital gains are taxed at the corporation income tax rate, and profit derived from the sales of movable and immovable assets related to the commercial enterprise are subject to the normal income tax rate. A switch-over from declining balance to straight-line is allowed. Trading stock in inventories is valued at cost price and determined by FIFO. Turkey has three major investment incentives. For example, investment allowance is provided at 30–100 percent for investment over TL 1 billion (TL 250 million in priority areas), export incentives exempt 18 percent of certain export profit from the corporate profit tax, and free zones are allowed for exemption from import duties and taxes on imported machinery and equipment. In addition, an investment fund can be reserved to set up for investment: the corporation can deposit 25 percent of its profits in an account at the Central Bank, and if invested in government securities an interest rate of 20 percent is paid. The withholding tax rate on interest is 10 percent, and the average rates of income tax on dividends and capital gains are 10 percent and 27 percent respectively.

In the early 1980s the *United Kingdom* experienced a temporary shift from an income-based tax system to an expenditure-based tax system. In 1981 immediate expensing of 75 percent of investment in industrial buildings and structures was introduced in along with 100 percent expensing of manufacturing plant and machinery previously incorporated into U.K. tax law. However, the course of the U.K. tax system was abruptly reversed in 1984, and the trend towards an expenditure-based corporate tax system was abandoned in favor of a return to an income-based system. Here we note that the most obvious consequences were a progressive reduction in the marginal corporate tax rate from 52 percent to 35 percent (33 percent in 1991), a phasing-out of the expenditure treatment of investments, and a further reduction in the marginal personal tax rates to 25 percent for a low income and 40 percent for a high income. For the year 1991–92 the government cut poll tax level, financed by a rise in the standard rate of value added tax from 15 percent to 17.5 percent. The U.K. has a partial imputation system of corporate tax, and the shareholder can credit part of the corporate tax imposed on distributed profits against his personal income tax liability. The system of taxing capital gains (formally separate from the income tax) experienced radical change over the decade. Since the abolition of all higher rates of income tax above the first 40 percent in 1988, capital gains of an individual are added to income and taxed at each individual's marginal income tax rate of either 25 percent or 40 percent, where previously it was 30 percent. Machinery is depreciated at 25 percent by a declining balance rate, and buildings are depreciated at 4 percent by a straight-line method. Accelerated depreciation can be used for plant and buildings employed in scientific research, and the taxpayer is allowed to depreciate any expenditure at 100 percent in the year they occur. Inventories are valued at the lower of cost price or market price, and determined by FIFO. In particular, a new tax-exempt form of savings aimed at small savers was effective in 1991. The personal income tax rates are simplified into 25 percent and 40 percent. The estimated average marginal tax rate on interest, dividends, and capital gains are 24 percent, 32 percent, and 33 percent respectively.

In the *United States* tax rules have changed almost yearly since 1980. In particular, the Economic Recovery Tax Act of 1981 reduced marginal tax rates and introduced a 10 percent investment tax credit with adoption of the Accelerated Cost Recovery System, while the Tax Reform Act of 1986 reduced marginal tax rates, repealed the investment tax credit, and lengthened depreciation lifetimes. The overall corporate tax rate was lowered from 49.5 percent to 38.3 percent by the 1986 Act, while the top statutory corporate tax rate was reduced from 46 percent to 34 percent. Further, the personal income tax rates (combined federal and state marginal tax rates) on wage, interest, and dividends were also lowered to 27.1 percent, 22.4 percent, and 32 percent respectively in 1990. The federal income tax rate is 15 percent, 28 percent, or 31 percent, according to the income level, where state and local income taxes add approximately 5 percentage points. Since personal and corporation income taxes are not integrated in the United States, dividends are taxed as ordinary income. In addition, capital gains are also taxed as ordinary income, and inventories are valued at cost price, selling value or replacement value. Cost price can be determined by FIFO, where the LIFO method is permitted. The taxpayer may switch over from declining balance to straight-line. The average marginal rates of personal income tax on dividends, interest, and capital gains are 31 percent, 28 percent, and 7 percent respectively.

Related to our discussions on tax schemes in OECD countries, we would like to abstract some characteristics of Korean tax schemes. Korea doesn't have the imputation system, and thereby the personal tax rate on dividends (10–30 percent) is much lower than the average tax rate on them in OECD countries. Although interest receipts are included in taxable income, the personal tax rate on interest is also taxed at a rate of 10–20 percent lower than that in OECD countries. However, the overall corporate tax in Korea, 45 percent in the 1960s, 53 percent in the 1970s and 43.8 percent in the 1980s, belongs to the higher group of OECD countries. Wealth taxes and capital gains taxes on shares transactions have not been imposed, and machinery and buildings are depreciated by declining balance. Inventories are valued at cost price or market price. Cost price can be determined by FIFO, and the LIFO method is also permitted.

6.3 The analytic model

Since the framework to present the cost of capital approach to the analysis of tax policy for capital income was developed by Jorgenson in 1963, there has been widespread use of the cost of capital approach integrated into the marginal effective tax rate. This methodology has been pervasively used for the evaluation of domestic tax policy related to tax reform and the international comparison of corporate and personal tax policy. The first successful international comparison of the taxation of income from capital was compiled by King and Fullerton (1984). The analytic model in this chapter has extended their models to include the country-specific tax system.

6.3.1 Cost of capital according to sources of finance

We will first derive the formulas of cost of capital according to sources of finance, which take into account taxes on personal capital income. Now, we assume that investors expect a minimum rate of return (ρ^*) to their investment. The investors receive from the firm the dividend income D and the capital gains. Dividend and capital gains are assumed to be taxed at the rates θ and c, respectively. New shares amounting to V^N are assumed to be issued or repurchased, and the capital gains received by the investors are equal to $\dot{V} - V^N$, where $\dot{V}$ is the derivative of the value of the firm (V) w.r.t. time t.

Investor's portfolio choice will yield the following equation:

$$\rho V = (\dot{V} - V^N) + (1 - \theta)D \qquad (6.1)$$

Solving this first-order differential equation of V,

$$V = (1 - \theta) \int_0^\infty e^{-\rho^* t} (D - \frac{1}{1 - \theta} V^N) dt \qquad (6.2)$$

The economic value of capital stock, K is to depreciate at the rate δ. Hence, net capital increase at time t is given by

$$\dot{K} = I - \delta K \qquad (6.3)$$

where I is the gross investment.

The dividend distributed by the firm at t, D is expressed by

$$D_t = (1-\tau)\Pi(K_t) - \left(1 - k_t - \tau \int_0^\infty \hat{\delta} e^{-\hat{\delta}(s-t)} e^{-\rho^*(s-t)} ds\right) P_t I_t$$

$$+ \left(1 - e^{-\rho^* t} - i(1-\tau) \int_t^{t+\iota} e^{-\rho^*(s-t)} ds\right) B_t + V_t^N \qquad (6.4)$$

where ρ^* : the rate of return to investment after tax,
$\Pi(K)$: the corporate income before tax,
k : the rate of investment tax credit,
$\hat{\delta}$: the rate of depreciation in tax law,
P : the price of investment goods,
B : the funds raised by issuing bonds,
ι: the maturity of bond,
i : the rate of interest paid by the firm.

As for the sources of financing investment, the fractions of investment, α_1 and α_2 are financed by issuing bonds and new shares respectively. So the fraction, $\alpha_3 = 1 - \alpha_1 - \alpha_2$ is financed by retained earnings (R_t).
    That is,

$$B_t = \alpha_1 P_t I_t$$

$$V_t^N = \alpha_2 P_t I_t$$

The problem of optimization at the time of corporate establishment is to maximize the value of the firm,

$$V = (1-\theta) \int_0^\infty e^{-\rho^* t}((1-\tau)\Pi(K_t) - (1 - k - \tau z - s\alpha_1$$

$$+ \frac{\theta}{1-\theta}\alpha_2)P_t I_t)dt \qquad (6.5)$$

subject to $\dot{K} = I - \delta K$,
where

$$z = \int_0^\infty \hat{\delta} e^{-(\rho^* + \hat{\delta})t} dt = \frac{\hat{\delta}}{\rho^* + \hat{\delta}}$$

$$s = 1 - e^{-\rho^* \iota} - \frac{i(1-\tau)(1 - e^{-\rho^* \iota})}{\rho^*}$$

In this optimization the tax bill saving due to depreciations on existing capital installed before time 0 is ignored, as it will be irrelevant for investment decisions from time 0 onward, The Hamiltonian for this problem is

$$H_t = e^{-\rho^* t}[1 - \theta\left((1-\tau)\Pi(K_t) - (1 - k - \tau z - s\alpha_1 + \frac{\theta}{1-\theta}\alpha_2)P_t I_t\right)$$
$$+ q_t^*(I_t - \delta K_t)]$$

where q_t^* is the shadow price of installed capital. This dynamic optimization problem can be solved using the Pontryagin maximum principle. Solving the first order conditions $\partial H_t/\partial I_t = 0$, where $P_t I_t = B_t + V_t^N + R_t$ and $\partial H_t/\partial K_t = q_t^*$, the formula of the cost of capital for each asset in an industry can be derived as

$$C = \alpha_1 C^B + \alpha_2 C^N + \alpha_3 C^R \tag{6.6}$$

where

$$C^B = \frac{1 - s - k - \tau z}{1 - \tau}(\rho^* + \hat{\delta} - \frac{\dot{P}}{P}) \tag{6.7}$$

$$C^N = \frac{1 + \frac{\theta}{1-\theta} - k - \tau z}{1 - \tau}(\rho^* + \hat{\delta} - \frac{\dot{P}}{P}) \tag{6.8}$$

$$C^R = \frac{1 - k - \tau z}{1 - \tau}(\rho^* + \hat{\delta} - \frac{\dot{P}}{P}) \tag{6.9}$$

C^B, C^N and C^R are each capital cost financed by borrowing, new shares and retained earnings, respectively. Equation (6) implies that the cost of capital for each asset in an industry is the weighted average of each cost of capital under the three modes of finances with weights being the fractions of investment financed by the corresponding financial sources. By the way, in this work we will use the cost of capital net of depreciation by subtracting the depreciation rate from the cost of capital derived above, that is $C^i - \hat{\delta}$. This concept was already used as the social rate of return by Jorgenson and the pretax rate of return net of depreciation by King and Fullerton.

The solution to the optimization problem must also satisfy the transversality condition

$$\lim_{t \to \infty} q_t^* e^{-\rho^* t} = 0$$

One of important variables affecting the cost of capital is the discount rate (ρ^*) shown in equations (6.7)–(6.9), representing the rate of return to investment. With perfect certainty and no tax, the discount rate would be equal to the market interest rate. Under distortionary taxes, however, the discount rate will differ from the market interest rate and in general will depend upon the source of finance. For debt finance, since nominal interest income is taxed and nominal interest payments are tax deductible, the rate at which firms will discount after-tax cash flow is the net of tax interest rate. In other words, for the case of debt finance

$$\rho^* = i(1 - \tau)$$

where i is the weighted average interest rate of the short-term interest rate, the long-term interest rate, and the interest rate in the private loan market.

For the two other sources of finance, the discount rate depends on both the personal tax system and the corporate tax system, affecting the dividend payout decision. In the corporate tax system King and Fullerton introduce the tax discrimination variable between retention and distribution. The variable is defined as the opportunity cost of retained earnings in terms of gross dividends foregone. Under a classical system of corporate tax (such as that in Korea) no additional corporate tax is collected or refunded when dividends are paid out, so the value of the tax discrimination variable is unity. For new share issues the net of tax dividend yield, $(1 - \theta)\rho^*$, must be equal to the investor's opportunity cost rate of return, $(1 - m)i$, where m is the marginal personal tax rate on interest income. Hence the discount rate for new share issues is given by

$$\rho^* = i(\frac{1 - m}{1 - \theta})$$

Similarly, for financing through retained earnings the net retained earnings yield, $(1 - c)\rho^*$, must be equal to the investor's opportunity cost rate of return, $(1 - m)i$. Then the discount rate for retained earnings is

$$\rho^* = i(\frac{1 - m}{1 - c})$$

To aggregate the cost of capital net of depreciation over different types of asset, sources of finance, or industries, we make a weighted average of each cost of capital. In particular, the average cost of capital resulting from all the possible combinations of assets, and sources of finance in this work is derived from King and Fullerton's definition, which is a weighted average of the cost of capital net of depreciation for the individual projects:

$$\bar{C} = \sum_{i=1}^{n} \tilde{C}_i \alpha_i$$

where $\tilde{C}_i$ is the cost of capital net of depreciation $(C^i - \hat{\delta})$ on the ith project and α_1 is the share of the ith project.

6.3.2 Effective tax rate

The statutory rate of corporate income tax does not represent the real tax burden, for various special treatments like the investment tax credit, special depreciation, tax holidays, and tax-free reserves reduce tax liabilities. On the other hand, the idea of effective tax rate is essentially to seek such a rate of corporate income tax that would realize by itself the cost of capital which prevails under the existing tax system. In this sense, the effective tax rate is the condensed rate of corporate income tax.

To be specific, let's consider the cost of capital under all preferential taxes mentioned above and the rate of economic depreciation.

Then, the effective tax rate (τ^E) is the marginal rate of corporate income tax to bring about the marginal cost of capital that emerges under all preferential taxes and the rate of economic depreciation:

$$\frac{(1 - \tau^E z^E)\tilde{S}}{1 - \tau^E} = \tilde{C}$$

where z^E is the present value of the stream of economic depreciation of a unit-value worth of investment, and $\tilde{C}$ on the right hand side is the cost of capital net of depreciation.

Thus, the effective tax rate is

$$\tau^E = \frac{\tilde{C} - \tilde{S}}{\tilde{C}} = 1 - \frac{\tilde{S}}{\tilde{C}}$$

which is defined to be the tax wedge divided by the before tax rate of return, net of depreciation.

6.4   International comparison of cost of capital and effective tax rate

In this section we present a detailed international comparison of the cost of capital and the marginal effective tax rate in 1989 or 1990 for Korea and OECD countries. The estimates of the cost of capital and the effective tax rate are based on the extended version of the King-Fullerton methodology derived in the previous section. While the cost of capital is simple in concept, it is quite complex in practice. It depends on the rates of return demanded by shareholders and bondholders, the tax system confronting corporations and individuals, and a variety of auxiliary aspects of corporate behaviors. Any attempt to estimate the cost of capital must rely on a variety of assumptions about corporate financing and investment practice. Moreover, data for firms in different nations are rarely comparable, requiring further assumptions and approximation. Fortunately, an extensive set of international comparisons of the tax wedge has been given by the OECD (1991) for 24 OECD countries. The OECD study covers the manufacturing sector of each country and classifies investment projects by type of asset and source of finance. Here we calculate the cost of capital and the effective tax rate of OECD countries by using the basic data exposed in the study. In this section, the cost of capital and the effective tax rate in the manufacturing sector are compared in Table 6.1 and Table 6.2.

The overall average effective tax rates in 1990 for Canada, Turkey, Sweden, Denmark, Netherlands, Finland, and Spain were high, while those of Greece, and Belgium were very low. The higher effective tax rates in Canada, Sweden, Denmark, Netherlands, Finland, and Spain were due to relatively high tax rates on interest income, but in Turkey high inflation caused the high effective tax rate in spite of a low tax rate on interest. Greece totally exempting the tax on interest income and Belgium with low tax rate on interest had low effective tax rates under high post-tax return to investors. In this context, the personal tax rates on interest and dividends, and inflation as well as the corporate tax, were important variables in affecting the effective tax rates.

In the average effective tax rates according to sources of finance, debt was the most tax efficient form of finance in the majority of countries. The deduction from tax of nominal interest payments significantly reduced the marginal tax rate on investment through debt. In particular, Belgium, Finland, France, Iceland, Italy, Japan, Korea, and Turkey had negative effective tax rates on debt. In contrast, Australia, Ireland, Spain, and the United Kingdom had higher effective tax rates on debt than on other sources of

Table 6.1: Cost of capital in OECD countries

	average for each source of finance			average for each type of asset			overall average
	r.e.	n.s.	d	B	M	I	
Australia	2.2	2.2	4.5	2.7	3.7	4.1	3.0
Austria	2.4	4.0	3.4	2.9	1.8	5.4	2.9
Belgium	5.8	9.1	2.8	5.0	3.9	8.0	5.1
Canada	4.1	5.9	3.6	3.9	3.4	6.0	4.1
Denmark	2.4	5.3	3.8	3.2	2.9	3.8	3.2
Finland	11.5	13.6	2.6	8.3	7.5	11.3	8.5
France	7.3	11.0	4.5	6.7	5.8	8.6	6.7
Germany	3.0	3.4	2.5	3.1	2.9	2.5	2.8
Greece	8.5	14.4	-2.8	5.1	5.6	4.3	5.2
Iceland	10.1	16.6	4.2	10.0	7.6	9.8	8.7
Ireland	2.5	4.5	5.8	3.7	3.8	4.2	3.9
Italy	8.1	6.5	2.8	6.7	6.2	5.3	6.1
Japan	7.6	11.4	2.7	6.8	5.7	7.1	6.3
Korea	7.4	12.6	4.7	7.7	6.5	19.9	7.2
Luxembourg	4.2	10.1	5.6	5.6	4.4	6.9	5.3
Netherlands	1.8	7.8	4.2	3.5	3.1	3.3	3.2
New Zealand	4.1	4.1	4.1	4.0	3.7	5.1	4.1
Norway	5.0	2.3	2.6	3.5	2.9	6.6	3.9
Portugal	3.0	8.1	-0.4	2.6	2.5	1.4	2.3
Spain	2.2	4.8	5.5	3.0	3.2	5.4	3.6
Sweden	4.5	4.4	1.5	3.0	2.6	6.0	3.5
Switzerland	2.7	8.0	4.1	3.9	3.7	3.7	3.8
Turkey	21.8	13.3	-15.5	-1.7	2.5	32.4	22.4
United Kingdom	3.5	2.9	4.0	3.2	3.1	5.4	3.6
United States	5.9	8.0	3.1	5.9	4.7	5.3	5.2

(1) The cost of capital is measured on the basis of the pretax real interest rate of 5 percent, country-specific inflation, average marginal personal tax rate, and average weights.
(2) r.e.: retained earnings; n.s.: new shares; d: debt
(3) B: building; M: machinery; I: inventory

Table 6.2: Effective tax rate in OECD countries

	average for each source of finance			average for each type of asset			overall average
	r.e	n.s.	d	B	M	I	
Australia	31.4	31.4	66.7	44.4	44.4	63.4	50.0
Austria	33.4	60.0	52.9	44.8	11.1	70.4	44.8
Belgium	27.6	53.8	-50.0	16.0	-76.9	47.5	17.6
Canada	92.7	94.9	91.7	92.3	91.2	95.0	92.7
Denmark	54.2	79.2	71.1	65.6	62.1	71.1	65.6
Finland	65.2	69.2	-53.8	51.8	46.7	64.6	56.3
France	36.9	58.2	-2.2	31.3	20.7	46.5	31.3
Germany	60.0	47.1	28.0	41.9	37.9	28.0	35.7
Greece	41.2	65.3	27.8	20.0	10.7	16.3	15.4
Iceland	50.5	69.9	-19.0	50.0	34.2	48.9	42.5
Ireland	20.0	62.5	65.5	45.9	47.4	52.4	48.7
Italy	55.6	44.6	-28.6	46.3	41.9	32.1	41.0
Japan	53.9	69.3	-29.6	50.8	38.6	50.7	44.4
Korea	42.8	75.7	-83.7	45.8	45.2	26.6	46.2
Luxembourg	28.6	70.3	46.4	46.4	31.8	56.5	43.4
Netherlands	27.8	83.3	69.0	62.9	58.1	90.6	59.4
New Zealand	47.6	47.6	47.6	46.3	42.1	56.9	47.4
Norway	70.0	34.8	42.3	57.1	48.3	77.3	61.5
Portugal	63.3	86.4	37.5	57.7	56.0	21.4	52.2
Spain	27.3	66.7	70.9	35.0	50.0	70.4	55.6
Sweden	80.0	79.5	40.0	70.0	65.4	85.0	74.3
Switzerland	22.2	73.8	51.2	46.5	43.2	43.2	44.7
Turkey	97.2	95.5	-103.2	-135.3	76.0	98.1	95.4
United Kingdom	54.3	44.8	60.0	50.0	48.4	70.4	55.6
United States	62.7	72.5	29.0	62.7	53.2	58.5	57.7
average	49.9	65.5	21.1	41.9	41.1	57.7	51.1

finance. And Australia, Finland, New Zealand, and Turkey under the full integration system between personal and corporation income taxes did not discriminate between uses of retained earnings and new equity, resulting in almost the same effective tax rates between them. In addition, Norway was a typical country where the effective tax rate on retained earnings was much higher than on debt and new equity due to higher capital gains tax rates on shares (40 percent).

In the category of asset specific effective tax rate, most countries, except for Ireland, Spain, and Turkey, had the lowest effective tax rate on machinery. Because investment allowance for machinery and high depreciation rates for machinery and buildings were in effect in many countries.

As we have discussed, the cost of capital and the effective tax rate were substantially different between countries. Although trying to find some common underlying cause for either high or low average effective marginal tax rates across countries is not easy, differences between them depend on considerable heterogeneity of tax system, sources of finance, inflation, interest rate, and the tax treatment to types of asset and depreciation.

Compared with OECD countries, Korea in recent years suffered from inflation and a relatively high interest rate. The overall corporate tax rate remains at a high level, while the personal tax rates on dividends and interest are still low. In the actual weight of asset in 1989, the weight of machinery (68.8 percent) was higher than the average weight (50 percent) in OECD countries. In the actual weight of each source of finance, Korean industries were more heavily dependent on debt (42 percent) than OECD countries (35 percent), while their dependence on retention (55 percent) was on average higher than Korea's (32 percent). These complex compositions of tax schemes and financial structures put the effective tax rate in Korea into the middle group of OECD countries.

6.5 International perspective on the Korean tax reform

In this work we have discussed comprehensively how Korea and OECD countries have changed their tax schemes in order to mitigate the problems in personal and corporate tax systems, which are criticized because of their alleged adverse effects on investment and saving, creating distortions in the international allocation of capital, complexity, and lack of neutrality between corporate and noncorporate sectors.

The common characteristics of reforms to resolve such problems were to

curtail investment incentives, to broaden the base for income taxes, and to
reduce statutory tax rates at the corporate and personal levels in the 1980s.
This international new approach to tax reform of lowering tax rates and
broadening the tax base was pervasive to many OECD countries and Korea,
for example, Australia in 1988, Canada in 1986, France in 1985, Germany
in 1986, Japan in 1989, Korea in 1982 and 1986, Sweden in 1985, the U.K.
budget for 1984, and the U.S Tax Reform Act of 1986.

Compared with OECD countries, Korea has imposed high corporate tax
rates (inclusive of surcharges), 45 percent in the 1960s, 53 percent in the
1970s, and 43.8 percent in the 1980s, while the personal income tax on dividends and interests has stayed at low rates of 10–25 percent. The personal
and corporation income taxes are not integrated. Instead, Korea had introduced extensive tax incentives in capital formation and key industries in the
1960s and the 1970s. In 1990, the new tax system relating to land-ownership
was put into effect in Korea, as explained in Chapter 4.

Our estimates of the cost of capital and the effective tax rate show they
were substantially different among OECD countries and Korea. Although
trying to find some common underlying cause for either high or low average effective marginal tax rates across countries is not easy, differences in
them are analyzed to depend on a considerable heterogeneity of tax system,
sources of finance, inflation, interest rate, and the tax treatment to types of
asset and depreciation. In the overall average effective tax rate in 1989 or
1990, Canada, Turkey, Sweden, Denmark, Netherlands, Finland, and Spain
showed high effective tax rates, while that of Greece and Belgium was very
low. As Korea in recent years has suffered from inflation, high corporate tax
rate, and relatively high interest rate, its overall effective tax rate belonged
to the middle group of OECD countries' effective tax rates.

In the category of the average effective tax rates according to sources of
finance, debt was the most efficient form of finance in the majority of countries. The deduction from tax on nominal interest payments significantly
reduced the marginal tax rate on investment through debt. Australia, Finland, New Zealand, and Turkey have the full integration system between
personal and corporation income tax rates and so had almost the same effective tax rates between retained earnings and new shares. In particular,
Norway was a typical country where the effective tax rate on retained earnings was much higher than on debt and new equity due to higher capital
gains tax rates on shares (40 percent). Looking at the asset-specific effective tax rates, in most countries, except for Ireland, Spain, and Turkey, the
effective tax rate on machinery was lowest among three assets.

From the international perspective on the Korean tax reform, in both the 1960s and 1970s Korea experienced an expenditure-based tax system. During the period under the shortage of domestic capital formation, the extensive tax incentives (tax holidays, investment tax credits, accelerated capital consumption allowance, tax-free reserves to investment) had been given to investment at the corporate level, while the low personal tax rate on interest income and the tax-free account had been allowed to stimulate savings. This expenditure-based tax system contributed to lowering the cost of capital in the Korean economy, but was analyzed to heighten the discrepancies of tax burdens among different assets, sources of finance, and industries. These discrepancies gave rise to concern about the impact of tax-induced distortions on the efficiency of capital allocation, which led to the tax reforms in 1982 and 1986. They were evaluated as a sharp change in the direction of Korean policy for taxation of income from capital, and closely resembled the international new approach of tax reforms. As we showed from Table 4.1 to Table 4.4, both tax reforms of the 1980s lowered the cost of capital and improved the efficiency of capital allocation.

7 Estimates of capital stock

7.1 Introduction

Capital stock is a basic variable in determining investment, consumption, production, and long-term economic growth. In recent years, repeated attempts have been made in Korea to measure the stock of fixed assets of industries or of the whole economy. However, they could not generate conclusive results in estimating capital stock. There have still been research requirements for estimating the consistent and sectorally disaggregated capital stock in order to carry out a wide spectrum of empirical economic analyses. In particular, such a disaggregated capital stock is indispensable to the analysis of sectoral profitability and productivity, calculations of the degree of utilization of individual sectors, and estimates of sectoral production and investment functions. Because Korea has experienced rapid changes in economic structure, capital stock estimates by industries and assets are very relevant to the current discussion related to the structural adjustment of industries. The present study is to estimate gross and net capital stocks for 37 industries, which together cover the entire Korean economy.

The problem of measuring capital stocks have been studied extensively by Usher and Von Furstenberg, and Ward was concerned with the problems of measuring capital in less developed countries. Since the perpetual-inventory method was originated by Goldsmith, and the benchmark-year method was applied by Aukrust and Bjerke, alternative methods of capital stock estimates have been proposed. Some examples are the polynomial benchmark method by Nishimizu, the Box-Cox power transformation method by Hulten and Wykoff, the Almon-type modified perpetual-inventory method by Hahn and Schmoranz, and the simultaneous estimation of production functions and capital stock by Dadkhah and Zahedi. The availability of data constrains the choice of methods to be applied to the particular country.

In this work we apply the polynomial benchmark method to estimating both gross capital stock and net capital stock in Korea, because of the availability of three national wealth surveys in 1968, 1977, and 1987. The polynomial benchmark method as a variation of the perpetual inventory method requires capital stock estimates from at least two benchmark years. It has been, for example, applied to generating net capital stocks of Japanese corporate industries by Nishimizu and the United States housing stock by Leigh. In Korea, Pyo estimated capital stock classified by 26 aggregate industries on the basis of the polynomial benchmark method. However, there are two limitations in his estimation: (i) it treated the retirement rates and the depreciation rates as constant between the two benchmark years; (ii) both retirement rates and depreciation rates were negative in most of the industries. This study attempts to overcome these limitations and generate more realistic capital stock estimates.

The next section explains the underlying data involved in the present calculation, including the definition for "capital". The third section presents the capital stock estimate model, and the results of the estimation are shown in the fourth section. The fifth section computes the average capital coefficients of industries. Finally, some conclusions are drawn in the final section.

7.2   The concept of capital and data

7.2.1   Concept of capital

The capital stock measures here are based on a production-oriented concept of capital. Capital is defined as the sum total of all durable, reproducible, and tangible assets. This definition of capital largely coincides with the concept of fixed assets like buildings, machines, and vehicles. It excludes such assets as land, natural resources, and inventory stocks. Although land and natural resources are durable and tangible, and contribute to future income, they are not reproducible and thus they are not regarded as forming part of the stocks of real capital. On the other hand, inventory stocks are tangible and reproducible, but they are not durable for the most part. The estimates of inventory stocks are made separately from this work.

In empirical capital stock calculations, the heterogeneity of capital goods can only be taken into account insofar as to include institutionalized conceptual differentiations. Apart from this, the fiction that capital goods are homogenous must be used, homogeneity being particularly assumed with respect to disembodied technical progress.

The distinction between the gross and the net capital stock is one of the most important differentiations in empirical analysis. The gross capital stock reflects the maximum available production capacity fixed assets at a given point of time. The net capital stock is computed as the gross capital minus depreciation. Since this work aims at estimating both the gross capital stock and the net capital stock, finding the realistic depreciation rate and the reliable retirement rate is crucial.

7.2.2 Data

The availability of data in Korea is somewhat better than that in most developing countries. In addition to capital formation data from National Income Accounts, there have been three National Wealth Surveys conducted in 1968, 1977, and 1987, and frequent Industrial Surveys since 1966. However, there have been no systematic surveys for capital stocks in Korea until the middle of 1960s, although the domestic capital formation series published by the Bank of Korea dates back to 1953. The present study is therefore covering the period starting from 1968 in estimating capital stocks.

The first national wealth survey in 1968 was implemented by complete and sampling survey methods, covering enterprise and household assets held by the government and the private sectors. The second national wealth survey in 1977 and the third national survey in 1987 were more comprehensive in coverage and scope. For example, they included information on the dates and the costs of asset acquisition. In addition, while the 1968 survey reported values of assets by ownership only, the 1977 and 1987 surveys reported values of assets by both ownership and use.

The alternative sources of capital stock estimates and the acquisition of tangible fixed assets on book value are the industrial censuses, conducted ten times since 1955, and the mining and manufacturing survey, conducted sixteen times since 1966. However, the capital stock estimation using these two sources is naturally limited to the mining and manufacturing sector.

Since the national wealth survey has been evaluated as being more reasonable in coverage and methodology than the industrial survey, we use the adjusted data on the mining and manufacturing survey to the national wealth survey on the basis of industrial sectors and types of assets in order to maintain consistency in data on capital stock and capital formation in a benchmark year. Further, since the decomposition of data on gross domestic capital formation in the national income account was different from that in the national wealth survey, we adjusted data on the former to conform to the latter in decomposition.

7.3   Method of capital stock estimation

Using as a basis the three benchmark-year estimates of durable and reproducible tangible assets from national wealth surveys, we link them with
gross capital formation data from national income accounts. The polynomial benchmark method is used in estimating capital stocks for the period
between the benchmark years. The method differs from the perpetual-
inventory method in the sense that it requires the estimates of capital
stocks from at least two benchmark years. And either the retirement rate or
the depreciation rate is endogenously determined rather than exogenously
assumed. Here, we cover 9 aggregate industries and 28 sub-manufacturing
industries (Appendix A), whose assets are classified by buildings and structures, machinery and equipment, and transportation equipment. In addition, we estimate both nominal capital stock and real capital stock at 1985
constant prices.

First, let's consider the model for estimating gross capital stocks. Since
a given stock of capital continues to provide services until the time of retirement, but the flow of its services declines over time, finding the realistic
retirement rate is the most important factor in estimating gross capital stock.

Let us denote the gross stock of i asset at the end of year t in a given
industry as GK_t^i. This is equal to the sum of the stock as of the end of the
preceding year (GK_{t-1}^i) and the gross investment in the year (I_t^i) deducted
by the amount of the capital stock retired in the same year (R_t^i):

$$GK_t^i = GK_{t-1}^i + I_t^i - R_t^i \qquad (7.1)$$

Let the fraction (r_t^i) of the gross stock be subject to retirement from the
previous stock:

$$R_t^i = r_t^i GK_{t-1}^i \qquad (7.2)$$

Substituting (7.2) into (7.1), the following polynomial equation on gross
capital stock can be derived:

$$\begin{aligned} GK_t^i &= GI_t^i + (1 - r_t^i)I_{t-1}^i + (1 - r_t^i)(1 - r_{t-1}^i)I_{t-2}^i + \cdots \\ &+ (1 - r_t^i)\cdots(1 - r_{t-s+1}^i)GK_{t-s}^i \end{aligned} \qquad (7.3)$$

where GK_{t-s}^i indicates the first benchmark year's estimates of the gross
capital stock. Given two benchmark estimates $(GK_{t-s}^i$ and GK_t^i) and the

investment series, the above polynomial equation can be used for estimating r_t^i. On the basis of the estimated retirement rate, gross capital stock is calculated by linking the gross capital stock at the benchmark year to the capital formation of each year from the following model:

$$GK_t^i = (1 - r_t^i)GK_{t-1}^i + I_t^i \qquad (7.4)$$

Second, the model and the method to estimate the net capital stock is identical to the above model except that we use the net capital stock of i asset at the end of year t NK_t^i instead of the gross capital stock, and the estimated depreciation rate (d_t^i) instead of the retirement rate. The corresponding equations for the net capital stock are as follows:

$$NK_t^i = NK_{t-1}^i + I_t^i - D_t^i \qquad (7.5)$$

$$D_t^i = d_t^i NK_{t-1}^i \qquad (7.6)$$

$$\begin{aligned} NK_t^i &= I_t^i + (1 - d_t^i)I_{t-1}^i + (1 - d_t^i)(1 - d_{t-1}^i)I_{t-2}^i + \cdots \\ &+ (1 - d_t^i)\cdots(1 - d_{t-s+1}^i)NK_{t-s}^i \end{aligned} \qquad (7.7)$$

where D_t^i is the depreciation amount of i asset at time t in a given industry. Given the estimates of the net capital stocks (NK_{t-s}^i and NK_t^i) and the investment series, the above polynomial equation can be used for estimating d_t^i. On the basis of the estimated depreciation rate, net capital stock is calculated by linking the net capital stock at the benchmark year to the capital formation of each year from the following model:

$$NK_t^i = (1 - d_t^i)NK_{t-1}^i + I_t^i \qquad (7.8)$$

The difference between this work and the previous studies in generating Korean capital stocks lies in the way they estimate the retirement rate and the depreciation rate. All previous studies estimated capital stocks of aggregate industries under the assumption that capital objects wear out and depreciate at the constant rate during the period (10 years) between the different benchmark years. Obviously this assumption is unrealistic, since

Table 7.1: Depreciation rate(d), retirement rate(r), and service life of asset(l)

	d(%)	r(%)	l(%)
Buildings & structures	3.32–6.98	2.62–2.82	35.50–38.20
Machinery & equipment	14.05–30.13	9.83–15.72	6.40–10.20
Transportation equipment	17.12–32.85	8.63–11.10	9.00–11.60

(The service life of asset (l) is calculated on the basis of 10 percent of the survival rate)

different assets follow quite different patterns of retirement and depreciation. They are variable as economic environments change. Even more of a serious problem arising from the assumption was that the estimates of both the retirement rate and the depreciation rate were negative in the majority of industries[1]. To get realistic results, we take three steps here. In the first step, we estimate the retirement rate and the depreciation rate of the benchmark year by using the relationship between the retirement rate and the service life of the asset, and the relationship between the depreciation rate and the service life of the asset. The service life of the asset is based on the national wealth survey. In the second step, we estimate the rates between the two different benchmark years such that the sum of the capital stock in the previous benchmark year and the subsequent annual investments between the benchmark years is equal to the capital stock in the next benchmark year. In the third step, we make an interpolation of estimates by comparing the depreciation rate and the retirement rate found from the second step with those obtained from the first step. Through these complex procedures, we have more realistic estimates of the asset-specific retirement rate and the depreciation rate in each industry, showing reasonable variations on the time horizon from 1968 to 1989.

The range of the estimated depreciation rate in Korea is 3.32–6.98 percent for buildings and structures, 14.05–30.13 percent for machinery and equipment, and 17.12–32.85 percent for transportation equipment, which compares with estimates in the United States of 3.01–7.85 percent, 16.49–27.58 percent, and 17.82–25.18 percent respectively, according to Hulten

---

[1]According to estimates from Pyo, either retirement rate or depreciation rate was negative and constant in Agriculture, Foresty and Fishing, Mining and Quarraying, Manufacturing, Construction, Wholesale and Retail, Trade, Restaurants and Hotal, Financing, Insurance, Real estate and Business Service.

and Wykoff's results. As for the sectoral comparison with the Japanese and the United States corporate industries, the average depreciation rates of the service sectors (e.g. wholesale, financing, insurance, business service, and social service) in Korea are much lower than those of agriculture, mining, and manufacturing sectors. A pattern similar to the United States and Japanese industrial sectors, according to Hulten and Wykoff, and Nishimizu's results.

The range of the estimated retirement rate in Korea is 2.62–2.82 percent for buildings and structures, 9.83–15.72 percent for machinery and equipment, and 8.63–11.10 percent for transportation equipment, whose standard deviations are much less than those of the depreciation rate. The estimated result of the retirement rate is quite close to it in the tax law. The retirement rates of agriculture, mining, and manufacturing sectors are much higher than those in the service sectors.

The range of the service life of assets in Korea is 35.50–38.20 years for buildings and structures, 6.40–10.20 years for machinery and equipment, and 9.0–11.60 years for transportation equipment, which compares with estimates in the United States of 50 years for buildings and structures, and 15–22 years for machinery and equipment, according to Ward's result. The service life of assets in Korea is estimated to be on average shorter than that in the developed countries (e.g. United States, United Kingdom).

Another difference of this study from the other works is in the estimates of the aggregate capital stock on the basis of three types of assets. We estimate in advance the capital stock of each type of assets, buildings and structures, machinery and equipment, and transportation equipment, and then aggregate the capital stock from the three different assets in each industry at a given time. In contrast, the other studies just allocate the estimated aggregate capital stock into three types of assets for the entire period by uniformly applying the percentage shares obtained at the benchmark year in each industry.

7.4   Estimates of capital stocks

We apply the benchmark estimates of capital stocks from the national wealth survey and the capital formation data from the national income account, both in 1985 prices, to the polynomial benchmark model. The resulting estimates of the real gross and net capital stocks by industry as well as for the three types of assets are presented in Appendix K. Of course, the nominal gross and net capital stocks were estimated, too. Let's abstract some interesting points on the structure of capital in Korea.

Table 7.2: Structure and growth of real gross capital stock

	aggregate	buildings	machinery	trans-portation
100 billion Won				
1968	349	290(76.4)	64(16.7)	26(6.9)
1983	2,604	1,649(63.3)	751(28.9)	204(7.8)
1989	4,773	3,103(65.0)	1,262(26.4)	407(8.6)
aggregate growth rate				
1968–83	13.8	12.1	18.1	14.9
1983–89	10.6	10.4	9.1	12.2
1968–89	12.6	11.6	13.0	14.2

First, as in Table 7.2, gross capital stock has grown at the rate of 12.9 percent on average since 1968, which exceeds the average economic growth rate of 9.7 percent. The gross capital stock in 1989 amounts to 12.6 times that in 1968.

Second, during the period of 1968–83 the average growth rate of machinery and equipment was higher than the rate of the other assets, but it was lower than that of other assets since 1983. This implies that the capital formation has skewed toward buildings and structures, and transportation equipment relative to machinery and equipment since 1983. According to the decomposition of capital stock, the proportion of buildings and structures has been lower since 1968, while those of machinery and equipment, and transportation equipment have been higher.

Third, the real net capital stock has grown at the rate of 13.1 percent on average from 1968 (185,128 hundred million Won) to 1989 (2,432,744 hundred million Won), which is higher than that of real gross capital stock. Comparing the ratio of the real net capital stock to the real gross capital stock according to assets, we could find structural changes of assets during the period of 1968–89 as in Table 7.3.

While the ratio of the net capital stock to the gross capital stock for buildings and structures has been increasing (46.1 percent to 56.3 percent) from 1968 to 1990, the ratios for machinery and equipment, and the ratios for transportation equipment have been declining (60.7 percent to 40.5 percent, and 52.6 percent to 40.2 percent). These changes in the ratios imply that the deterioration of buildings and structures has improved, but the deterio-

Table 7.3: Ratio of net capital to gross capital(%)

	buildings	machinery	transportation
1968	46.1	60.7	52.6
1983	56.6	44.4	41.3
1989	56.3	40.5	40.2

Table 7.4: Decomposition of capital stock(1987)

	Korea	Japan	United States
residential buildings	21.5(%)	22.8(%)	36.5(%)
buildings & structures	49.5(%)	59.7(%)	38.0(%)
machinery & plant	29.0(%)	17.5(%)	25.5(%)

rations of other assets have rather deepened. Such structural changes of net capital stock would cause a bottleneck in sustaining future economic growth in Korea.

Fourth, comparing the international decomposition of capital stock, as in Table 7.4, buildings and structures have highest proportion in all three countries. The proportion of residential buildings is almost the same between Korea and Japan, which is much lower than that in the United States. On the other hand, the proportion of buildings and structures in Korea and Japan is much higher than that in the United States. This implies that Korea and Japan put more emphasis on investing in buildings and structures relative to the United States, but the latter invested more in residential buildings.

Table 7.5: Capital-output ratio

	Korea	Japan
1968	1.77	2.17
1979	2.82	1.45
1989	3.72	2.15

7.5   Capital coefficients

The estimates of capital stocks enable us to generate capital-output ratios. The capital-output ratios can be defined differently, depending on the category of capital stock and output. Here, we measure two kinds of capital-output ratios, the aggregate capital-output ratio and the net capital-output ratio. The aggregate capital-output ratio is derived from the ratio of the real gross capital stock to the real GNP, and the net capital-output ratio is calculated from the ratio of the real net capital stock to the real GNP. The resulting estimates of both capital coefficients are presented in Appendix L. In Korea both capital-output ratios for the entire economy have increased to 3.72 and 1.89 in 1989. This implies that the productivity of capital has decreased since 1968. According to the distribution of capital-output ratios among industries, the construction industry has shown highest productivity of capital, while the electricity, gas and water industry have been the lowest.

Our estimates of the aggregate capital-output ratio are compared with those of Japan for the period of 1968–89. From OECD reports of nonresidential private gross capital stock and the GNP data for Japan, Table 7.5 presents some comparisons in the aggregate capital-output ratios between Korea and Japan. The range for the capital-output ratio in Japan has remained at 1.45–2.17 and in Korea at 1.77–3.72 since 1968.

From the Table, Japan seems to have achieved more gains in the productivity of capital than Korea. The overall rising pattern of Korea's capital-output ratio suggests the main source of the high growth should come from capital accumulation, and the share of income to the owners of capital has been shrinked under the assumption of constant returns to scale.

7.6 Estimates of inventory stock

Inventory stocks are also fixed and reproducible assets but they are not durable assets. In this sense, the method of inventory stock estimation is different from that of durable asset estimation, and the depreciation rate on durable asset is no longer applied. Instead of the depreciation rate we introduce the rate of loss as an adjustment coefficient into the polynomial benchmark method. In Korea the national wealth surveys include inventory stocks (e.g., semi-manufactured goods, manufactured goods, raw materials, stored goods), and the inventory investments are reported in the national income account. Here we estimate inventory stocks of the whole industry, the mining industry, the manufacturing sector with 28 sub-manufacturing industries, and other industries (Appendix A) from 1968–89.

The model to estimate inventory stocks is based on the modified polynomial benchmark method,

$$IS_t^i = C^i x(II_t^i + II_{t-1}^i + \cdots + II_{t-s+1}^i) + IS_{t-s}^i$$

$$= IR_t^i + IR_{t-1}^i + \cdots + IR_{t-s+1}^i + IR_{t-s}^i$$

where IS_t^i is inventory stock of industry i at time t, II_t^i inventory investment, C^i the rate of loss of industry i, and IR_t^i is net inventory investment. The rate of loss on inventory investment is assumed to be applied to current investment because of a short life of inventory stock, while the depreciation rate of fixed reproducible and durable asset is applicable to past asset. After estimating the rate of loss in the above model, the annual inventory stock is measured by

$$IS_t^i = IR_t^i + IS_{t-i}^i$$

where $IR_t^i = C^i x II_t^i$.

The inventory stock in the benchmark year comes from three national wealth surveys conducted in 1968, 1977, and 1988, and GNP deflator is used as a price index. The estimated results of inventory stocks in 1985 prices are shown in Table 7.6. The inventory stocks of the whole industry in 1989 were 18.3 times the stocks in 1968. The growth of the inventory stocks in the manufacturing sector, in particular, showed the same magnitude as that of the whole industry during 1968–89, which implied the manufacturing sector had led the increase in the inventory stocks. Among the manufacturing sector, manufacture of textiles (321), manufacture of machinery except electrical (382), and manufacture of electrical machinery, apparatus, appliances and supplies (383) represented large inventory stocks.

Table 7.6: Inventory stocks and fixed capital stock
(Unit: 100 Million Won)

year	inventory stocks (A)	fixed gross capital stock (B)	fixed capital & inventory stock (A+B)	A/B	A/A+B
1968	45,157	379,248	424,405	0.119	0.106
1970	44,319	481,693	526,012	0.092	0.084
1975	147,726	888,081	1,028,807	0.168	0.144
1980	334,014	1,938,090	2,272,104	0.172	0.147
1985	379,864	3,147,160	3,527,024	0.121	0.108
1989	826,045	4,772,589	5,598,634	0.173	0.148

The proportion of inventory stocks among fixed gross capital stock and the reproducible tangible assets (fixed gross capital stock plus inventory stocks) increased to 17.3 percent and 14.8 percent respectively in 1989. Hence, inventory stocks in Korea have stayed at less than 15 percent of the (non-residential) reproducible tangible assets.

7.7   Estimates of human capital stock

The concept of human capital started with the assumption that individuals decide on their education, training, medical care, and other additions to knowledge and health by weighting the benefits and costs. Benefits include cultural and other nonmonetary gains along with improvement in earnings and occupations, whereas costs usually depend mainly on the forgone value of the time spent on these investments.

In Korea there has been no estimate of human capital stock, and the availability of the basic data related to human capital is very limited. Fortunately the data on training expenditures and health expenditures in both private and public sectors is available, and statistics are listed in the industrial survey of labor cost, the mining and manufacturing survey, the comprehensive report on public sector's training, and medical insurance statistics. Here the main purpose is to estimate human capital stock directly related to production in order to analyze the effect of human capital on the economic growth. In this work, human capital stock is estimated according to industries and public sector, consisting of training expenditures and health expenditures.

Table 7.7: Aggregate human capital stock
(Unit: 100 Million Won)

	Total		Industry		Public Sector	
	E	M	E	M	E	M
1968	294	1270	68	560	226	710
1975	1220	3019	298	850	922	2169
1980	1975	5406	573	1289	1402	4117
1985	3421	8685	1062	1830	2359	6885
1989	5779	13719	1714	2618	4065	10561

(E: training, M: health)

I first estimate the average annual real expenditures per head, and then multiply this by all workers. The basic model for estimating human capital consisting of training and health expenditures is

$$GH_t = N_t E_t + (1 - u_t)GH_{t-1}$$

$$NH_t = N_t E_t + (1 - d_t)NH_{t-1}$$

where GH is aggregate human capital, NH is net human capital, N is the number of workers, E is per capita training expenditures or per capita health expenditures, u is the retirement rate, and d is the depreciation rate.

According to the age distribution of workers, more than 90 percent of workers were aged 20–49, and thereby it is assumed that the average working period is 30 years, and the enduring period of new technology is 15 years. The estimated human capital stock (1985 constant price) is summarized in Table 7.7.

Human capital consisting of training and health expenditures is estimated as 1,959.8 billion Won in 1989 and 156.4 billion Won in 1968. Human capital grew in a rapid growth rate with an average annual growth rate of 12.5 percent, which exceeded the economic growth rate during the period 1968–89.

7.8   Concluding remarks

In this work, we presented estimates of capital stocks by industry for Korea based on the polynomial benchmark-year method. The primary emphasis of our study was on estimating more realistic values for the retirement rate and the depreciation rate. According to the above estimates, the gross capital stock and the net capital stock expanded by an average rate of 12.9 percent and 13.1 percent respectively between 1968 and 1989. They are consistent with the nature of a fast-growing economy. Among the industries, the capacity expansion (as measured by the gross of real assets) was faster in the manufacturing industry and the construction industry, but was slower in service sectors and the mining industry.

Both the aggregate capital-output ratio and the net capital-output ratio for the entire economy increased from 1.77 to 3.72 and from 0.86 to 1.89, for the period 1968–89, exhibiting a slightly increasing trend. The aggregate capital-output ratio was higher in the electricity, gas and water industry, transport, storage and communication industry, and the manufacturing industry, but was lower in the construction industry, wholesale and retail trade, and the restaurant and hotel industry.

According to the analysis of the real net capital stock-the real gross capital stock ratio, the deterioration of buildings and structures has improved, but the deterioration in machinery and equipment, and transportation equipment has somewhat worsened.

Hence, changes in the structure of capital stock over the past two decades reflect some characteristics of a fast-growing economy experiencing structural adjustments.

8 Q model of investment

8.1 Introduction

In this chapter we incorporate the tax policy analysis based on the cost of capital into a q model of investment. This framework is particularly useful for analyzing the relationship between capital cost and capital formation. In past researches of investment, there have been arguments between the traditional investment theory and the neoclassical investment theory. In the traditional investment theory, investment and the cost of capital are either uncorrelated or only weakly correlated. These relationships might appear to suggest that business fixed investment can be best explained by an accelerator model of investment, whereby investment responds to changes in the desired capital stock, itself determined by the demand for output. By contrast, the neoclassical theory of investment views output as the consequence of firms' choice of capital stock and other factors, not the cause. Put another way, the latter implies that firms should use prices and not quantities as signals in making their investment decisions.

Tobin defined q as the ratio of the market value of existing capital to the replacement cost of capital. Subsequent empirical studies of investment by Ciccolo, Von Furstenberg, Abel, and Hayashi have examined the role of q as a determinant of investment behavior. The observation that investment and output are strongly correlated while the cost of capital has little correlation with investment weighs against the neoclassical model.

In this paper, through a rigorous foundation of the q theory of investment based on intertemporal optimization by firms, we will develop a q model of investment in the Korean economy. Our analytic framework is different from previous ones in the sense that marginal q derived from a profit function and the cost of capital are considered as a determinant of investment behavior, where marginal q reflects the comprehensive tax policy related to investment. Most of the past works in the analysis of investment were based on average

119

q rather than marginal q, which are different under taxation. Our result
will show that there remains an important role for the cost of capital in
determining investment.

In the next section the theoretical q model of investment subject to extensive tax incentives is explained. The tax-adjusted marginal q of each industry
is estimated in Section 3, and both investment behavior and capital stock
are related to the tax-adjusted marginal q and/or the cost of capital in
Section 4. In the final section we abstract our analytic results.

8.2   A Q model of investment

We assume that investors expect a minimum rate of return (ρ^*) to their
investment. The investors receive from the firm the dividend income D and
the capital gains. Dividend is assumed to be taxed at the rate θ. New shares
amounting to V^N are assumed to be issued or repurchased, and the capital
gains received by the investors are equal to $\dot{V} - V^N$, where $\dot{V}$ is the derivative
of the value of the firm (V) w.r.t. time t.

An investor's portfolio choice will yield the following equation:

$$\rho V = (\dot{V} - V^N) + (1 - \theta)D \tag{8.1}$$

Solving this first-order differential equation of V,

$$V = (1 - \theta) \int_0^\infty e^{-\rho^* t}(D - \frac{1}{1 - \theta}V^N)d_t \tag{8.2}$$

The economic value of capital stock K is to depreciate at the rate δ. Hence,
net capital increase at time t is given by

$$\dot{K} = I - \delta K \tag{8.3}$$

where I is the gross investment.

The dividend distributed by the firm at t, D is expressed by

$$
\begin{aligned}
D_t =\ & (1 - \tau)\Pi(K_t) - \left(1 - k_{t'} - \tau \int_0^\infty \hat{\delta}e^{-\hat{\delta}(s-t)}e^{-\rho^*(s-t)}ds\right)A(I_t) \\
& + \left(1 - e^{-\rho^* t} - i(1 - \tau)\int_t^{t+\iota} e^{-\rho^*(s-t)}ds\right)B_t + V_t^N
\end{aligned} \tag{8.4}
$$

where ρ^* : the rate of return to investment after tax,
$\Pi(K)$: the corporate income before tax,
k : the rate of investment tax credit,
$\hat{\delta}$: the rate of depreciation in tax law,
$A(I_t)$: the cost of purchasing and installing capital,
B : the funds raised by issuing bonds,
ι : the maturity of bond,
i : the rate of interest paid by the firm.

As for the sources of financing investment, the fractions of investment, α_1 and α_2 are financed by issuing bonds and new shares, respectively. So the fraction,$\alpha_3 = 1 - \alpha_1 - \alpha_2$ is financed by retained earnings (R_t).
  That is,

$$B_t = \alpha_1 A(I_t)$$
$$V_t^N = \alpha_2 A(I_t)$$

The problem of optimization at the time of corporate establishment is to maximize the value of the firm,

$$V = (1-\theta)\int_0^\infty e^{-\rho^* t}((1-\tau)\Pi(K_t) - (1-k-\tau z - s\alpha_1$$
$$+\frac{\theta}{1-\theta}\alpha_2)A(I_t))dt \qquad (8.5)$$

subject to $\dot{K} = I - \delta K$,
where

$$z = \int_0^\infty \hat{\delta}e^{-(\rho^*+\hat{\delta})t}dt = \frac{\hat{\delta}}{\rho^*+\hat{\delta}}$$

$$s = 1 - e^{-\rho^* \iota} - \frac{i(1-\tau)(1-e^{-\rho^* \iota})}{\rho^*}$$

In this optimization the tax bill saving due to depreciations on existing capital installed before time 0 is ignored, since it will be irrelevant for investment decisions from time 0 onward. The Hamiltonian for this problem is

$$H_t = \int_0^\infty e^{-\rho^* t}[1 - \theta((1-\tau)\Pi(K_t) - (1-k-\tau z - s\alpha_1$$
$$+\frac{\theta}{1-\theta}\alpha_2)A(I_t))dt + \lambda_t^*(I_t - \delta K_t)]$$

where λ_t^* is the shadow price of installed capital. This dynamic optimization problem can be solved using the Pontryagin maximum principle.

Solving the first order condition $\partial H_t/\partial I_t = 0$, we obtain

$$(1 - k - \tau z - s\alpha_1 + \frac{\theta}{1-\theta}\alpha_2)A'(I_t) = \lambda_t^* \qquad (8.6)$$

which implies the rate of gross investment is determined to equate the net marginal cost of investment with the shadow price of capital. This relation can be rewritten as

$$I_t = A^{-1}(q_t) \qquad (8.7)$$

where

$$q_t = \lambda_t^*/(1 - k - \tau z - s\alpha_1 + \frac{\theta}{1-\theta}\alpha_2) \qquad (8.8)$$

Note that q_t is the ratio of the shadow price of installed capital to the net marginal cost of uninstalled capital. From the necessary condition, $(\partial/\partial t)(\lambda_t^* e^{-\rho^* t}) = -\partial H_t/\partial K_t$, the time path of the shadow price is

$$\dot{\lambda}_t^* = (\rho^* + \hat{\delta})\lambda_t^* - (1 - \tau)\Pi'(K_t) \qquad (8.9)$$

suggesting that the shadow return from holding and using capital, $\dot{\lambda}_t^* + (1 - \tau)\Pi'(K_t)$ is equal to the required return to capital $(\rho^* + \hat{\delta})\lambda_t^*$.

The solution to the firms' optimization problem must also satisfy the transversality condition

$$\lim_{t \to \infty} \lambda_t^* e^{-\rho^* t} = 0 \qquad (8.10)$$

Solving the equation of motion for λ_t^* in (8.9) and using the transversality condition, we obtain

$$\lambda_t^* = \int_t^\infty (1 - \tau)\Pi'(K_s)e^{-(\rho^* + \hat{\delta})(s-t)}ds$$

Thus, λ_t^* is the present value of after tax marginal profit. To have the dynamic path of q_t , differentiate q_t in (8.7) w.r.t. time, and using (8.9),

$$\dot{q}_t = (\rho^* + \hat{\delta})q_t - \frac{1}{1 - k - \tau z - s\alpha_1 + \frac{\theta}{1-\theta}\alpha_2} \left((1 - \tau)\Pi'(K_t) + \dot{k} + \dot{\tau}z + \tau\dot{z} + \dot{s}\alpha_1 \right)$$

Solving the above differential equation and applying the transversality condition, we can derive a q model

$$q_t = \int_t^{\infty} (1 - \tau)\Pi'(K_s)e^{-(\rho^* + \hat{\delta})(s-t)}ds/(1 - k - \tau z - s\alpha_1 + \frac{\theta}{1-\theta}\alpha_2) \tag{8.11}$$

When the profit function is linear $(\Pi(K_s) = \alpha + \beta K_s)$ and $A(I_t) = P_t I_t$, q_t is represented as

$$q_t = \beta / \frac{1 - k - \tau z - s\alpha_1 + \frac{\theta}{1-\theta}\alpha_2}{1 - \tau}(\rho^* + \hat{\delta} - \dot{P}/P) \tag{8.12}$$

where the denominator of (8.12) is the cost of capital. Thus q_t is the ratio of the marginal profit to the cost of capital. Since the extensive tax incentives (tax holidays, investment tax credit, accelerated depreciation system, tax-free reserves for investment and export) have given to capital formation in Korea, the tax-adjusted marginal q is derived as

$$q_t = \beta / \frac{1 - (k + (\tau z)^*)(1 - f') - uzf' - s\alpha_1 + \frac{\theta}{1-\theta}\alpha_2}{(1 - u^*) + (B_{XR} + B_{IR})(1 - f')}(\rho^* + \hat{\delta} - \dot{P}/P) \tag{8.13}$$

where $(\tau z)^*$ is the rate of depreciation under tax holidays, u the average tax rate, f' the increased defense tax rate, u^* the average tax rate under surtax and tax holidays, B_{XR} the tax benefit under the tax-free reserves for export, and B_{IR} the tax-free reserves to machinery and equipment.

8.3   Estimates of tax-adjusted marginal Q

As we derived the tax-adjusted marginal q in (8.12) and (8.13), it is necessary to regress the profit function on capital stock for estimating the marginal q. This work estimates the profit functions of 9 aggregate industries and the profit function of the whole corporate sector, as in Table 8.1. According to results, these profit functions are to be estimated as linear forms of capital stock,

$$\Pi(K_s) = \alpha + \beta K_s + \varepsilon_s \tag{8.14}$$

Since K_s is correlated to ε_s, we use the lagged net cost of capital $(\tilde{C}_{s-1})$ as an instrument variable in estimating the profit function, which is distinctive feature of our analysis. The estimated results are summarized in Table 8.1.

Table 8.1: Profit function

industry	α	β	R^2	D.W.
0		0.25(33.10)	0.99	1.67
1	7,632.09	0.36(13.32)	0.90	0.69
2	1,150.36	0.18(4.56)	0.98	1.79
3	2,782.35	0.29(19.14)	0.99	1.53
4		0.18(12.25)	0.99	0.95
5	754.51	0.99(37.32)	0.99	1.46
6		0.55(15.35)	0.99	1.01
7	137.46	0.20(24.04)	0.99	1.18
8	-7,882.82	0.14(14.60)	0.99	0.69
9		0.06(16.67)	0.99	1.33

(The number in parenthesis is t value)

On the basis of the estimated results of the profit functions and the cost of capital (Table 8.1), the tax-adjusted marginal q of each industry could be calculated as in Table 8.2. A striking feature of this table is the sustained increase in the marginal q value except for the period 1975–80. The value of marginal q actually peaked in 1974. Except for construction, trade, and hotel and restaurant industries, it appears that marginal q averages less than its theoretical equilibrium value of unity because of tax incentives. Marginal q values of mining and service industries have been on average low. The highest marginal q value in the construction industry due to a low cost of capital supports rapid growth of capital formation in the industry.

8.4 Cost of capital, marginal Q, and capital formation

As already discussed, neoclassical and neo-Keynesian theories of investment give primary explanatory power for changes in investment to changes in the factor prices and investor's required rate of return. In theories based on Tobin's q, the ratio of the market value to the replacement cost of capital is likewise the key determinant of investment. Indeed, the neoclassical theory is equivalent to the q theory when the production functions are such as constant returns to scale.

In equation (8.7) we derived a q model of investment such that investment is a function of marginal q. As we pointed out, average q was considered not to be a significant variable in determining investment in most of the researches done in the past. However, this work shows the tax-adjusted marginal q has a strong explanatory power and is statistically significant for investment, and therefore the important role for the cost of capital in determining capital stock is discovered.

The estimated result of a q model of investment function by using the lagged investment (I_{t-1}) as an instrument variable is

$$I_t = 418,734.4\, q_t + \varepsilon_t \qquad (8.15)$$
$$(7.56)$$
$$(R^2 = 0.90,\ D.W. = 1.81)$$

Thus the tax-adjusted marginal q turns out to be a significant factor for investment. Increases in marginal q have significantly positive effects on capital formation. The result in (8.15) provides evidence that the inclusion of tax effects, profit, and the cost of capital into marginal q contributes to the explanatory power of the q theory. The above estimated result can be considered as stronger evidence of the q theory of investment than results done in other works.

Further the estimated result of capital function is

$$K_t = 1.30\, K_{t-1} - 839,940.8\, \tilde{C}_{t-1} + \varepsilon_t \qquad (8.16)$$
$$(43.27) \qquad (-2.56)$$
$$(R^2 = 0.99,\ D.W. = 1.70)$$

which implies that the cost of capital has significant negative effects on

capital stock. This result also provides evidence that the cost of capital has
to be considered as an important signal in determining capital stock.

8.5   Concluding remarks

This work incorporates the cost of capital into the marginal q model of
investment. The model described above features joint movements of the
tax-adjusted marginal q and investment in which firms' profit and the cost
of capital have an important role. In the model, firms maximize the present
value of net profit, and we introduce the extensive tax policies in deriving marginal q. The tax-adjusted marginal q is derived as the ratio of
the marginal profit to the cost of capital. In this context, this marginal q
approach is distinctive from the average q approaches used in other works.

In Korea marginal q had been widely distributed across industries because
of different cost of capital and tax incentives. Marginal q in the majority of
industries had been less than one under the extensive tax incentives to investment, while the construction industry showed highest marginal q values
of greater than one.

In this paper we find evidence that the tax-adjusted marginal q is a significant variable in determining investment, and the cost of capital is also an
important factor in making a decision of capital stock. Hence, these results
are in contrast to those induced from an accelerator model of investment.

Table 8.2: Tax-adjusted marginal q-1

	Tobin 0	Tobin 1	Tobin 2	Tobin 3	Tobin 4
1966: 1	.63900	.78884	.42155	.67657	.51350
1967: 1	.68260	.86083	.44069	.72149	.53830
1968: 1	.60888	.79558	.34663	.63987	.41270
1969: 1	.62867	.83119	.35776	.66126	.42543
1970: 1	.67872	.90179	.38413	.71345	.45867
1971: 1	.65994	.87864	.37513	.69453	.44382
1972: 1	.99694	1.3442	.55381	1.0743	.64384
1973: 1	1.0164	1.3736	.56313	1.0995	.64887
1974: 1	1.0587	1.4055	.58152	1.1407	.68324
1975: 1	.84556	.99912	.54356	.91380	.66490
1976: 1	.76633	.91005	.49409	.82835	.59926
1977: 1	.72911	.87885	.46697	.78668	.56187
1978: 1	.77116	.91646	.49547	.83301	.60268
1979: 1	.59978	.78889	.43403	.61406	.52442
1980: 1	.62617	.76154	.41063	.66502	.49981
1981: 1	.71928	.88382	.44132	.77851	.53249
1982: 1	.77706	1.0262	.40645	.83773	.49390
1983: 1	.89691	1.1649	.46470	.97791	.56249
1984: 1	.81358	1.1245	.44957	.86042	.53009
1985: 1	.82915	1.1447	.45511	.87949	.53740
1986: 1	.85545	1.1864	.46886	.91222	.54755
1987: 1	.83474	1.1621	.45394	.88533	.54143
1988: 1	.91762	1.2789	.49309	.97396	.59238
1989: 1	.91506	1.2789	.49294	.97221	.59060

Table 8.3: Tax-adjusted marginal q-2

	Tobin 5	Tobin 6	Tobin 7	Tobin 8	Tobin 9
1966: 1	2.1405	1.3335	.47340	.29012	.12811
1967: 1	2.3795	1.4204	.50890	.30764	.13719
1968: 1	2.2324	1.3716	.48610	.29618	.12865
1969: 1	2.3737	1.3911	.49636	.30031	.13169
1970: 1	2.5963	1.5053	.53561	.32400	.14221
1971: 1	2.5250	1.4496	.51604	.31417	.13816
1972: 1	3.5940	2.1766	.71493	.44026	.19334
1973: 1	3.6394	2.2041	.71513	.44658	.19603
1974: 1	3.6704	2.3879	.76835	.47721	.20666
1975: 1	2.5464	1.7547	.59449	.38130	.16352
1976: 1	2.3367	1.5701	.53648	.34381	.14816
1977: 1	2.2295	1.4915	.51380	.32806	.14337
1978: 1	2.3235	1.5895	.54516	.34646	.15044
1979: 1	2.0136	1.3628	.47121	.29903	.12995
1980: 1	1.9669	1.3345	.46364	.29082	.12615
1981: 1	2.3248	1.4453	.50702	.31590	.14025
1982: 1	2.6428	1.6553	.57515	.36507	.16286
1983: 1	3.0469	1.8429	.64424	.40851	.18246
1984: 1	2.9640	1.7614	.61899	.39096	.17508
1985: 1	3.0348	1.7774	.62589	.39398	.17695
1986: 1	3.2336	1.7846	.62994	.39340	.17920
1987: 1	3.1168	1.7846	.62708	.39332	.17813
1988: 1	3.4016	1.9775	.68909	.43400	.19628
1989: 1	3.4665	1.9435	.68154	.42728	.19451

9 Summary and conclusions

The key points of this work were focused on analyzing interdependence among tax policies, cost of capital, and capital formation during the last three decades (1960–1990). In particular, this interdependence is analyzed according to three types of assets: buildings and structures, machinery and equipment, transportation equipment; three sources of finance: debt, new shares, retained earnings; and industries classified into 26 or 37 categories, as well as an aggregate economy. Such a disaggregated analytic approach is very important because tax policies in Korea have been implemented for industry-specific and asset-specific objectives.

According to Rostow's definition of the take-off stage of economic development, and to Kuznets' definition of modern economic growth, Korea entered a phase of modern economic growth in 1963, when there was a tendency for growth to accelerate and for structural change to become rapid. Since then the Korean economy grew rapidly at an average rate of 10 percent a year between 1962, with the beginning the first five-year economic development plan, and 1991, with the ending the seventh five-year development plan. This rapid economic growth has been driven by exports and investment on the demand side and the accumulation of capital on the supply side. The estimated result of the capital stock during 1968–1989 indicates that the annual growth rate of capital stock exceeded that of economic growth. Such rapid capital accumulation and capital formation was not due to the pure market oriented mechanism, but rather to public policies. In particular, fiscal policy based on extensive tax incentives directed to capital formation and for supporting key industries.

The Korean government introduced extensive tax incentives in the process of economic development through a series of tax reforms. Major tax reforms were carried out in 1974, 1976, 1982, and 1986. Beginning with the introduction of tax holidays in 1949, special depreciation in 1961, and the investment tax credit in 1967, Korean tax policy incorporated a series of tax

129

preferences for specific forms of capital income. They could stimulate capital formation by reducing the cost of capital. However, these tax incentives also heightened the discrepancies among tax burdens born by different types of capital. Such tax-induced distortions led to the tax reforms of 1982 and 1986 and a sharp change in the direction of Korean policy for taxation of income from capital. Statutory tax rates were lowered in 1983, but the tax base was broadened by a gradual elimination of tax preferences for corporations. For example, the 1982 tax reform repealed tax holidays and lowered the investment tax credit to 6 percent, and the 1986 tax reform abolished special treatments for key industries.

The 1980s Korean tax reforms were carried out in close connection with international tax reform. Especially the U.K. budget for 1984 and the U.S. Tax Reform Act of 1986 halted the erosion of income tax base by curtailing investment incentives and broadening the base for income taxes. This international new approach to tax reform by lowering tax rates and broadening the tax base was common in many OECD countries since the mid-1980s: for example, Australia in 1988, Canada in 1986, France in 1985, Germany in 1986, Japan in 1988, and Sweden in 1985. Hence, in this work Korean tax reform was investigated from both the international and the domestic capital formation aspects.

The tax incentives introduced by tax reforms, in particular tax holidays, the investment tax credit, and special depreciation, were found to lower the cost of capital, but resulted in increasing tax wedges among different assets, sources of finance, and industries. In types of assets the cost of capital and the effective tax rate of machinery and equipment were in general lower than those of other assets. In sources of finance the cost of capital and the effective tax rate from debt were lower than those of other sources of finance, while retained earnings lowered the cost of capital and effective tax rate more than new share issues did. Out of 26 industries, the construction industry had a low effective tax rate as well as a low cost of capital in the 1980s, whereas for the mining industry the reverse was true. In our analysis of tax wedges, the tax wedge of transportation equipment is greater than those of other assets. Through our work we have found that the personal tax wedges and therefore the effective personal tax rates of all three assets were negative. These results were different from those of all OECD countries. They were due to high interest rates under excess demand in the capital market, the dual structure of capital market, and low personal income tax rates to stimulate saving. In this context there were severe distortions in taxation between the corporate income and the personal income originating in the corporate sector. However, the 1982 and 1986 tax reforms had special meaning for the cost of capital and the tax wedge. Because these tax reforms curtailing tax incentives for capital formation broadened the base for income tax, the cost of capital and the tax wedge were noticeably reduced, and the gap in the cost of capital and the effective tax rate between the highest and the lowest industries was narrowed. The reduction of the tax wedge through the tax reforms improved economic efficiency in resource allocation between saving and investment, resulting in excess saving to domestic capital formation and capital exports in 1986–89 with trade surplus.

The international comparison of the cost of capital and the effective tax rate were substantially different among OECD countries and Korea. Although trying to find some common underlying cause for either high or low average effective marginal tax rates across countries is not easy, differences in them are analyzed to depend on the considerable heterogeneity of the tax system, sources of finance, inflation, the interest rate, and the tax treatment to types of assets and depreciation. In the overall average effective tax rate in 1989 or 1990, Canada, Turkey, Sweden, Denmark, the Netherlands, Finland, and Spain showed high effective tax rates, while Greece and Belgium had very low rates. Because Korea in recent years has suffered from inflation, a high corporate tax rate, and a relatively high interest rate, its overall effective tax rate belongs to the middle group of OECD countries' effective tax rates. In the category of average effective tax rates according to sources of finance, debt was the most efficient form of finance in the majority of countries. The deduction from tax on nominal interest payments significantly reduced the marginal tax rate on investment through debt. Australia, Finland, New Zealand, and Turkey have the full integration system between personal and corporation income tax rates and so had almost identical effective tax rates between retained earnings and new shares. In particular, Norway was typical in that the effective tax rate on retained earnings was much higher than on debt and new equity, due to higher capital gains tax rates on shares (40 percent). Looking at the asset-specific effective tax rates, in most countries, except for Ireland, Spain, and Turkey, the effective tax rate on machinery was lowest among three assets.

In order to analyze the effect of tax policies on capital formation, we estimate capital stock in 37 industries for Korea based on the polynomial benchmark-year method. The primary emphasis of our study was put on estimating a more realistic value of the retirement rate and the depreciation rate. According to the above estimates the gross capital stock and the net capital stock expanded by an average rate of 12.9 percent and 13.1 percent respectively between 1968 and 1989. This verifies the nature of a fast-growing economy. Among the industries, capacity expansion (as measured by the gross of real assets) was faster in the manufacturing industry and the construction industry, but was slower in service sectors and the mining industry. Both the aggregate capital-output ratio and the net capital-output ratio for the total economy amounted to 1.77–3.72 and 0.86–1.89, for the period 1968-89 respectively, exhibiting a slightly increasing trend. The aggregate capital-output ratio was higher in the electricity, gas and water industry, the transport, storage and communication industry, and the manufacturing industry, but was lower in the construction industry, and the wholesale and retail trade, the restaurant and hotel industry. According to the analysis of the real net capital stock-the real gross capital stock ratio, the deterioration of buildings and structures has improved, but the deteriorations of machinery and equipment, and transportation equipment have rather deepened. Hence, changes in the structure of capital stock over the past two decades reflect some characteristics of a fast-growing economy experiencing structural adjustments.

Finally, this work incorporates the cost of capital into the marginal q model of investment. The model developed above features joint movements of the tax-adjusted marginal q and investment in which firm's profits and the cost of capital have an important role. In the model, firms maximize the present value of net profit, and we introduce the extensive tax policies in deriving marginal q. The tax-adjusted marginal q is derived as the ratio of the marginal profit to the cost of capital. In this context, this marginal q approach is distinct from the average q approache used in other works. In Korea the marginal q values were very different among industries because of different costs of capital and tax incentives. Marginal q in the majority of industries had been less than one under the extensive tax incentives to investment, while the construction industry showed highest marginal q values greater than one. In this paper we find evidence that the tax-adjusted marginal q is a significant variable in determining investment, and the cost of capital is also an important indicator in making a decision about capital stock. In this context, these results are contrasted with ones induced from an accelerator model of investment.

Hence, through an expenditure-based tax system in the 1960s and 1970s, and a sharp change in the direction of Korean tax policy resembling the international new approach to tax reforms, the cost of capital and the tax wedge have been lowered, and the accumulation of capital stock and capital formation has increased rapidly. Such rapid capital formation has accelerated economic growth in Korea.

Finally as we discussed, the change in the cost of capital was closely related to tax policies, and human capital as well as physical capital grew at rapid rates in the process of the economic growth. In this section our analytic point is to simulate the effect of the change in the cost of capital on economic growth, and to estimate the causal relationship between human capital and economic growth. Lucas (1993) already developed the endogenous growth model, including human capital stock, and further pointed out that human capital would play a key role in Korean economic growth.

First, it is simulated how the dynamic changes of the cost of capital affect the economic growth. Here we use our macroeconomic model (1993), consisting of 137 equations and including the capital accumulation equation (16) estimated in Chapter 8 as the simulation model. We have an historic simulation in order to trace out the effect of annual decrease in the cost of capital by 1 (SIM1), 2 (SIM2), 3(SIM3), 4(SIM4), 5 (SIM5), or 10 (SIM10) percent on the annual economic growth and the annual capital accumulation growth. The simulated results are summarized in the following Table 9.1 and Table 9.2. Although the decrease in the cost of capital was simulated to increase the annual capital accumulation by less than 1 percent, it increased the capital accumulation by 1 to 2 trillion Won in absolute amount. And the decrease in the cost of capital was also simulated to increase the annual economic growth (the annual GDP growth rate) in the short run by less than 1 percent, but to level up the annual economic growth rate by 1 to 2 percent in the long run through the steady capital accumulation.

Table 9.1: The annual capital accumulation growth (%)

	SIM1	SIM2	SIM3	SIM4	SIM5	SIM10
1985	0.05	0.10	0.14	0.19	0.24	0.47
1986	0.04	0.10	0.13	0.17	0.21	0.42
1987	0.04	0.08	0.11	0.14	0.18	0.35
1988	0.03	0.07	0.10	0.13	0.16	0.33
1989	0.03	0.07	0.08	0.10	0.13	0.26

Second, as we mentioned above, human capital as well as physical capital have been counted as key sources of sustained economic growth, and in particular Lucas (1993) pointed out the important role of human capital in the Korean economic growth. Our estimated result supports his conjecture, according to the regression of GDP on human capital and physical capital. GDP, human capital($HUMK_t$), and physical capital(K_t) have unit roots, but these variables turn out to be cointegrated. Hence, the estimated

Table 9.2: The annual economic growth (%)

	SIM1	SIM2	SIM3	SIM4	SIM5	SIM10
1985	0.02	0.05	0.07	0.09	0.12	0.23
1986	0.02	0.04	0.06	0.08	0.10	0.21
1987	0.02	0.03	0.05	0.07	0.09	0.17
1988	0.02	0.03	0.05	0.07	0.08	0.16
1989	0.01	0.03	0.04	0.05	0.06	0.13

result is

$$\log GDP = 0.41 \log K_t + 0.53 \log HUMK_t$$
$$(2.65) \qquad\qquad (2.24)$$
$$(R^2 = 0.99, \ D.W. = 1.81)$$

The above estimated outcome suggests human capital had significant contributions to the economic growth in Korea.

Appendix A Classification of industries and types of assets

1. Classification of industries

(0) All industries
(1) Agriculture, Forestry, and Fishing
(2) Mining and Quarrying
(3) Manufacturing
(4) Electricity, Gas and Water
(5) Construction
(6) Wholesale and Retail Trade, Restaurants, and Hotels
(7) Transport, Storage, and Communication
(8) Financing, Insurance, Real Estate, and Business Services
(9) Community, Social, and Personal Services

331. Food Manufacturing
313. Beverage Industries
314. Tobacco Manufacturers
321. Manufacture of Textiles
322. Manufacture of Wearing, Apparel, except for Footwear
323. Manufacture of Leather, Products of Leather, and Leather Finishing
324. Manufacture of Footwear
331. Manufacture of Wood and Cork Products, except Furniture
332. Manufacture of Furniture and Fixtures, except Primary Metal
341. Manufacture of Paper and Paper Products
342. Printing, Publishing, and Allied Industries
351. Manufacture of Industrial Chemicals
352. Manufacture of Other Chemical Products
353. Petroleum Refineries
354. Manufacture of Miscellaneous Products of Petroleum and Coal
355. Manufacture of Rubber Products
356. Manufacture of Plastic Products, N. E. C.
361. Manufacture of Pottery, China, and Earthenware
362. Manufacture of Glass and Glass Products
369. Manufacture of Other Non-Metallic Mineral Products
371. Iron and Steel Basic Industries
372. Non-Ferrous Metal Basic Industries
381. Manufacture of Fabricated Metal Products except Machinery and Equipment

382. Manufacture of Machinery except Electrical
383. Manufacture of Electrical Machinery, Apparatus, Appliances, and Supplies
384. Manufacture of Transport Equipment
385. Manufacture of Professional Scientific and Measuring Equipment, N. E. C.
390. Other Manufacturing

2. Types of Assets

· Buildings and Structures (B)
· Machinery and Equipment (M)
· Transportation Equipment (T)

Appendix B   Economic depreciation rate

	B	M	T
1	0.0581	0.1644	0.0920
2	0.0568	0.1728	0.2082
331-3	0.0525	0.1275	0.2315
321	0.0497	0.1274	0.2286
323-4	0.0527	0.1271	0.2156
331-2	0.0501	0.1276	0.1827
341	0.0530	0.1273	0.2464
342	0.0490	0.1283	0.2275
351-2	0.0487	0.1275	0.2244
353	0.0501	0.1273	0.2464
354	0.0486	0.1303	0.2276
355	0.0505	0.1286	0.2256
369	0.0493	0.1282	0.2081
371	0.0484	0.1255	0.1993
381	0.0489	0.1267	0.2316
382	0.0501	0.1266	0.2265
383	0.0502	0.1281	0.2313
384	0.0495	0.1302	0.1868
385	0.0501	0.1276	0.2266
390	0.0495	0.1216	0.1977
4	0.0389	0.1930	0.1903
5	0.0387	0.1317	0.2231
6	0.0346	0.1666	0.1493
7	0.0382	0.1524	0.2257
8	0.0321	0.1390	0.1734
9	0.0411	0.1352	0.1567

Appendix C   Estimate of α_1, α_2 and α_3

	Buildings and structures (B)			Machinery and equipment (M)			Transportation equipment (T)		
	α_1	α_2	α_3	α_1	α_2	α_3	α_1	α_2	α_3
1	.523	.297	.179	.309	.185	.506	.277	.165	.557
2	.515	.371	.114	.506	.359	.135	.508	.358	.134
331-3	1.516	.868	-1.38	1.234	.711	-.944	1.105	.637	-.742
321	.268	.600E-01	.672	.294	.796E-01	.626	.257	.651E-01	.678
323-4	.389	.175	.436	.193	.749E-01	.731	.662E-01	.704E-02	.927
331-2	.303	-.398E-01	.737	.151	-.101	.950	.226E-01	-.162	1.140
341	-.119	-.142	1.260	.567E-02	-.764E-01	1.071	.103E-01	-.670E-01	1.057
342	.144E-01	.157	.829	.195	.221	.584	.240	.231	.529
351-2	.901E-01	.205	.705	.118	.202	.680	.118	.199	.683
353	-1.707	-.868	3.574	-1.206	-.626	2.832	-1.096	-.575	2.671
354	.137	.733E-01	.789	.260	.140	.600	.242	.131	.626
355	1.972	1.156	-2.129	1.582	.930	-1.512	1.425	.839	-1.264
369	.350	.177	.472	.398	.195	.407	.390	.192	.419
371	.383	.174	.442	.386	.164	.450	.390	.160	.450
381	.162	.137	.701	.200	.162	.638	.190	.165	.646
382	.809	.454	-.264	.590	.366	.440E-01	.528	.333	.138
383	.986	.488	-.474	.716	.353	-.698E-01	.614	.300	.858E-01
384	.499	-.412	.889E-01	.533	.425	.416E-01	.558	.418	.241E-01
385	.245E-01	.239	.737	.441	.434	.125	.501	.462	.364E-01
390	.271	.166	.563	.476	.254	.270	.511	.269	.220
4	.620	.134	.246	.624	.151	.226	.616	.150	.235
5	-.132	-.157	1.288	-.175	-.173	1.347	-.216	-.195	1.411
6	.912	.426	-.338	.915	.446	-.362	.830	.401	-.230
7	.739	.257	.401E-02	.615	.211	.174	.517	.162	.321
8	1.220	.768	-.988	1.057	.660	-.717	1.005	.631	-.637
9	.821	.565	-.386	.884	.588	-.472	.924	.611	-.534

α_1 : Borrowing α_2 : New shares α_3 : Retained earnings

Appendix D The overall average of α_1, α_2 and α_3

	B	M	T
α_1	0.445	0.434	0.405
α_2	0.252	0.244	0.226
α_3	0.303	0.322	0.369

Appendix E The weight of assets(overall average)

	B	M	T
66	21.8	66.6	11.6
70	22.0	66.9	11.1
75	23.4	67.0	9.6
80	23.8	67.2	7.0
85	25.9	67.1	7.0
89	23.1	68.8	8.1

Appendix F Discount rate and expected inflation

	$i(1-m)$	$i(1-\tau)$	$i(1-m)/(1-\theta)$	$i(1-m)/(1-c)$	m	$\tau(1+l+f)$	π
1966	0.365	0.264	0.487	0.406	0.150	0.385	0.145
1970	0.317	0.205	0.423	0.352	0.150	0.450	0.156
1975	0.286	0.141	0.381	0.317	0.050	0.530	0.156
1980	0.341	0.169	0.455	0.379	0.050	0.530	0.149
1985	0.167	0.104	0.222	0.185	0.100	0.438	0.042
1989	0.146	0.092	0.195	0.163	0.100	0.438	0.047

Appendix G   Cost of capital by assets

YEAR	CCT1	CCT1B	CCT1M	CCT1T
1966:01	0.356090	0.342760	0.361060	0.364450
1967:01	0.317520	0.306620	0.321660	0.324280
1968:01	0.352190	0.333000	0.369780	0.353800
1969:01	0.332150	0.315600	0.349480	0.331370
1970:01	0.296360	0.281630	0.315890	0.297570
1971:01	0.308950	0.295680	0.324420	0.306750
1972:01	0.165650	0.175950	0.161530	0.159460
1973:01	0.159860	0.171780	0.155660	0.152130
1974:01	0.153840	0.159820	0.151990	0.149700
1975:01	0.259070	0.229820	0.281820	0.265580
1976:01	0.294680	0.267160	0.316280	0.300600
1977:01	0.308870	0.290650	0.315780	0.320180
1978:01	0.291890	0.288890	0.302350	0.304420
1979:01	0.356040	0.333800	0.364330	0.369980
1980:01	0.372580	0.343550	0.389510	0.384690
1981:01	0.306550	0.287960	0.319790	0.311890
1982:01	0.249460	0.237730	0.257280	0.253370
1983:01	0.207270	0.203750	0.216690	0.201370
1984:01	0.218500	0.216230	0.227470	0.211800
1985:01	0.212790	0.210320	0.222190	0.205870
1986:01	0.201630	0.200650	0.210920	0.193330
1987:01	0.208020	0.206300	0.217330	0.200440
1988:01	0.179450	0.174950	0.190240	0.173160
1989:01	0.179450	0.174190	0.193940	0.170230

YEAR	C311-3	C311-3B	C311-3M	C311-3T
1966:01	0.334990	0.339790	0.335150	0.323630
1967:01	0.312710	0.321230	0.311870	0.298990
1968:01	0.288820	0.312180	0.273320	0.326230
1969:01	0.297860	0.307510	0.287830	0.333950
1970:01	0.267960	0.274970	0.259040	0.303480
1971:01	0.280980	0.291120	0.270780	0.316930
1972:01	0.143580	0.165390	0.127950	0.185100
1973:01	0.139680	0.157060	0.124410	0.188780
1974:01	0.119000	0.137700	0.105710	0.153950
1975:01	0.195840	0.174470	0.194880	0.247670
1976:01	0.231060	0.210100	0.229060	0.287870
1977:01	0.247600	0.233820	0.242340	0.307420
1978:01	0.227560	0.209070	0.224200	0.286790
1979:01	0.280920	0.264990	0.276530	0.345540
1980:01	0.298100	0.271930	0.299110	0.374660
1981:01	0.273180	0.253700	0.273250	0.351170
1982:01	0.221950	0.214610	0.217890	0.275530
1983:01	0.201030	0.200180	0.196920	0.231210
1984:01	0.216010	0.215740	0.212200	0.248700
1985:01	0.214520	0.212570	0.211240	0.249740
1986:01	0.215360	0.211660	0.212020	0.262590
1987:01	0.217840	0.211500	0.216340	0.256430
1988:01	0.185760	0.177160	0.185240	0.224300
1989:01	0.192990	0.182350	0.192860	0.235990

YEAR	CCT2	CCT2B	CCT2M	CCT2T
1966:01	0.271820	0.267000	0.278500	0.269970
1967:01	0.253870	0.249980	0.258900	0.252140
1968:01	0.362100	0.381440	0.318420	0.386430
1969:01	0.346320	0.360800	0.305340	0.372830
1970:01	0.312490	0.323540	0.274940	0.338980
1971:01	0.323510	0.337680	0.283540	0.349310
1972:01	0.172060	0.198030	0.118620	0.201520
1973:01	0.166770	0.191590	0.110330	0.198400
1974:01	0.156880	0.182860	0.102270	0.185510
1975:01	0.178050	0.160300	0.188230	0.185620
1976:01	0.210460	0.191960	0.221000	0.218430
1977:01	0.231180	0.214580	0.240550	0.238400
1978:01	0.209490	0.191070	0.219700	0.217690
1979:01	0.259800	0.240700	0.270750	0.287940
1980:01	0.282920	0.254000	0.297000	0.297750
1981:01	0.253090	0.224730	0.265270	0.269280
1982:01	0.287330	0.289040	0.258220	0.314720
1983:01	0.233020	0.232900	0.214380	0.251770
1984:01	0.245850	0.246100	0.226560	0.264890
1985:01	0.241010	0.239460	0.222660	0.260900
1986:01	0.229660	0.225040	0.208020	0.255910
1987:01	0.242000	0.231860	0.234660	0.259490
1988:01	0.211210	0.198580	0.205550	0.229490
1989:01	0.211320	0.196880	0.206380	0.230690

YEAR	C321	C321B	C321M	C321T
1966:01	0.324310	0.320310	0.325300	0.323790
1967:01	0.285400	0.281310	0.286410	0.284930
1968:01	0.293530	0.311680	0.287660	0.328900
1969:01	0.276700	0.292520	0.271370	0.312730
1970:01	0.245900	0.258710	0.241320	0.281590
1971:01	0.258050	0.274320	0.252690	0.292230
1972:01	0.121770	0.153770	0.112180	0.165870
1973:01	0.118100	0.151330	0.108120	0.164430
1974:01	0.108880	0.138840	0.099740	0.154090
1975:01	0.210620	0.218640	0.205890	0.278360
1976:01	0.244450	0.257150	0.238520	0.314010
1977:01	0.258310	0.282420	0.249340	0.333980
1978:01	0.239880	0.258600	0.232180	0.316600
1979:01	0.298360	0.324990	0.288260	0.379690
1980:01	0.314740	0.331910	0.305210	0.396560
1981:01	0.260090	0.273360	0.251520	0.334250
1982:01	0.212950	0.226850	0.205430	0.271090
1983:01	0.181120	0.191900	0.175890	0.211760
1984:01	0.191560	0.203990	0.186630	0.222920
1985:01	0.186580	0.197320	0.181570	0.218000
1986:01	0.172310	0.183740	0.166760	0.210150
1987:01	0.182970	0.190130	0.178360	0.215320
1988:01	0.155280	0.159190	0.152510	0.188010
1989:01	0.154550	0.157790	0.151960	0.187250

YEAR	C323-4	C323-4B	C323-4M	C323-4T
1966:01	0.358320	0.342460	0.362350	0.383130
1967:01	0.310060	0.301260	0.312450	0.323150
1968:01	0.340900	0.334210	0.336630	0.377280
1969:01	0.310490	0.313880	0.302150	0.337590
1970:01	0.291650	0.285410	0.286090	0.332390
1971:01	0.291110	0.291540	0.281440	0.331850
1972:01	0.160190	0.175130	0.136560	0.222760
1973:01	0.160220	0.175260	0.142270	0.197930
1974:01	0.159330	0.164970	0.141860	0.220030
1975:01	0.273430	0.246170	0.269980	0.361060
1976:01	0.294770	0.276920	0.289200	0.366520
1977:01	0.308930	0.307180	0.292850	0.383270
1978:01	0.288830	0.278370	0.278280	0.362460
1979:01	0.364930	0.365750	0.354300	0.445910
1980:01	0.382240	0.373130	0.376540	0.469340
1981:01	0.312030	0.303630	0.307970	0.393000
1982:01	0.250490	0.246770	0.243280	0.326760
1983:01	0.200900	0.204470	0.195030	0.230300
1984:01	0.214670	0.218640	0.207920	0.239470
1985:01	0.205570	0.208810	0.199020	0.229680
1986:01	0.194340	0.197790	0.189100	0.217570
1987:01	0.204110	0.206070	0.199280	0.227030
1988:01	0.173330	0.171550	0.170250	0.198760
1989:01	0.173590	0.172790	0.169460	0.202080

YEAR	C341	C341B	C341M	C341T
1966:01	0.334460	0.336190	0.332100	0.345440
1967:01	0.289660	0.288750	0.288190	0.301120
1968:01	0.316780	0.335280	0.305230	0.355210
1969:01	0.293440	0.310190	0.282580	0.330910
1970:01	0.261160	0.274770	0.251260	0.298580
1971:01	0.272650	0.289690	0.262050	0.307860
1972:01	0.139140	0.171500	0.120820	0.194140
1973:01	0.135950	0.171150	0.116470	0.192860
1974:01	0.130880	0.161370	0.112420	0.190530
1975:01	0.242340	0.254160	0.227680	0.314490
1976:01	0.277090	0.294380	0.250730	0.349390
1977:01	0.294250	0.320090	0.274850	0.369300
1978:01	0.276270	0.297120	0.258060	0.353530
1979:01	0.335520	0.369190	0.318180	0.419830
1980:01	0.345890	0.377630	0.334280	0.434750
1981:01	0.279550	0.301470	0.267210	0.356680
1982:01	0.228550	0.248190	0.219640	0.292270
1983:01	0.188330	0.203000	0.183440	0.223160
1984:01	0.199790	0.214140	0.192980	0.232550
1985:01	0.192330	0.206170	0.186390	0.225720
1986:01	0.174390	0.187480	0.168280	0.210940
1987:01	0.189000	0.196490	0.184240	0.219850
1988:01	0.161660	0.166070	0.157770	0.193710
1989:01	0.157830	0.162080	0.154070	0.188780

YEAR	C331-2	C331-2B	C331-2M	C331-2T
1966:01	0.277780	0.271270	0.279540	0.278200
1967:01	0.241200	0.237310	0.242680	0.240320
1968:01	0.255080	0.259100	0.245350	0.277780
1969:01	0.238190	0.244010	0.229110	0.257740
1970:01	0.209420	0.213180	0.201140	0.228450
1971:01	0.222070	0.230070	0.213120	0.239590
1972:01	0.093720	0.118320	0.074890	0.124480
1973:01	0.090870	0.117660	0.071260	0.121980
1974:01	0.081400	0.101640	0.062740	0.115130
1975:01	0.184590	0.170870	0.171080	0.231170
1976:01	0.217030	0.207330	0.202010	0.264480
1977:01	0.235610	0.232530	0.217890	0.285060
1978:01	0.216400	0.207480	0.199980	0.266990
1979:01	0.267100	0.267750	0.253290	0.327250
1980:01	0.273950	0.271490	0.267060	0.337310
1981:01	0.227080	0.226290	0.216690	0.274000
1982:01	0.178200	0.189540	0.177720	0.224580
1983:01	0.158920	0.163620	0.152010	0.172660
1984:01	0.170560	0.175490	0.161890	0.182010
1985:01	0.163820	0.169500	0.156550	0.175840
1986:01	0.150720	0.158940	0.142550	0.164420
1987:01	0.160290	0.163720	0.155510	0.171460
1988:01	0.133550	0.134030	0.129930	0.146120
1989:01	0.132560	0.134150	0.128880	0.143180

YEAR	C342	C342B	C342M	C342T
1966:01	0.418340	0.422340	0.417640	0.412060
1967:01	0.368890	0.369620	0.368960	0.365590
1968:01	0.396540	0.424110	0.385290	0.423280
1969:01	0.371170	0.394240	0.361030	0.401350
1970:01	0.334730	0.353850	0.325770	0.365870
1971:01	0.344820	0.366670	0.335090	0.374760
1972:01	0.193240	0.230690	0.176370	0.246720
1973:01	0.187230	0.225760	0.169670	0.244550
1974:01	0.184500	0.221480	0.167660	0.239250
1975:01	0.307950	0.327220	0.296230	0.368470
1976:01	0.345810	0.370570	0.332280	0.406940
1977:01	0.358380	0.396180	0.340000	0.427040
1978:01	0.341780	0.375140	0.324740	0.411350
1979:01	0.427940	0.456150	0.390990	0.483040
1980:01	0.432670	0.469960	0.412920	0.504020
1981:01	0.355850	0.377110	0.336230	0.423350
1982:01	0.288570	0.308510	0.275070	0.345590
1983:01	0.237580	0.251290	0.230140	0.270880
1984:01	0.255660	0.263350	0.240950	0.282370
1985:01	0.245390	0.254750	0.234490	0.276470
1986:01	0.226800	0.235690	0.220440	0.263430
1987:01	0.234260	0.246460	0.228380	0.270840
1988:01	0.204950	0.213000	0.199800	0.241740
1989:01	0.201180	0.207480	0.196260	0.238840

YEAR	C351-2	C351-2B	O351-2M	C351-2T
1966:01	0.274770	0.277560	0.274030	0.273870
1967:01	0.253540	0.255930	0.252850	0.253510
1968:01	0.370540	0.423320	0.349880	0.448210
1969:01	0.345030	0.394340	0.325460	0.421470
1970:01	0.310430	0.354060	0.292550	0.384720
1971:01	0.319180	0.366930	0.300250	0.392790
1972:01	0.155720	0.217970	0.132800	0.229260
1973:01	0.146930	0.210810	0.123170	0.222860
1974:01	0.146590	0.207760	0.123610	0.222550
1975:01	0.200660	0.197920	0.200500	0.214530
1976:01	0.229680	0.227860	0.229260	0.243350
1977:01	0.248090	0.248490	0.247020	0.261940
1978:01	0.230020	0.228580	0.229460	0.244240
1979:01	0.279430	0.278610	0.278410	0.292620
1980:01	0.301950	0.295590	0.302420	0.323620
1981:01	0.254970	0.250000	0.255400	0.279130
1982:01	0.287140	0.307070	0.281320	0.363980
1983:01	0.240290	0.251230	0.234490	0.283380
1984:01	0.250880	0.263490	0.244950	0.294100
1985:01	0.244050	0.255100	0.238060	0.287130
1986:01	0.218640	0.234060	0.212630	0.271230
1987:01	0.234650	0.244400	0.229600	0.280830
1988:01	0.205150	0.211090	0.201300	0.251820
1989:01	0.200570	0.205940	0.196930	0.246620

YEAR	C354	C354B	C354M	C354T
1966:01	0.351310	0.357750	0.338810	0.361540
1967:01	0.310400	0.313070	0.300190	0.319310
1968:01	0.333690	0.353470	0.290840	0.369240
1969:01	0.314810	0.329880	0.273010	0.350390
1970:01	0.282920	0.293560	0.243350	0.317380
1971:01	0.293000	0.308110	0.252610	0.327260
1972:01	0.165930	0.184870	0.115830	0.206400
1973:01	0.162830	0.182110	0.110300	0.207470
1974:01	0.155860	0.172330	0.105390	0.199200
1975:01	0.278000	0.260180	0.240060	0.317050
1976:01	0.313850	0.300590	0.273810	0.353870
1977:01	0.332600	0.326030	0.289640	0.373900
1978:01	0.315430	0.303270	0.273170	0.357270
1979:01	0.375910	0.375450	0.333800	0.424080
1980:01	0.390660	0.384930	0.352930	0.442570
1981:01	0.327350	0.312370	0.289600	0.372070
1982:01	0.258050	0.257430	0.236530	0.302810
1983:01	0.211600	0.213610	0.200130	0.236820
1984:01	0.224640	0.225590	0.210970	0.248060
1985:01	0.215500	0.218100	0.205350	0.242670
1986:01	0.202740	0.203700	0.194710	0.231840
1987:01	0.213320	0.211930	0.200800	0.238040
1988:01	0.184960	0.179910	0.173170	0.210040
1989:01	0.183040	0.176810	0.171450	0.208280

YEAR	C353	O353B	C353M	C353T
1966:01	0.426970	0.433350	0.422810	0.470940
1967:01	0.352670	0.348890	0.351470	0.396580
1968:01	0.420790	0.464360	0.404420	0.491500
1969:01	0.368730	0.412260	0.353000	0.427410
1970:01	0.329590	0.367940	0.315360	0.388360
1971:01	0.337220	0.379160	0.322180	0.391350
1972:01	0.160080	0.225400	0.137490	0.228470
1973:01	0.150750	0.224890	0.125890	0.213500
1974:01	0.186090	0.232250	0.142370	0.251450
1975:01	0.362860	0.425110	0.338510	0.482250
1976:01	0.400440	0.474050	0.373060	0.514510
1977:01	0.418300	0.501770	0.387910	0.534980
1978:01	0.403990	0.482910	0.374640	0.526060
1979:01	0.498620	0.582750	0.450620	0.609380
1980:01	0.527430	0.599460	0.466350	0.613310
1981:01	0.379970	0.442290	0.340490	0.459050
1982:01	0.330270	0.355400	0.286980	0.391500
1983:01	0.253710	0.263340	0.223730	0.281040
1984:01	0.250240	0.270950	0.228040	0.282380
1985:01	0.227640	0.257220	0.215030	0.266250
1986:01	0.173710	0.216200	0.167270	0.218080
1987:01	0.211190	0.236840	0.196840	0.245410
1988:01	0.186310	0.207380	0.173530	0.223080
1989:01	0.169420	0.191990	0.156920	0.198430

YEAR	C355	C355B	C355M	C355T
1966:01	0.331900	0.343240	0.330770	0.316600
1967:01	0.315880	0.332570	0.313960	0.298000
1968:01	0.299850	0.307970	0.297580	0.316960
1969:01	0.306490	0.308460	0.304630	0.333320
1970:01	0.276810	0.276580	0.275340	0.303450
1971:01	0.290410	0.292940	0.288410	0.317980
1972:01	0.150630	0.166960	0.145390	0.192650
1973:01	0.147230	0.156340	0.142730	0.198510
1974:01	0.121520	0.133780	0.117510	0.154410
1975:01	0.181270	0.154090	0.183430	0.227330
1976:01	0.216030	0.188400	0.217900	0.268710
1977:01	0.230170	0.211570	0.230160	0.288120
1978:01	0.210630	0.186420	0.211740	0.266210
1979:01	0.259850	0.238060	0.261440	0.322560
1980:01	0.282560	0.244370	0.287070	0.355130
1981:01	0.271060	0.241400	0.273400	0.346980
1982:01	0.215490	0.206320	0.215910	0.269070
1983:01	0.201170	0.200050	0.199530	0.232100
1984:01	0.218260	0.216760	0.216470	0.251730
1985:01	0.218470	0.214810	0.217170	0.254890
1986:01	0.229240	0.220160	0.228790	0.274370
1987:01	0.223520	0.217680	0.222790	0.264090
1988:01	0.190430	0.181860	0.190580	0.230430
1989:01	0.200900	0.189410	0.201610	0.246590

YEAR	C369	C369B	C369M	C369T
1966:01	0.256430	0.262460	0.257920	0.250580
1967:01	0.235570	0.240860	0.236680	0.230810
1968:01	0.322360	0.339180	0.307910	0.341060
1969:01	0.306480	0.319010	0.292220	0.327000
1970:01	0.274630	0.283730	0.261270	0.295190
1971:01	0.286160	0.298710	0.272230	0.306030
1972:01	0.143820	0.171100	0.120130	0.173960
1973:01	0.139460	0.166890	0.114870	0.171880
1974:01	0.129640	0.156180	0.106680	0.159460
1975:01	0.153980	0.145170	0.152620	0.160970
1976:01	0.184190	0.175060	0.182690	0.191610
1977:01	0.205090	0.196920	0.204040	0.211180
1978:01	0.184040	0.174170	0.183110	0.190760
1979:01	0.228830	0.220920	0.230200	0.237620
1980:01	0.244580	0.231670	0.246210	0.263690
1981:01	0.216560	0.202670	0.216810	0.236680
1982:01	0.235360	0.245250	0.222700	0.278520
1983:01	0.201570	0.207230	0.190840	0.220870
1984:01	0.213170	0.219690	0.202200	0.232960
1985:01	0.205550	0.212940	0.197390	0.228620
1986:01	0.192480	0.198760	0.184500	0.222820
1987:01	0.204020	0.205490	0.196860	0.226830
1988:01	0.175200	0.173630	0.168940	0.198420
1989:01	0.174840	0.171940	0.168770	0.198980

YEAR	C381	C381B	C381M	C381T
1966:01	0.373940	0.377250	0.370830	0.397140
1967:01	0.330090	0.331250	0.327950	0.350090
1968:01	0.365940	0.373780	0.359660	0.407830
1969:01	0.342900	0.349080	0.337160	0.385500
1970:01	0.308000	0.311650	0.303160	0.350750
1971:01	0.319000	0.325730	0.313210	0.359760
1972:01	0.173720	0.198450	0.159760	0.234930
1973:01	0.168750	0.194750	0.154080	0.233030
1974:01	0.163790	0.186240	0.150380	0.228230
1975:01	0.278940	0.277310	0.273150	0.356170
1976:01	0.315880	0.318410	0.308530	0.393870
1977:01	0.333240	0.343830	0.322770	0.413930
1978:01	0.315570	0.321520	0.306610	0.398190
1979:01	0.384300	0.395710	0.371460	0.468630
1980:01	0.398970	0.406420	0.388520	0.488300
1981:01	0.327270	0.329980	0.316740	0.408450
1982:01	0.262770	0.271510	0.258960	0.333640
1983:01	0.221060	0.224830	0.216980	0.260270
1984:01	0.234830	0.237000	0.227740	0.271320
1985:01	0.227120	0.229350	0.221490	0.265250
1986:01	0.209990	0.211550	0.204390	0.252750
1987:01	0.223120	0.220170	0.220020	0.260490
1988:01	0.193730	0.187930	0.191480	0.231980
1989:01	0.190480	0.184410	0.188320	0.228680

YEAR	C371	C371B	C371M	C371T
1966:01	0.228890	0.232220	0.228450	0.224440
1967:01	0.211620	0.215270	0.211110	0.207410
1968:01	0.281270	0.327910	0.270580	0.321940
1969:01	0.266300	0.308840	0.256320	0.308610
1970:01	0.236690	0.274200	0.227730	0.277620
1971:01	0.247650	0.289450	0.237860	0.288800
1972:01	0.101330	0.159240	0.088140	0.149900
1973:01	0.082050	0.125170	0.072390	0.114620
1974:01	0.069610	0.110900	0.060550	0.096290
1975:01	0.145810	0.138200	0.147040	0.150810
1976:01	0.175620	0.168070	0.176820	0.181090
1977:01	0.194780	0.190090	0.195420	0.200700
1978:01	0.173570	0.166990	0.174540	0.180100
1979:01	0.219780	0.213310	0.220740	0.226120
1980:01	0.236570	0.223190	0.239240	0.250430
1981:01	0.209310	0.196270	0.210910	0.224970
1982:01	0.216550	0.250270	0.206060	0.262210
1983:01	0.179650	0.201130	0.175750	0.208210
1984:01	0.192320	0.213620	0.186730	0.220150
1985:01	0.188630	0.207070	0.182120	0.215890
1986:01	0.171020	0.193770	0.164700	0.210590
1987:01	0.190770	0.200040	0.188310	0.214310
1988:01	0.162500	0.168360	0.160810	0.186260
1989:01	0.162260	0.167110	0.160790	0.187080

YEAR	C382	C382B	C382M	O382T
1966:01	0.280130	0.268700	0.285500	0.275920
1967:01	0.260230	0.252580	0.263900	0.256220
1968:01	0.314720	0.330570	0.301900	0.372590
1969:01	0.301800	0.316250	0.289410	0.361370
1970:01	0.270390	0.281920	0.259430	0.328380
1971:01	0.281740	0.297300	0.269100	0.339100
1972:01	0.132400	0.165540	0.112550	0.186210
1973:01	0.126310	0.158970	0.106270	0.184010
1974:01	0.116650	0.146510	0.098400	0.168620
1975:01	0.156150	0.123130	0.167990	0.179430
1976:01	0.188790	0.155500	0.200690	0.212550
1977:01	0.206790	0.179540	0.215890	0.232480
1978:01	0.183740	0.153390	0.193970	0.211500
1979:01	0.234560	0.201910	0.244040	0.261290
1980:01	0.256450	0.210620	0.268980	0.291880
1981:01	0.223310	0.193940	0.240820	0.266460
1982:01	0.235780	0.246190	0.229530	0.307240
1983:01	0.201430	0.205400	0.196920	0.245750
1984:01	0.214770	0.219060	0.209040	0.259110
1985:01	0.211080	0.213670	0.205050	0.255640
1986:01	0.201690	0.204530	0.198490	0.252490
1987:01	0.220610	0.208650	0.222460	0.255090
1988:01	0.189930	0.175780	0.192590	0.225330
1989:01	0.190830	0.176680	0.193370	0.227550

YEAR	C383	C383B	C383M	C383T
1966:01	0.318010	0.316520	0.318340	0.321230
1967:01	0.288660	0.290660	0.287980	0.288530
1968:01	0.268590	0.295860	0.256180	0.325210
1969:01	0.250710	0.285960	0.248890	0.319290
1970:01	0.232040	0.253760	0.221540	0.288550
1971:01	0.243980	0.270030	0.232000	0.300420
1972:01	0.106540	0.146570	0.089900	0.160500
1973:01	0.101780	0.140830	0.085230	0.160410
1974:01	0.088720	0.124720	0.073620	0.139890
1975:01	0.193580	0.178870	0.194850	0.263220
1976:01	0.227480	0.215070	0.227770	0.300700
1977:01	0.239100	0.239440	0.234590	0.320480
1978:01	0.219940	0.214740	0.217300	0.301700
1979:01	0.273620	0.273330	0.269960	0.362710
1980:01	0.290280	0.279120	0.291590	0.384670
1981:01	0.252660	0.247280	0.252040	0.339220
1982:01	0.206820	0.208190	0.203420	0.271110
1983:01	0.182320	0.187600	0.179340	0.218410
1984:01	0.195000	0.201540	0.192010	0.232230
1985:01	0.191850	0.197020	0.188940	0.229850
1986:01	0.182820	0.191400	0.179370	0.230850
1987:01	0.190160	0.193680	0.187810	0.231170
1988:01	0.160920	0.161200	0.159630	0.201900
1989:01	0.164230	0.163900	0.163100	0.206440

YEAR	C385	C385B	O385M	C385T
1966:01	0.430550	0.453840	0.423160	0.438870
1967:01	0.384510	0.398430	0.379750	0.394590
1968:01	0.422440	0.457500	0.410250	0.451000
1969:01	0.399050	0.425470	0.388930	0.434660
1970:01	0.361440	0.383260	0.352600	0.398070
1971:01	0.371230	0.395300	0.361770	0.407300
1972:01	0.212870	0.252890	0.197250	0.271120
1973:01	0.206150	0.246660	0.190040	0.269550
1974:01	0.202330	0.244600	0.186190	0.258410
1975:01	0.325860	0.356700	0.312820	0.385840
1976:01	0.364830	0.401240	0.350040	0.426550
1977:01	0.379030	0.426840	0.360510	0.446560
1978:01	0.362720	0.406560	0.345350	0.430380
1979:01	0.438090	0.491100	0.413170	0.503300
1980:01	0.476170	0.506910	0.442440	0.529250
1981:01	0.390900	0.406780	0.367410	0.455060
1982:01	0.309260	0.332180	0.298970	0.369160
1983:01	0.257840	0.269740	0.251710	0.294600
1984:01	0.270730	0.282020	0.263910	0.308150
1985:01	0.264520	0.273090	0.258220	0.303790
1986:01	0.251220	0.252480	0.246550	0.295900
1987:01	0.257800	0.264090	0.253210	0.300510
1988:01	0.226670	0.229790	0.222770	0.269340
1989:01	0.224050	0.223480	0.220740	0.269630

YEAR	C384	O384B	C384M	O384T
1966:01	0.310780	0.305300	0.319120	0.294370
1967:01	0.287930	0.283660	0.294620	0.274660
1968:01	0.366700	0.398790	0.344690	0.391420
1969:01	0.349600	0.376170	0.328800	0.377470
1970:01	0.315530	0.337700	0.296360	0.343150
1971:01	0.325660	0.351320	0.305060	0.353410
1972:01	0.166510	0.206460	0.137550	0.201460
1973:01	0.159500	0.198480	0.129910	0.197140
1974:01	0.152510	0.192020	0.124720	0.184820
1975:01	0.187780	0.169650	0.195160	0.187250
1976:01	0.220620	0.201480	0.228250	0.220470
1977:01	0.241010	0.224040	0.247830	0.240730
1978:01	0.219430	0.200910	0.226630	0.219770
1979:01	0.270720	0.251580	0.279170	0.270890
1980:01	0.289000	0.265640	0.302020	0.299710
1981:01	0.252560	0.233080	0.266800	0.270740
1982:01	0.283530	0.299300	0.266720	0.314690
1983:01	0.231010	0.240490	0.221880	0.253080
1984:01	0.243820	0.253710	0.234000	0.266370
1985:01	0.233690	0.246700	0.229370	0.262320
1986:01	0.220880	0.230970	0.216530	0.257180
1987:01	0.241970	0.238550	0.242300	0.260810
1988:01	0.211030	0.204780	0.212010	0.230350
1989:01	0.210180	0.202350	0.211470	0.231530

YEAR	C390	C390B	C390M	C390T
1966:01	0.336960	0.362600	0.321460	0.333420
1967:01	0.300310	0.319840	0.288410	0.298610
1968:01	0.328940	0.356510	0.311250	0.335590
1969:01	0.311680	0.334250	0.296490	0.324400
1970:01	0.278640	0.297920	0.265350	0.292840
1971:01	0.290970	0.312460	0.276420	0.304080
1972:01	0.156800	0.187810	0.134550	0.188490
1973:01	0.152830	0.184270	0.129950	0.188190
1974:01	0.142850	0.173990	0.120730	0.172360
1975:01	0.238130	0.258240	0.222440	0.271580
1976:01	0.274290	0.298420	0.256040	0.308540
1977:01	0.292710	0.323700	0.270050	0.328690
1978:01	0.273540	0.300910	0.253040	0.310360
1979:01	0.339280	0.372250	0.311010	0.373180
1980:01	0.353940	0.381880	0.329640	0.392240
1981:01	0.294390	0.312980	0.276070	0.338280
1982:01	0.240330	0.258330	0.224610	0.273100
1983:01	0.202100	0.216210	0.193110	0.219050
1984:01	0.214530	0.228560	0.204830	0.231850
1985:01	0.207890	0.221410	0.200240	0.228190
1986:01	0.202120	0.208140	0.193420	0.223990
1987:01	0.206380	0.215780	0.197440	0.226580
1988:01	0.176650	0.183320	0.169270	0.197660
1989:01	0.176210	0.180830	0.169700	0.199750

YEAR	CCT 4	CCT 4B	CCT 4M	CCT 4T
1966:01	0.217550	0.214940	0.222130	0.215580
1967:01	0.201000	0.199280	0.204550	0.199170
1968:01	0.305030	0.291630	0.323630	0.299820
1969:01	0.291730	0.275010	0.311790	0.288380
1970:01	0.260360	0.242220	0.280460	0.258400
1971:01	0.273780	0.258270	0.292970	0.270090
1972:01	0.145010	0.138280	0.155710	0.141050
1973:01	0.142820	0.134540	0.154780	0.139130
1974:01	0.128540	0.121360	0.139810	0.124440
1975:01	0.135960	0.118030	0.150670	0.139180
1976:01	0.166260	0.147480	0.181790	0.169520
1977:01	0.186700	0.169750	0.201020	0.189320
1978:01	0.164520	0.145950	0.179390	0.168230
1979:01	0.210080	0.190760	0.225790	0.213700
1980:01	0.227350	0.197650	0.248080	0.236310
1981:01	0.204770	0.175460	0.225020	0.213840
1982:01	0.231760	0.221160	0.230310	0.243800
1983:01	0.186340	0.180050	0.184330	0.194630
1984:01	0.206330	0.192410	0.219910	0.206670
1985:01	0.201610	0.186260	0.215810	0.202760
1986:01	0.195250	0.177320	0.210370	0.198070
1987:01	0.199060	0.182580	0.213660	0.200830
1988:01	0.169830	0.151230	0.185100	0.173170
1989:01	0.170770	0.150990	0.186480	0.174840

YEAR	CCT 6	CCT 6B	CCT 6M	CCT 6T
1966:01	0.223180	0.305410	0.17341	0.190710
1967:01	0.197420	0.279650	0.14765	0.164950
1968:01	0.200380	0.282610	0.15061	0.167910
1969:01	0.188850	0.271080	0.13908	0.156380
1970:01	0.157030	0.239260	0.10726	0.124560
1971:01	0.173220	0.255450	0.12345	0.140750
1972:01	0.053150	0.135380	0.00338	0.020680
1973:01	0.046730	0.128960	-0.00304	0.014260
1974:01	0.032680	0.114910	-0.01709	0.000211
1975:01	0.092370	0.174600	0.04260	0.059900
1976:01	0.130710	0.212940	0.08094	0.098240
1977:01	0.157840	0.240070	0.10807	0.125370
1978:01	0.129970	0.212200	0.08020	0.097500
1979:01	0.191460	0.273690	0.14169	0.158990
1980:01	0.191970	0.274200	0.14220	0.159500
1981:01	0.159600	0.241830	0.10983	0.127130
1982:01	0.124240	0.206470	0.07447	0.091770
1983:01	0.094800	0.177030	0.04503	0.062330
1984:01	0.108190	0.190420	0.05842	0.075720
1985:01	0.103210	0.185440	0.05344	0.070740
1986:01	0.096540	0.178770	0.04677	0.064070
1987:01	0.099510	0.181740	0.04974	0.067040
1988:01	0.067520	0.149750	0.01775	0.035050
1989:01	0.069440	0.151670	0.01967	0.036970

YEAR	CCT 5	CCT 5B	CCT 5M	CCT 5T
1966:01	0.335170	0.325930	0.328150	0.351420
1967:01	0.288300	0.279610	0.282830	0.302450
1968:01	0.315940	0.323170	0.264980	0.359670
1969:01	0.289320	0.298450	0.240720	0.328790
1970:01	0.253300	0.263260	0.200780	0.295870
1971:01	0.264120	0.278410	0.209440	0.304510
1972:01	0.146560	0.162600	0.083760	0.193320
1973:01	0.143100	0.161870	0.077130	0.190300
1974:01	0.140790	0.151350	0.076740	0.194280
1975:01	0.260810	0.241040	0.218780	0.322620
1976:01	0.296000	0.281290	0.249900	0.356820
1977:01	0.316530	0.307170	0.265300	0.377130
1978:01	0.298430	0.283830	0.249520	0.361940
1979:01	0.364540	0.355500	0.307890	0.430230
1980:01	0.376300	0.363340	0.323790	0.441780
1981:01	0.298190	0.288440	0.253540	0.352800
1982:01	0.245520	0.237230	0.210690	0.291630
1983:01	0.196430	0.194040	0.175700	0.219540
1984:01	0.205600	0.205220	0.184150	0.227420
1985:01	0.197740	0.197320	0.176920	0.218970
1986:01	0.177510	0.179360	0.154500	0.198680
1987:01	0.189070	0.188090	0.168470	0.210660
1988:01	0.162270	0.157710	0.143750	0.185350
1989:01	0.156770	0.154030	0.139080	0.177210

YEAR	CCT 7	CCT 7B	CCT. 7M	CCT. 7T
1966:01	0.286350	0.280430	0.277730	0.300880
1967:01	0.256740	0.253760	0.249390	0.267070
1968:01	0.275230	0.260120	0.280430	0.285150
1969:01	0.266710	0.248820	0.272860	0.278460
1970:01	0.236990	0.218140	0.243360	0.249460
1971:01	0.251230	0.235010	0.256950	0.261720
1972:01	0.142750	0.126430	0.148170	0.153660
1973:01	0.142670	0.123240	0.148860	0.155900
1974:01	0.123170	0.105110	0.128950	0.135460
1975:01	0.199770	0.162580	0.209090	0.227630
1976:01	0.236370	0.200560	0.245260	0.263300
1977:01	0.252930	0.227800	0.247880	0.283120
1978:01	0.230390	0.199570	0.227620	0.263990
1979:01	0.288350	0.259870	0.283260	0.321910
1980:01	0.295310	0.259270	0.288380	0.340270
1981:01	0.258170	0.227150	0.249750	0.297610
1982:01	0.211160	0.193960	0.201700	0.237820
1983:01	0.173630	0.164580	0.166080	0.190220
1984:01	0.186370	0.177490	0.178550	0.203070
1985:01	0.182780	0.172430	0.175630	0.200290
1986:01	0.180710	0.167660	0.175110	0.199370
1987:01	0.182180	0.170660	0.175700	0.200180
1988:01	0.153290	0.139350	0.148190	0.172330
1989:01	0.156530	0.141290	0.152110	0.176180

YEAR	CCT 8	CCT 8B	CCT 8M	CCT 8T
1966:01	0.354380	0.387080	0.349960	0.346090
1967:01	0.327660	0.341240	0.323010	0.318740
1968:01	0.344800	0.342930	0.347180	0.344280
1969:01	0.338410	0.329850	0.343000	0.342380
1970:01	0.305290	0.294830	0.310490	0.310560
1971:01	0.318430	0.309630	0.323030	0.322620
1972:01	0.194380	0.182710	0.199500	0.200920
1973:01	0.189960	0.172530	0.197060	0.200300
1974:01	0.170420	0.159560	0.175490	0.176210
1975:01	0.242160	0.213470	0.253180	0.259820
1976:01	0.281080	0.253150	0.291740	0.298350
1977:01	0.300090	0.280060	0.301860	0.318340
1978:01	0.278070	0.253270	0.282130	0.298810
1979:01	0.340380	0.318870	0.342330	0.359930
1980:01	0.353220	0.322620	0.353930	0.383120
1981:01	0.316070	0.285700	0.316960	0.345540
1982:01	0.258020	0.242670	0.254930	0.276470
1983:01	0.218380	0.209620	0.214850	0.230670
1984:01	0.233350	0.224020	0.229780	0.246250
1985:01	0.230660	0.219010	0.228040	0.244940
1986:01	0.231170	0.213500	0.230980	0.249040
1987:01	0.231250	0.216910	0.229700	0.247130
1988:01	0.198820	0.182280	0.198610	0.215560
1989:01	0.203740	0.183880	0.204780	0.222570

YEAR	CCTO	CCTOB	CCTOM	CCTOT
1966:01	0.277690	0.273680	0.265230	0.263290
1967:01	0.252430	0.248690	0.239680	0.238710
1968:01	0.296870	0.296300	0.266260	0.303740
1969:01	0.283590	0.280640	0.254440	0.292010
1970:01	0.253910	0.249890	0.226930	0.263800
1971:01	0.264570	0.263100	0.236420	0.273400
1972:01	0.135410	0.150560	0.108850	0.155530
1973:01	0.130420	0.143680	0.103390	0.151830
1974:01	0.120700	0.133030	0.094390	0.140070
1975:01	0.179930	0.169800	0.173630	0.193030
1976:01	0.210880	0.201240	0.202830	0.223120
1977:01	0.228030	0.222730	0.214490	0.240940
1978:01	0.208950	0.201460	0.197730	0.223550
1979:01	0.292920	0.259380	0.247900	0.315920
1980:01	0.286570	0.268770	0.260050	0.314210
1981:01	0.238110	0.226690	0.220740	0.261940
1982:01	0.214760	0.220010	0.224920	0.238070
1983:01	0.172380	0.179490	0.163010	0.180060
1984:01	0.196570	0.196090	0.178320	0.205400
1985:01	0.191110	0.188800	0.176760	0.202370
1986:01	0.181240	0.178820	0.166670	0.197910
1987:01	0.188830	0.181700	0.174570	0.200140
1988:01	0.161420	0.153000	0.149320	0.174440
1989:01	0.162070	0.152820	0.150330	0.175860

YEAR	CCT 9	CCT 9B	CCT 9M	CCT 9T
1966:01	0.370050	0.385090	0.366520	0.358540
1967:01	0.338220	0.350300	0.335330	0.329040
1968:01	0.368120	0.370110	0.378060	0.356180
1969:01	0.357010	0.352180	0.368710	0.350130
1970:01	0.322370	0.315410	0.334230	0.317480
1971:01	0.335110	0.329670	0.346730	0.328940
1972:01	0.207780	0.199320	0.217190	0.206830
1973:01	0.203430	0.191370	0.214450	0.204460
1974:01	0.187230	0.180310	0.196610	0.184780
1975:01	0.265940	0.253270	0.273540	0.271000
1976:01	0.305010	0.283700	0.312050	0.309280
1977:01	0.318890	0.319440	0.307760	0.329470
1978:01	0.298690	0.295400	0.290200	0.310470
1979:01	0.363300	0.365410	0.351090	0.373390
1980:01	0.377570	0.373520	0.364230	0.394950
1981:01	0.328470	0.317990	0.317480	0.349930
1982:01	0.267440	0.284950	0.255630	0.281750
1983:01	0.226790	0.224610	0.222180	0.233590
1984:01	0.241030	0.238410	0.236270	0.248420
1985:01	0.237320	0.232390	0.233430	0.246130
1986:01	0.232930	0.220790	0.230440	0.247560
1987:01	0.235000	0.226300	0.231180	0.247530
1988:01	0.203000	0.192330	0.200590	0.216090
1989:01	0.205870	0.191890	0.204610	0.221100

Notes
Ci: the overall average of the cost
    of capital in sub-manufacturing
    industry i
Cij: the cost of capital of asset j
    in sub-manufacturing industry i

Appendix H   Cost of capital by industries

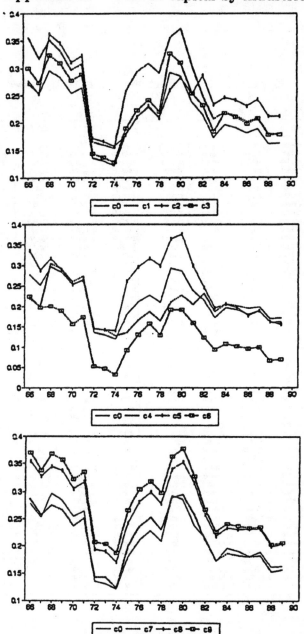

Appendix I   Effective tax rate by assets

YEAR	ES1	TE1B	TE1N	TE1T
1966:01	0.459830	0.439230	0.467660	0.472610
1967:01	0.451280	0.432110	0.458680	0.463050
1968:01	0.518580	0.491770	0.542320	0.521660
1969:01	0.520660	0.496400	0.545220	0.520360
1970:01	0.532580	0.505890	0.559480	0.532360
1971:01	0.507880	0.486540	0.532030	0.505070
1972:01	0.441510	0.475220	0.428370	0.420950
1973:01	0.439860	0.480180	0.426350	0.413040
1974:01	0.487150	0.506750	0.481330	0.473380
1975:01	0.565540	0.513810	0.603520	0.579290
1976:01	0.541430	0.496720	0.574870	0.552690
1977:01	0.506780	0.476820	0.518450	0.525060
1978:01	0.539260	0.501490	0.556640	0.559660
1979:01	0.517790	0.486720	0.529730	0.536930
1980:01	0.548990	0.512430	0.589960	0.564570
1981:01	0.537700	0.508850	0.557730	0.546530
1982:01	0.483610	0.458770	0.499900	0.492170
1983:01	0.438610	0.429500	0.463560	0.422760
1984:01	0.427370	0.421870	0.450450	0.409780
1985:01	0.435570	0.429500	0.460000	0.417200
1986:01	0.434950	0.432910	0.460500	0.411430
1987:01	0.434680	0.430590	0.459500	0.413940
1988:01	0.469790	0.457120	0.500760	0.451500
1989:01	0.469520	0.455250	0.510740	0.442570

YEAR	E311-3	T311-3B	T311-3M	T311-3T
1966:01	0.426130	0.434350	0.426510	0.406100
1967:01	0.442950	0.457950	0.441680	0.417640
1968:01	0.411020	0.457870	0.380800	0.481220
1969:01	0.465090	0.483160	0.447810	0.524080
1970:01	0.479310	0.493930	0.462800	0.541470
1971:01	0.458130	0.478480	0.439310	0.520950
1972:01	0.343530	0.441710	0.278340	0.501150
1973:01	0.346440	0.431440	0.282250	0.526990
1974:01	0.323110	0.427500	0.254280	0.487930
1975:01	0.424020	0.359570	0.428660	0.548850
1976:01	0.413550	0.360040	0.412980	0.532910
1977:01	0.381930	0.349660	0.372530	0.505350
1978:01	0.406250	0.358850	0.402110	0.532600
1979:01	0.386750	0.353430	0.380440	0.504170
1980:01	0.434300	0.384000	0.439980	0.552900
1981:01	0.479290	0.442530	0.482410	0.597260
1982:01	0.417740	0.400460	0.409490	0.533020
1983:01	0.420520	0.419340	0.409720	0.497260
1984:01	0.420300	0.420550	0.410910	0.497350
1985:01	0.439610	0.435550	0.432000	0.519560
1986:01	0.470090	0.462400	0.463320	0.566670
1987:01	0.459600	0.444610	0.457020	0.541910
1988:01	0.487110	0.463910	0.487280	0.576570
1989:01	0.506470	0.479620	0.508000	0.597920

YEAR	ES2	TE2B	TE2N	TE2T
1966:01	0.292680	0.280120	0.309850	0.288060
1967:01	0.313440	0.303460	0.327440	0.309410
1968:01	0.528950	0.556310	0.468500	0.562050
1969:01	0.537550	0.559490	0.479470	0.573700
1970:01	0.551080	0.569890	0.493870	0.589490
1971:01	0.526770	0.550400	0.464550	0.565370
1972:01	0.427920	0.533720	0.208250	0.541790
1973:01	0.424820	0.533910	0.190650	0.549910
1974:01	0.457700	0.568890	0.229150	0.575050
1975:01	0.369140	0.302980	0.406400	0.398040
1976:01	0.358520	0.299530	0.391600	0.384440
1977:01	0.340440	0.291340	0.367850	0.362140
1978:01	0.357510	0.298420	0.389860	0.384240
1979:01	0.338660	0.288210	0.367200	0.360570
1980:01	0.404660	0.340530	0.438010	0.437430
1981:01	0.437430	0.370660	0.466840	0.474780
1982:01	0.549250	0.554850	0.501720	0.591170
1983:01	0.499010	0.500910	0.457790	0.538320
1984:01	0.489450	0.492050	0.448230	0.528080
1985:01	0.500060	0.498940	0.461130	0.540110
1986:01	0.500910	0.494370	0.453000	0.555350
1987:01	0.513370	0.493380	0.499410	0.547320
1988:01	0.548600	0.521720	0.537950	0.586140
1989:01	0.548980	0.518040	0.540230	0.588670

YEAR	E321	T321B	T321M	T321T
1966:01	0.407310	0.399930	0.409140	0.406400
1967:01	0.389860	0.381030	0.392040	0.388890
1968:01	0.422600	0.457010	0.411660	0.485430
1969:01	0.424810	0.456670	0.414320	0.491780
1970:01	0.433330	0.462110	0.423360	0.505820
1971:01	0.410750	0.446560	0.399180	0.480480
1972:01	0.227540	0.399510	0.176880	0.443320
1973:01	0.227760	0.409910	0.174080	0.456950
1974:01	0.260630	0.432190	0.209580	0.488390
1975:01	0.467810	0.488960	0.457300	0.598600
1976:01	0.448350	0.477120	0.436290	0.571800
1977:01	0.408610	0.461560	0.390150	0.544700
1978:01	0.438750	0.481640	0.422580	0.576600
1979:01	0.423340	0.472810	0.405630	0.548770
1980:01	0.466170	0.495320	0.451170	0.577600
1981:01	0.454060	0.482620	0.437700	0.576860
1982:01	0.393180	0.432810	0.373660	0.525370
1983:01	0.356540	0.394290	0.339140	0.451080
1984:01	0.345990	0.387170	0.330180	0.439220
1985:01	0.355480	0.391830	0.339180	0.449600
1986:01	0.337320	0.380690	0.317670	0.458540
1987:01	0.356920	0.382170	0.345070	0.454450
1988:01	0.387240	0.403380	0.377250	0.494840
1989:01	0.384940	0.398640	0.375580	0.493250

YEAR	E323-4	T323-4B	T323-4M	T323-4T
1966:01	0.462890	0.438760	0.469560	0.498330
1967:01	0.438120	0.422020	0.442720	0.461160
1968:01	0.502810	0.493610	0.497250	0.551430
1969:01	0.487440	0.493640	0.473980	0.529200
1970:01	0.521690	0.512450	0.513600	0.581350
1971:01	0.477020	0.479240	0.480540	0.542500
1972:01	0.406170	0.472740	0.323820	0.585490
1973:01	0.433780	0.490480	0.372330	0.548850
1974:01	0.494910	0.522140	0.444280	0.641730
1975:01	0.585850	0.546120	0.586140	0.690540
1976:01	0.540450	0.514440	0.535060	0.633150
1977:01	0.504140	0.504970	0.480750	0.603250
1978:01	0.532340	0.518450	0.518300	0.630180
1979:01	0.529340	0.531560	0.516430	0.615770
1980:01	0.560290	0.551080	0.555150	0.643100
1981:01	0.544880	0.534190	0.540760	0.640130
1982:01	0.483290	0.478600	0.471100	0.606240
1983:01	0.419860	0.431510	0.404000	0.495280
1984:01	0.416580	0.428240	0.398780	0.477980
1985:01	0.415200	0.425380	0.397120	0.477600
1986:01	0.413570	0.424680	0.398280	0.477010
1987:01	0.423670	0.429950	0.410550	0.482590
1988:01	0.450970	0.446380	0.442150	0.522150
1989:01	0.452010	0.450850	0.440040	0.530440

YEAR	E341	T341B	T341M	T341T
1966:01	0.425230	0.428290	0.421240	0.445200
1967:01	0.398770	0.396980	0.395800	0.421760
1968:01	0.464140	0.495240	0.445530	0.523550
1969:01	0.456670	0.487620	0.437550	0.519690
1970:01	0.465310	0.493550	0.446160	0.533950
1971:01	0.441280	0.475910	0.420640	0.506850
1972:01	0.313420	0.461590	0.235770	0.524380
1973:01	0.316540	0.478250	0.233300	0.536980
1974:01	0.373570	0.511460	0.298800	0.586240
1975:01	0.534180	0.560370	0.509240	0.644710
1976:01	0.510390	0.543250	0.484290	0.615160
1977:01	0.477990	0.524940	0.446740	0.588230
1978:01	0.509600	0.548840	0.480560	0.620830
1979:01	0.485890	0.535930	0.461520	0.591910
1980:01	0.513700	0.556420	0.498900	0.614700
1981:01	0.490750	0.530860	0.470700	0.603480
1982:01	0.434220	0.481570	0.414200	0.559760
1983:01	0.380950	0.427400	0.366350	0.479140
1984:01	0.372250	0.416230	0.352220	0.462450
1985:01	0.374360	0.418020	0.356270	0.468440
1986:01	0.345090	0.393060	0.323820	0.460570
1987:01	0.377170	0.402180	0.352410	0.465920
1988:01	0.411080	0.428110	0.398020	0.509690
1989:01	0.397340	0.414560	0.384110	0.497360

YEAR	E331-2	T331-2B	T331-2M	T331-2T
1966:01	0.30798	0.291470	0.31240	0.309110
1967:01	0.27805	0.266270	0.28250	0.275450
1968:01	0.33481	0.346820	0.31020	0.390750
1969:01	0.33112	0.348660	0.30620	0.383350
1970:01	0.33369	0.347250	0.30810	0.390860
1971:01	0.31461	0.340110	0.28760	0.366320
1972:01	-0.04248	0.219630	-0.23290	0.258250
1973:01	-0.04863	0.241080	-0.25310	0.267940
1974:01	-0.04286	0.224430	-0.25640	0.315250
1975:01	0.38502	0.346090	0.34690	0.516650
1976:01	0.37283	0.351480	0.33430	0.491610
1977:01	0.34690	0.346050	0.30200	0.466560
1978:01	0.37187	0.353920	0.32960	0.497940
1979:01	0.35381	0.360100	0.32350	0.476460
1980:01	0.38602	0.383010	0.37270	0.503400
1981:01	0.37377	0.374980	0.34730	0.483820
1982:01	0.27771	0.321150	0.27600	0.427080
1983:01	0.26685	0.289590	0.23530	0.326780
1984:01	0.26545	0.287650	0.22780	0.313180
1985:01	0.26604	0.292130	0.23350	0.317660
1986:01	0.24220	0.284070	0.20170	0.307940
1987:01	0.26620	0.282530	0.24460	0.314900
1988:01	0.28768	0.291380	0.26900	0.350020
1989:01	0.28321	0.292650	0.26370	0.337300

YEAR	E342	T342B	T342M	T342T
1966:01	0.540540	0.544910	0.539790	0.533550
1967:01	0.527980	0.528910	0.528070	0.523730
1968:01	0.572410	0.600950	0.560750	0.600180
1969:01	0.571040	0.596850	0.559770	0.603990
1970:01	0.583560	0.606730	0.572840	0.619660
1971:01	0.558880	0.585940	0.546930	0.594890
1972:01	0.514060	0.599730	0.476450	0.625750
1973:01	0.513780	0.604470	0.473710	0.634880
1974:01	0.564820	0.644060	0.529820	0.670510
1975:01	0.635710	0.658540	0.622810	0.696770
1976:01	0.609640	0.637150	0.595340	0.669590
1977:01	0.573040	0.616180	0.552760	0.643920
1978:01	0.605420	0.642670	0.587210	0.674130
1979:01	0.597050	0.624400	0.561800	0.643310
1980:01	0.611060	0.643570	0.594340	0.667660
1981:01	0.600770	0.624960	0.579360	0.665930
1982:01	0.552120	0.582940	0.532240	0.627680
1983:01	0.509510	0.537440	0.494930	0.570890
1984:01	0.510010	0.525320	0.481190	0.557290
1985:01	0.510000	0.529010	0.488310	0.566020
1986:01	0.496950	0.517220	0.483810	0.568050
1987:01	0.497280	0.523380	0.485650	0.566280
1988:01	0.535260	0.554100	0.524650	0.607110
1989:01	0.526970	0.542660	0.516530	0.602720

YEAR	E351-2	T351-2B	T351-2M	T351-2T
1966:01	0.300480	0.307530	0.298600	0.298190
1967:01	0.313220	0.319640	0.311370	0.313150
1968:01	0.539590	0.600210	0.516300	0.622410
1969:01	0.535510	0.596960	0.511660	0.622900
1970:01	0.547880	0.606970	0.524500	0.638300
1971:01	0.520000	0.586230	0.494350	0.613480
1972:01	0.376740	0.576390	0.303650	0.597230
1973:01	0.355790	0.576410	0.275030	0.599310
1974:01	0.431740	0.620550	0.362230	0.645770
1975:01	0.443040	0.435470	0.442730	0.479180
1976:01	0.414460	0.409900	0.413500	0.447460
1977:01	0.386980	0.388050	0.384420	0.419470
1978:01	0.417140	0.413560	0.415820	0.451170
1979:01	0.386760	0.385050	0.384610	0.414490
1980:01	0.445180	0.433320	0.446110	0.482400
1981:01	0.445170	0.434280	0.446240	0.493310
1982:01	0.550780	0.580990	0.542620	0.646500
1983:01	0.515230	0.537330	0.504290	0.589810
1984:01	0.500750	0.525570	0.489660	0.574950
1985:01	0.507390	0.529660	0.495980	0.582130
1986:01	0.477830	0.513850	0.464850	0.580470
1987:01	0.498530	0.519360	0.488390	0.581720
1988:01	0.536240	0.550070	0.528190	0.622840
1989:01	0.526100	0.539250	0.518160	0.615250

YEAR	E354	T354B	T354M	T354T
1966:01	0.452350	0.462740	0.432710	0.468370
1967:01	0.438550	0.443810	0.419960	0.454690
1968:01	0.486080	0.521210	0.418110	0.541660
1969:01	0.487880	0.518200	0.417850	0.546400
1970:01	0.500200	0.525970	0.428180	0.561560
1971:01	0.473790	0.507250	0.398990	0.536080
1972:01	0.397830	0.500540	0.202800	0.556920
1973:01	0.399270	0.509640	0.190380	0.569590
1974:01	0.445450	0.542540	0.252030	0.604250
1975:01	0.590900	0.570550	0.534560	0.647580
1976:01	0.565160	0.552670	0.508940	0.620030
1977:01	0.536060	0.533600	0.474980	0.593310
1978:01	0.568070	0.558000	0.509290	0.624800
1979:01	0.538820	0.543670	0.486730	0.595990
1980:01	0.566530	0.564840	0.525380	0.621520
1981:01	0.561980	0.547230	0.511640	0.619880
1982:01	0.495800	0.500190	0.456020	0.575090
1983:01	0.447850	0.455840	0.419180	0.509160
1984:01	0.440520	0.445850	0.407460	0.496060
1985:01	0.440590	0.449850	0.415690	0.505560
1986:01	0.436240	0.441380	0.415610	0.509200
1987:01	0.446230	0.445710	0.415000	0.506520
1988:01	0.482750	0.472100	0.451550	0.547820
1989:01	0.477680	0.463330	0.446540	0.544410

YEAR	E353	T353B	T353M	T353T
1966:01	0.549610	0.556470	0.545400	0.591870
1967:01	0.505990	0.500930	0.504590	0.560940
1968:01	0.596120	0.635540	0.581530	0.655670
1969:01	0.566830	0.614480	0.549760	0.628140
1970:01	0.575640	0.621800	0.558750	0.641690
1971:01	0.547340	0.599580	0.528760	0.612060
1972:01	0.395560	0.590350	0.328400	0.595850
1973:01	0.369650	0.602920	0.290680	0.581740
1974:01	0.502060	0.660570	0.446290	0.686490
1975:01	0.688320	0.737160	0.669930	0.768310
1976:01	0.660060	0.716360	0.639570	0.738660
1977:01	0.631460	0.696950	0.607990	0.715760
1978:01	0.663580	0.722410	0.642200	0.745190
1979:01	0.650950	0.706000	0.619790	0.718850
1980:01	0.677370	0.720570	0.640820	0.726880
1981:01	0.621650	0.680230	0.584620	0.691900
1982:01	0.605450	0.637960	0.551650	0.671350
1983:01	0.539180	0.558600	0.480460	0.586390
1984:01	0.496560	0.538630	0.451810	0.557310
1985:01	0.469330	0.533530	0.442010	0.549360
1986:01	0.339980	0.473680	0.319740	0.478230
1987:01	0.439080	0.504020	0.403240	0.521340
1988:01	0.485720	0.542030	0.452680	0.574250
1989:01	0.434360	0.505760	0.395310	0.521820

YEAR	E355	T355B	T355M	T355T
1966:01	0.420730	0.440030	0.418920	0.392910
1967:01	0.448460	0.476430	0.445400	0.415690
1968:01	0.435620	0.450470	0.431290	0.466060
1969:01	0.481250	0.484750	0.478260	0.523180
1970:01	0.497070	0.496870	0.494600	0.541420
1971:01	0.476990	0.481740	0.473580	0.522540
1972:01	0.383730	0.446960	0.364890	0.520700
1973:01	0.390180	0.428820	0.374380	0.550160
1974:01	0.348140	0.410730	0.329170	0.489460
1975:01	0.379750	0.274890	0.390870	0.508490
1976:01	0.374520	0.286310	0.382920	0.499610
1977:01	0.337140	0.281270	0.339310	0.472230
1978:01	0.360620	0.280950	0.366920	0.496460
1979:01	0.338900	0.280310	0.344660	0.468840
1980:01	0.403430	0.314550	0.416500	0.528320
1981:01	0.474200	0.414110	0.482700	0.592390
1982:01	0.401670	0.376360	0.404070	0.521810
1983:01	0.421610	0.418960	0.417440	0.499180
1984:01	0.426630	0.423290	0.422510	0.503410
1985:01	0.450160	0.441450	0.447520	0.529260
1986:01	0.502630	0.483150	0.502640	0.585270
1987:01	0.473720	0.460360	0.472750	0.555210
1988:01	0.500160	0.477740	0.501630	0.587840
1989:01	0.526400	0.499040	0.529340	0.615200

YEAR	E369	T369B	T369M	T369T
1966:01	0.250270	0.257690	0.254800	0.232960
1967:01	0.260690	0.277070	0.264320	0.245610
1968:01	0.473690	0.501040	0.450360	0.503780
1969:01	0.480000	0.501790	0.456110	0.513960
1970:01	0.491750	0.509550	0.467400	0.528600
1971:01	0.467860	0.491740	0.442310	0.503900
1972:01	0.335700	0.460320	0.231330	0.469210
1973:01	0.334870	0.464950	0.222610	0.480480
1974:01	0.368160	0.495250	0.261040	0.505620
1975:01	0.273500	0.230300	0.267880	0.305850
1976:01	0.269340	0.231930	0.263980	0.298280
1977:01	0.258170	0.227810	0.254730	0.279940
1978:01	0.271020	0.230380	0.267930	0.297320
1979:01	0.250900	0.224470	0.255730	0.278960
1980:01	0.314290	0.276950	0.319660	0.364760
1981:01	0.345610	0.302140	0.347680	0.402450
1982:01	0.449680	0.475370	0.422240	0.538030
1983:01	0.421040	0.439090	0.390910	0.473720
1984:01	0.411450	0.430990	0.381770	0.463380
1985:01	0.414530	0.436540	0.392130	0.475170
1986:01	0.406280	0.427520	0.383250	0.489320
1987:01	0.422620	0.428360	0.403300	0.482140
1988:01	0.455950	0.453000	0.437830	0.521340
1989:01	0.455220	0.448150	0.437750	0.523140

YEAR	E381	T381B	T381M	T381T
1966:01	0.485850	0.490520	0.481680	0.516030
1967:01	0.472370	0.474350	0.469060	0.503910
1968:01	0.537070	0.547230	0.529450	0.585020
1969:01	0.536010	0.544690	0.528610	0.587710
1970:01	0.547670	0.553490	0.540990	0.603260
1971:01	0.523510	0.533910	0.515270	0.577990
1972:01	0.460740	0.534720	0.422030	0.606970
1973:01	0.461890	0.541480	0.420440	0.616800
1974:01	0.511190	0.576710	0.475760	0.654590
1975:01	0.597930	0.597080	0.590940	0.686290
1976:01	0.572970	0.577710	0.564190	0.658620
1977:01	0.542020	0.557740	0.528880	0.632630
1978:01	0.573620	0.583080	0.562800	0.663360
1979:01	0.552720	0.567040	0.538760	0.634400
1980:01	0.578850	0.587850	0.568860	0.656960
1981:01	0.568040	0.571400	0.553480	0.653730
1982:01	0.509210	0.526100	0.503150	0.614350
1983:01	0.473200	0.483000	0.464290	0.553400
1984:01	0.466200	0.472530	0.451100	0.539260
1985:01	0.470520	0.476850	0.458270	0.547650
1986:01	0.456290	0.462110	0.443260	0.549790
1987:01	0.472460	0.466480	0.466100	0.549050
1988:01	0.508390	0.494630	0.503980	0.590580
1989:01	0.500400	0.485450	0.496120	0.585030

YEAR	E371	T371B	T371M	T371T
1966:01	0.16023	0.172300	0.15860	0.143610
1967:01	0.17714	0.191160	0.17520	0.160470
1968:01	0.39499	0.483890	0.37450	0.474310
1969:01	0.39998	0.485380	0.37990	0.484990
1970:01	0.40887	0.492500	0.38890	0.498750
1971:01	0.38330	0.475490	0.36170	0.474290
1972:01	0.04010	0.420140	-0.04750	0.384030
1973:01	-0.13701	0.286590	-0.23360	0.220830
1974:01	-0.19339	0.289170	-0.30190	0.181260
1975:01	0.23327	0.191480	0.24010	0.259130
1976:01	0.23408	0.200000	0.23950	0.257510
1977:01	0.21922	0.200060	0.22180	0.242340
1978:01	0.22746	0.197250	0.23190	0.255710
1979:01	0.22032	0.198810	0.22380	0.242310
1980:01	0.29142	0.249480	0.29980	0.331130
1981:01	0.32380	0.279390	0.32940	0.371330
1982:01	0.40170	0.485890	0.37550	0.509300
1983:01	0.35132	0.422080	0.33860	0.441720
1984:01	0.34788	0.414800	0.33050	0.432170
1985:01	0.36173	0.420550	0.34110	0.444240
1986:01	0.33119	0.412760	0.30910	0.459650
1987:01	0.38382	0.412780	0.37610	0.451890
1988:01	0.41520	0.435890	0.40830	0.490100
1989:01	0.41495	0.432200	0.40980	0.492790

YEAR	E382	T382B	T382M	T382T
1966:01	0.313370	0.284680	0.326780	0.303400
1967:01	0.330620	0.310890	0.340190	0.320410
1968:01	0.460240	0.488030	0.439420	0.545770
1969:01	0.471280	0.497430	0.450820	0.560180
1970:01	0.483220	0.506410	0.463610	0.576240
1971:01	0.458700	0.489330	0.435820	0.552280
1972:01	0.275250	0.442200	0.179600	0.504130
1973:01	0.261920	0.438290	0.159740	0.514720
1974:01	0.295250	0.461910	0.198860	0.532490
1975:01	0.269620	0.092520	0.334890	0.377290
1976:01	0.277800	0.135330	0.330000	0.367400
1977:01	0.258940	0.153020	0.295650	0.345920
1978:01	0.281390	0.126120	0.308920	0.366210
1979:01	0.264480	0.151450	0.297950	0.344300
1980:01	0.339010	0.204700	0.377250	0.426100
1981:01	0.358960	0.270750	0.412710	0.469220
1982:01	0.452180	0.477370	0.439430	0.581220
1983:01	0.421300	0.434090	0.409730	0.527000
1984:01	0.416560	0.429350	0.401980	0.517540
1985:01	0.429550	0.438460	0.414850	0.530650
1986:01	0.434670	0.443650	0.426730	0.549330
1987:01	0.466410	0.437020	0.471960	0.539510
1988:01	0.498220	0.459670	0.506840	0.578500
1989:01	0.501010	0.462940	0.509290	0.582990

YEAR	E383	T383B	T383M	T383T
1966:01	0.395580	0.392760	0.39620	0.401650
1967:01	0.396770	0.400930	0.39530	0.396510
1968:01	0.366540	0.427980	0.33930	0.479600
1969:01	0.387170	0.444200	0.36140	0.502220
1970:01	0.397090	0.451620	0.37180	0.517750
1971:01	0.373970	0.437750	0.34550	0.494630
1972:01	0.087790	0.370030	−0.02710	0.424690
1973:01	0.072810	0.365910	−0.04760	0.443330
1974:01	0.056480	0.367920	−0.07070	0.436470
1975:01	0.419760	0.375340	0.42650	0.575510
1976:01	0.406650	0.374810	0.40960	0.552850
1977:01	0.361730	0.364930	0.35170	0.525510
1978:01	0.388000	0.375780	0.38310	0.555690
1979:01	0.372420	0.373180	0.36530	0.527640
1980:01	0.421600	0.399880	0.42550	0.564540
1981:01	0.438730	0.428040	0.43880	0.583070
1982:01	0.376060	0.381960	0.36740	0.525410
1983:01	0.361410	0.380400	0.35180	0.467810
1984:01	0.358220	0.379750	0.34890	0.461700
1985:01	0.373920	0.391000	0.36490	0.477990
1986:01	0.376440	0.405490	0.36560	0.507080
1987:01	0.381640	0.393490	0.37450	0.491870
1988:01	0.409110	0.410830	0.40500	0.529590
1989:01	0.421540	0.421050	0.41820	0.540360

YEAR	E385	T.385B	T385M	T385T
1966:01	0.553210	0.576490	0.545790	0.562050
1967:01	0.546960	0.562970	0.541480	0.558720
1968:01	0.598490	0.630080	0.587480	0.624740
1969:01	0.601030	0.626440	0.591350	0.634350
1970:01	0.614370	0.636920	0.605350	0.650430
1971:01	0.590310	0.615930	0.580330	0.627250
1972:01	0.560350	0.634870	0.531880	0.659420
1973:01	0.560180	0.637980	0.530120	0.668720
1974:01	0.604210	0.677700	0.576600	0.694930
1975:01	0.655610	0.686760	0.642820	0.710410
1976:01	0.629820	0.664890	0.615870	0.684770
1977:01	0.596320	0.643750	0.578200	0.659480
1978:01	0.628210	0.670290	0.611850	0.688540
1979:01	0.606280	0.651130	0.585330	0.659590
1980:01	0.646540	0.669560	0.621400	0.683500
1981:01	0.635660	0.652320	0.615060	0.689200
1982:01	0.582450	0.612660	0.569630	0.651460
1983:01	0.548380	0.569080	0.538210	0.605440
1984:01	0.537440	0.556740	0.526330	0.594320
1985:01	0.545650	0.560630	0.535330	0.605050
1986:01	0.546290	0.549320	0.538480	0.615450
1987:01	0.543560	0.555200	0.536080	0.609110
1988:01	0.580150	0.586680	0.573660	0.647380
1989:01	0.575570	0.575400	0.570140	0.648080

YEAR	E384	T.384B	T.384M	T.384T
1966:01	0.380860	0.370440	0.397700	0.347060
1967:01	0.394770	0.386150	0.408990	0.366040
1968:01	0.536340	0.575620	0.509010	0.567630
1969:01	0.543280	0.577490	0.516320	0.578940
1970:01	0.556890	0.587930	0.530460	0.594480
1971:01	0.531420	0.567850	0.502320	0.570410
1972:01	0.423990	0.552770	0.328730	0.541670
1973:01	0.415440	0.550100	0.312620	0.547050
1974:01	0.461060	0.589450	0.367940	0.573460
1975:01	0.403110	0.341400	0.427470	0.403280
1976:01	0.389020	0.332620	0.410920	0.390110
1977:01	0.368040	0.321280	0.386430	0.368320
1978:01	0.387680	0.332800	0.408510	0.390060
1979:01	0.365890	0.318990	0.386280	0.367520
1980:01	0.418190	0.369420	0.445370	0.441110
1981:01	0.437470	0.393210	0.469890	0.477620
1982:01	0.544490	0.570100	0.517590	0.591120
1983:01	0.495790	0.516660	0.476130	0.540710
1984:01	0.486250	0.507270	0.465770	0.530700
1985:01	0.485880	0.513650	0.476900	0.542800
1986:01	0.484130	0.507350	0.474490	0.557550
1987:01	0.514470	0.507580	0.515210	0.549600
1988:01	0.549790	0.536210	0.552020	0.587690
1989:01	0.548310	0.531070	0.551290	0.580180

YEAR	F390	T.390B	T390M	T.390T
1966:01	0.427740	0.469830	0.402080	0.423540
1967:01	0.418800	0.455590	0.396260	0.416900
1968:01	0.483370	0.525290	0.456260	0.495690
1969:01	0.488380	0.524500	0.463940	0.510060
1970:01	0.499030	0.532920	0.475580	0.524800
1971:01	0.476410	0.514110	0.450750	0.500710
1972:01	0.395010	0.508360	0.313740	0.510130
1973:01	0.397900	0.515410	0.312850	0.525490
1974:01	0.430140	0.546910	0.347010	0.542620
1975:01	0.527940	0.567320	0.497700	0.588570
1976:01	0.506790	0.549430	0.474840	0.564200
1977:01	0.476240	0.530230	0.436910	0.537360
1978:01	0.506170	0.554530	0.470250	0.568090
1979:01	0.490940	0.539740	0.449120	0.540890
1980:01	0.524000	0.561360	0.491850	0.572950
1981:01	0.517020	0.548110	0.487700	0.581910
1982:01	0.461510	0.501930	0.427150	0.528870
1983:01	0.423010	0.462390	0.398080	0.469340
1984:01	0.415520	0.453070	0.389700	0.460810
1985:01	0.421310	0.458090	0.400810	0.474190
1986:01	0.435640	0.453300	0.411700	0.491980
1987:01	0.429350	0.455550	0.405030	0.481570
1988:01	0.460960	0.481920	0.438920	0.519500
1989:01	0.460200	0.475270	0.440840	0.524960

YEAR	ES4	TE4B	TE4M	TE4T
1966:01	0.116310	0.105780	0.134730	0.108420
1967:01	0.133580	0.126220	0.148750	0.125770
1968:01	0.444090	0.419670	0.477070	0.435530
1969:01	0.453730	0.422070	0.490240	0.448870
1970:01	0.463600	0.425510	0.503830	0.461470
1971:01	0.443940	0.412150	0.481760	0.437880
1972:01	0.361550	0.332270	0.407010	0.345370
1973:01	0.372510	0.336290	0.423070	0.358170
1974:01	0.384340	0.350410	0.436130	0.366480
1975:01	0.169680	0.053380	0.258440	0.197220
1976:01	0.185160	0.088280	0.260360	0.206830
1977:01	0.181520	0.104210	0.243550	0.196800
1978:01	0.179170	0.081530	0.252770	0.203200
1979:01	0.180440	0.101860	0.241200	0.198250
1980:01	0.256150	0.152510	0.324780	0.291150
1981:01	0.301330	0.193920	0.371460	0.338610
1982:01	0.443920	0.418210	0.441320	0.472240
1983:01	0.375520	0.354400	0.369390	0.402770
1984:01	0.392320	0.350290	0.431550	0.395130
1985:01	0.402700	0.355820	0.444030	0.408250
1986:01	0.414310	0.358300	0.459110	0.425510
1987:01	0.407410	0.356620	0.450220	0.415380
1988:01	0.435810	0.371990	0.486900	0.451530
1989:01	0.440000	0.371570	0.491160	0.457280

YEAR	ES6	TE6B	TE6M	TE6T
1966:01	0.354340	0.370670	0.355480	0.336870
1967:01	0.360550	0.377350	0.361880	0.342420
1968:01	0.408510	0.401160	0.429180	0.395180
1969:01	0.433020	0.413680	0.461670	0.423700
1970:01	0.443480	0.418400	0.475660	0.436380
1971:01	0.425460	0.405670	0.455880	0.414840
1972:01	0.326560	0.317930	0.355460	0.306290
1973:01	0.332630	0.307550	0.372970	0.317370
1974:01	0.312380	0.313970	0.335490	0.287670
1975:01	0.432030	0.360060	0.480970	0.455070
1976:01	0.425690	0.368550	0.467690	0.440840
1977:01	0.400210	0.366600	0.417300	0.416720
1978:01	0.417800	0.368300	0.442380	0.442730
1979:01	0.406150	0.374000	0.421650	0.422800
1980:01	0.435150	0.389110	0.451220	0.465130
1981:01	0.465540	0.415160	0.488580	0.492870
1982:01	0.406910	0.376810	0.416920	0.426990
1983:01	0.365140	0.343400	0.373100	0.378930
1984:01	0.365360	0.343530	0.374640	0.377910
1985:01	0.381730	0.352990	0.395950	0.396250
1986:01	0.408790	0.363480	0.428690	0.434190
1987:01	0.390080	0.353640	0.402380	0.414210
1988:01	0.414600	0.365770	0.432820	0.445200
1989:01	0.431390	0.374380	0.457340	0.462450

YEAR	ES5	TE5B	TE5M	TE5T
1966:01	0.425880	0.410290	0.41428	0.453060
1967:01	0.395300	0.377260	0.38436	0.424290
1968:01	0.455700	0.476310	0.36133	0.529460
1969:01	0.441270	0.467470	0.33973	0.516600
1970:01	0.436010	0.471410	0.30693	0.529680
1971:01	0.410400	0.454680	0.27509	0.501430
1972:01	0.284050	0.432130	-0.10234	0.522370
1973:01	0.273800	0.448330	-0.15769	0.530760
1974:01	0.348670	0.479130	-0.02734	0.594230
1975:01	0.559810	0.536460	0.48929	0.653670
1976:01	0.535700	0.521980	0.46194	0.623170
1977:01	0.509520	0.504950	0.42682	0.596780
1978:01	0.540050	0.527730	0.46279	0.629640
1979:01	0.521120	0.518060	0.44354	0.601770
1980:01	0.547500	0.538980	0.48267	0.620840
1981:01	0.516910	0.509670	0.44218	0.598880
1982:01	0.468570	0.457620	0.38930	0.558790
1983:01	0.403320	0.400970	0.33844	0.470550
1984:01	0.387440	0.390860	0.32114	0.450310
1985:01	0.388600	0.391920	0.32183	0.452040
1986:01	0.352120	0.365580	0.26352	0.427270
1987:01	0.373540	0.375480	0.30275	0.442390
1988:01	0.406220	0.397780	0.33929	0.487580
1989:01	0.388750	0.383960	0.31774	0.464550

YEAR	ES7	TE7B	TE7M	TE7T
1966:01	0.327920	0.314610	0.307950	0.361190
1967:01	0.321220	0.313840	0.301800	0.348020
1968:01	0.384120	0.349370	0.396510	0.406480
1969:01	0.402660	0.361240	0.417510	0.429240
1970:01	0.410620	0.362080	0.428200	0.442170
1971:01	0.394340	0.353970	0.409140	0.419900
1972:01	0.348510	0.269640	0.376800	0.399090
1973:01	0.367580	0.275420	0.400120	0.427200
1974:01	0.352230	0.249960	0.388660	0.418060
1975:01	0.429160	0.312730	0.465610	0.509150
1976:01	0.423560	0.329580	0.451770	0.489320
1977:01	0.393970	0.332460	0.386550	0.462910
1978:01	0.410550	0.328320	0.411100	0.492220
1979:01	0.401210	0.340710	0.395160	0.467770
1980:01	0.425580	0.353930	0.415100	0.507720
1981:01	0.445290	0.377370	0.433710	0.524780
1982:01	0.385890	0.336630	0.362070	0.458980
1983:01	0.327600	0.293740	0.300120	0.388930
1984:01	0.326640	0.295670	0.299860	0.384400
1985:01	0.340650	0.304160	0.316840	0.400960
1986:01	0.366920	0.321330	0.350190	0.429250
1987:01	0.352090	0.311670	0.331420	0.413190
1988:01	0.375460	0.318420	0.359070	0.448880
1989:01	0.388680	0.328430	0.376180	0.461420

YEAR	ES8	TE8B	TE8M	TE8T
1966:01	0.457270	0.476400	0.450780	0.444640
1967:01	0.468130	0.489740	0.480940	0.453710
1968:01	0.509150	0.506490	0.512530	0.508420
1969:01	0.530200	0.518160	0.536630	0.535800
1970:01	0.543920	0.528020	0.551820	0.551920
1971:01	0.523020	0.509660	0.530000	0.529410
1972:01	0.524080	0.494640	0.537170	0.540440
1973:01	0.527830	0.482430	0.546860	0.554190
1974:01	0.536440	0.505940	0.550770	0.552620
1975:01	0.535070	0.476590	0.558670	0.569950
1976:01	0.519100	0.468850	0.539110	0.549330
1977:01	0.491870	0.457030	0.496240	0.522330
1978:01	0.515670	0.470740	0.524880	0.551400
1979:01	0.495400	0.462700	0.499520	0.523990
1980:01	0.523430	0.480780	0.526720	0.562780
1981:01	0.549810	0.504960	0.553780	0.590700
1982:01	0.499900	0.489790	0.495290	0.534610
1983:01	0.466840	0.445470	0.458970	0.496090
1984:01	0.463430	0.441970	0.455970	0.492340
1985:01	0.478720	0.452160	0.473850	0.510150
1986:01	0.505830	0.467040	0.507370	0.543090
1987:01	0.490580	0.458460	0.488600	0.524670
1988:01	0.520040	0.478940	0.521790	0.559390
1989:01	0.531420	0.483960	0.536640	0.573670

YEAR	ES0	TE0B	TE0M	TE0T
1966:01	0.326900	0.320820	0.312730	0.308070
1967:01	0.330650	0.324170	0.314070	0.311260
1968:01	0.434340	0.430120	0.389820	0.448360
1969:01	0.443570	0.434760	0.399570	0.459490
1970:01	0.453830	0.441580	0.408520	0.472730
1971:01	0.432240	0.426650	0.386010	0.451300
1972:01	0.315590	0.392780	0.206050	0.420580
1973:01	0.306790	0.383640	0.180130	0.422530
1974:01	0.328110	0.400170	0.194480	0.437180
1975:01	0.380380	0.334560	0.379320	0.414780
1976:01	0.369320	0.333120	0.365320	0.399750
1977:01	0.346710	0.325690	0.331490	0.379100
1978:01	0.365560	0.333710	0.354200	0.401100
1979:01	0.394900	0.332760	0.331950	0.441530
1980:01	0.410120	0.364510	0.381240	0.457020
1981:01	0.410770	0.375450	0.387970	0.455580
1982:01	0.413470	0.418220	0.424370	0.462970
1983:01	0.364050	0.374190	0.343010	0.392080
1984:01	0.384380	0.379230	0.349620	0.414240
1985:01	0.392100	0.381350	0.364040	0.426620
1986:01	0.390680	0.381770	0.360660	0.439870
1987:01	0.396710	0.374090	0.368330	0.431350
1988:01	0.425520	0.393130	0.398320	0.464960
1989:01	0.427840	0.393490	0.402100	0.468210

YEAR	ES9	TE9B	TE9M	TE9T
1966:01	0.480130	0.500880	0.475590	0.463920
1967:01	0.484830	0.502930	0.480740	0.470810
1968:01	0.539980	0.542730	0.552350	0.524850
1969:01	0.554570	0.548710	0.568940	0.546070
1970:01	0.558050	0.558810	0.583660	0.561690
1971:01	0.546680	0.539470	0.562130	0.538450
1972:01	0.555060	0.536750	0.574860	0.553560
1973:01	0.560070	0.533370	0.583590	0.563260
1974:01	0.578410	0.562790	0.599050	0.573380
1975:01	0.579350	0.558830	0.591530	0.587690
1976:01	0.558850	0.542190	0.569110	0.565250
1977:01	0.522770	0.523960	0.505900	0.538460
1978:01	0.550850	0.548220	0.538090	0.568250
1979:01	0.528090	0.531130	0.512000	0.541150
1980:01	0.555840	0.551550	0.540100	0.575880
1981:01	0.568530	0.555230	0.554520	0.595830
1982:01	0.518120	0.514370	0.496660	0.543320
1983:01	0.487230	0.482490	0.476820	0.502370
1984:01	0.481110	0.475650	0.470910	0.496780
1985:01	0.494070	0.483690	0.486000	0.512520
1986:01	0.510400	0.484620	0.506210	0.540370
1987:01	0.499420	0.480920	0.491890	0.525450
1988:01	0.531060	0.506190	0.526510	0.560470
1989:01	0.537530	0.505510	0.536240	0.570830

Notes

Ei: the overall average of the effective tax rate in sub-manufacturing
industry i

Tij: the effective tax rate of asset j
in sub-manufacturing industry i

Appendix J   Effective tax rate by industries

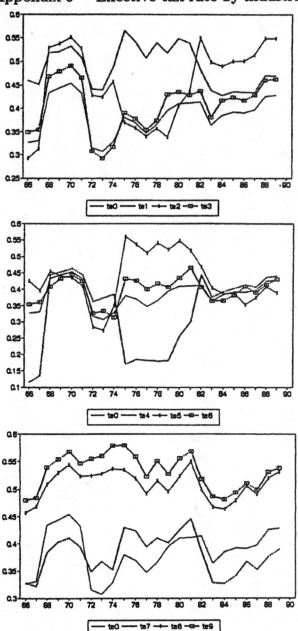

Appendix K   Real capital stock

YEAR	1	2	3
68	16845	2832	39371
69	23095	3062	47768
70	28788	3182	52789
71	35164	3526	62121
72	40628	3828	75767
73	45097	4247	110323
74	60824	4865	129019
75	63881	5373	152997
76	68037	6352	184645
77	75061	7692	219121
78	101860	10018	286684
79	138786	12173	409168
80	158508	13811	536747
81	165541	15711	610848
82	171210	17832	680202
83	185396	19915	733348
84	203381	22359	800206
85	217949	25037	873395
86	247878	27512	993371
87	271461	28612	1161800
88	312944	30487	1233450
89	415690	33234	1343500

YEAR	4	5	6
68	9674	3098	14893
69	12119	4184	19614
70	13992	5119	24490
71	17029	6253	29239
72	20616	7741	35696
73	24064	8783	42024
74	26828	10157	47692
75	30360	13072	54940
76	33587	18386	63840
77	41335	26565	72992
78	52357	30942	83456
79	66857	35411	91720
80	80013	39454	98963
81	93948	43284	107541
82	108399	48023	121953
83	126297	52003	131502
84	141306	57292	143643
85	156138	62124	157037
86	168136	66125	178483
87	175207	72342	204665
88	184132	79076	235746
89	198772	87409	268849

YEAR	7	8	9
68	63524	157787	71221
69	63934	183515	74364
70	63652	212108	77570
71	65109	235505	80865
72	69914	258904	83577
73	80547	288528	85970
74	95154	323671	88027
75	106280	362425	91752
76	129292	399869	95927
77	144746	432122	102316
78	160471	490060	137547
79	177888	549434	174520
80	197495	604028	209070
81	219543	642706	241739
82	239231	692317	280040
83	271644	758130	325455
84	302335	826366	377472
85	334443	887907	433130
86	387121	965047	487195
87	384052	.1058430	544098
88	417980	.1164760	612040
89	453368	.1285530	686428

YEAR	B	M	T
68	308593	63505	25912
69	352105	75900	29614
70	397202	86110	32671
71	441529	99852	36843
72	481350	116338	41177
73	532115	133539	47083
74	593337	161259	51940
75	657659	186037	57736
76	730074	214313	68189
77	829390	265627	79941
78	964484	371455	106978
79	1105400	466056	139051
80	1241710	544664	157028
81	1360830	624367	172387
82	1512210	687886	187557
83	1702890	751172	203770
84	1905440	825808	223516
85	2114630	891803	243058
86	2324830	964389	272921
87	2464300	1125410	310968
88	2746030	1188500	356855
89	3091750	1262290	407161

YEAR	311B	311M	311T	311
68	3181.03	1034.25	113.476	4328.76
69	3446.73	1121.15	117.140	4685.02
70	3842.88	1336.91	116.115	5295.91
71	4356.95	1616.05	114.310	6087.31
72	5580.63	2492.43	150.476	8223.54
73	7035.18	3292.20	336.919	10664.3
74	7507.78	3729.75	530.467	11768.0
75	8579.67	4528.64	590.061	13698.4
76	9593.32	5067.57	974.312	15635.2
77	10955.0	6349.61	946.067	18250.7
78	10916.5	7102.42	1032.11	19051.0
79	11119.7	9326.91	1307.27	21753.9
80	33257.7	29224.6	3457.83	65940.1
81	32466.4	28313.0	3284.45	64063.8
82	31798.6	28221.5	3277.25	63297.4
83	32034.6	28334.5	3379.68	63748.8
84	31715.6	28675.7	3382.11	63773.5
85	31408.8	29173.9	3377.11	63959.8
86	31360.9	31054.2	3443.12	65858.2
87	30625.0	33201.0	3600.00	67426.0
88	30241.7	34187.8	3678.77	68108.2
89	30037.1	34891.2	3691.25	68619.5

YEAR	313B	313M	313T	313
68	1869.77	334.268	34.5800	2238.62
69	1859.07	328.887	41.0670	2229.02
70	1913.16	362.034	53.2451	2328.44
71	2060.86	517.170	71.3471	2649.38
72	2089.76	571.729	83.8094	2745.30
73	2199.06	776.332	139.374	3114.77
74	2337.70	920.580	140.311	3398.59
75	2429.75	1063.15	191.999	3684.90
76	2599.18	1257.58	208.915	4065.67
77	2684.40	1392.52	261.562	4338.47
78	3432.25	2610.88	336.509	6379.64
79	5701.40	5904.98	381.731	11988.1
80	5975.37	6482.91	385.764	12844.0
81	7085.32	7679.28	429.149	15193.7
82	7656.31	8366.59	475.529	16498.4
83	9075.26	8256.35	575.312	17906.9
84	10117.4	8886.19	594.356	19598.0
85	11039.4	9422.19	598.785	21060.3
86	11658.5	10868.3	622.458	23149.2
87	13330.0	12401.0	675.000	26406.0
88	13335.5	11732.3	712.888	25780.7
89	13601.6	11461.8	707.692	25771.1

YEAR	314B	314M	314T	314
68	1574.53	211.199	4.02752	1789.76
69	1569.35	256.187	3.78656	1829.32
70	1588.24	428.087	4.13020	2020.45
71	1688.89	630.908	3.76309	2323.57
72	1636.99	750.804	3.64678	2391.44
73	1774.92	901.232	4.67511	2680.83
74	1819.41	1056.26	4.45321	2880.13
75	2090.94	1288.81	4.37788	3384.13
76	2136.79	1453.73	4.08666	3594.61
77	2175.67	1377.88	14.9940	3568.55
78	2244.73	1326.88	14.4632	3586.07
79	2531.41	1339.53	15.0823	3886.02
80	3272.40	1536.45	15.9969	4824.85
81	3170.11	1500.71	16.4081	4687.23
82	3092.58	1424.79	16.0988	4533.47
83	3281.70	2108.95	26.3624	5417.01
84	3239.23	2051.04	24.6209	5314.89
85	3211.07	1868.74	23.5054	5103.31
86	3303.45	1737.53	55.6837	5096.66
87	3478.00	1799.00	59.0000	5336.00
88	3408.54	1647.30	54.0460	5109.88
89	3357.82	1605.01	50.3396	5013.16

YEAR	321B	321M	321T	321
68	2853.06	3725.24	46.4535	6624.76
69	3052.80	3419.19	66.3728	7138.37
70	4169.60	3981.34	75.1301	8226.07
71	4571.35	5024.79	122.674	9718.82
72	4899.53	5611.61	143.490	10654.6
73	8829.50	9456.67	341.731	18627.9
74	10285.3	12697.7	356.493	23339.5
75	11327.8	15685.5	389.292	27402.6
76	13817.5	18904.8	497.929	33220.2
77	15660.1	22536.3	644.589	38841.0
78	18854.0	32926.1	991.061	52771.1
79	23428.6	47292.3	1476.60	72197.5
80	26147.1	51833.9	1628.73	79609.7
81	28719.8	57134.8	1904.49	87759.1
82	30933.3	62546.1	2131.92	95611.3
83	34059.7	65896.0	2530.05	102486.
84	36709.1	74794.9	2691.34	114195.
85	38921.4	80723.7	2811.41	122457.
86	42463.7	91651.1	3217.58	137332.
87	48977.0	115565.	4234.00	168776.
88	51767.7	115434.	4078.79	171280.
89	53587.0	117424.	4080.60	175092.

YEAR	322B	322M	322T	322
68	399.686	118.802	3.24700	521.734
69	464.797	153.967	4.04030	622.795
70	533.066	170.440	5.17950	708.685
71	588.402	228.423	8.76435	825.590
72	686.929	306.462	9.48606	1002.88
73	854.512	619.427	20.3025	1494.24
74	1115.03	786.981	22.2195	1924.23
75	1379.46	1079.60	28.6475	2487.71
76	1971.29	1475.06	101.675	3548.02
77	2329.25	1758.54	106.624	4194.42
78	2718.43	2023.06	142.446	4883.94
79	3200.55	2638.44	249.901	6088.89
80	3519.26	2821.98	283.568	6624.80
81	4041.26	3372.74	361.430	7775.43
82	4427.89	3699.80	378.844	8506.53
83	4870.97	3880.05	386.493	9137.51
84	5343.32	4188.90	419.633	9951.86
85	5902.92	4518.50	475.175	10896.6
86	6464.24	5084.72	576.740	12125.7
87	6862.00	5859.00	738.000	13459.0
88	7232.35	6160.98	938.571	14331.9
89	7599.66	6974.87	1411.55	15986.1

YEAR	323B	323M	323T	323
68	80.8631	38.3866	7.94770	127.197
69	85.9453	37.3113	7.60910	130.866
70	87.9184	36.2981	6.73759	130.954
71	94.4380	35.3821	6.02110	135.841
72	115.357	44.3894	5.98382	165.730
73	217.770	224.958	12.1617	454.890
74	255.136	342.810	13.8205	611.767
75	400.974	535.854	20.4352	957.263
76	628.613	815.260	30.4073	1474.28
77	815.875	964.480	43.6540	1824.01
78	930.631	972.082	58.8695	1961.58
79	1432.00	1032.34	77.8882	2542.23
80	1444.27	1016.16	82.7489	2543.18
81	1635.34	1180.66	118.464	2934.46
82	1753.54	1273.23	131.249	3158.02
83	1982.64	1376.59	138.234	3497.46
84	2193.35	1508.26	168.048	3869.65
85	2423.91	1635.94	216.038	4275.89
86	2970.85	2114.76	286.759	5372.37
87	3458.00	2669.00	388.000	6515.00
88	3984.06	2983.56	456.544	7424.16
89	4414.07	3418.49	568.439	8401.00

YEAR	324B	324M	324T	324
68	44.6326	15.5064	.292770	60.4318
69	51.1589	15.9287	.467953	67.5556
70	57.7457	19.1046	.483365	77.3337
71	67.4563	22.7555	.562927	90.7647
72	81.6981	27.9578	.707185	110.363
73	91.3403	38.0521	2.13126	131.524
74	98.8025	39.5933	2.61914	141.015
75	117.078	58.2956	5.09166	180.466
76	135.161	78.4090	5.85020	219.420
77	235.224	191.698	6.66400	433.586
78	1881.09	2050.46	203.440	4134.98
79	2284.43	2866.63	205.971	5357.03
80	2901.17	3559.89	205.127	6666.18
81	4011.38	4196.70	211.024	8419.10
82	4474.87	5431.15	223.579	10129.6
83	5080.95	6767.69	341.920	12190.6
84	5467.12	7326.88	347.729	13141.7
85	6149.75	8127.73	349.730	14627.2
86	6778.50	9499.48	382.940	16660.9
87	7955.00	10999.0	446.000	19400.0
88	7922.63	10049.9	414.861	18387.3
89	7838.89	9210.16	410.803	17459.9

YEAR	331B	331M	331T	331
68	762.114	1124.14	127.790	2014.04
69	877.511	1221.78	133.937	2233.23
70	1058.71	1548.36	144.987	2752.06
71	1214.12	1658.48	146.149	3018.74
72	1374.71	1773.98	160.778	3309.47
73	1838.85	2279.98	241.551	4360.38
74	2069.53	2311.52	245.725	4626.78
75	2235.50	2331.07	264.588	4831.16
76	2531.26	2502.49	342.353	5376.10
77	2677.22	2552.08	409.150	5638.45
78	2696.70	3031.88	778.654	6507.23
79	2867.11	4773.17	1352.41	8992.69
80	2871.20	5229.76	1350.27	9451.23
81	2936.24	5257.63	1417.87	9611.74
82	2901.22	4917.41	1384.39	9203.02
83	2972.58	4666.31	1373.95	9012.83
84	3003.81	4522.00	1431.71	8957.52
85	2985.72	4292.27	1422.19	8700.18
86	2969.91	4325.93	1479.99	8775.82
87	2899.00	4388.00	1647.00	8934.00
88	2881.04	4210.15	1543.46	8634.64
89	2860.99	4241.57	1493.13	8595.68

YEAR	332B	332M	332T	332
68	204.321	24.2071	1.43792	229.966
69	233.140	24.1239	1.29781	258.562
70	240.282	27.7021	1.17720	269.161
71	237.593	26.4640	1.05508	265.112
72	237.490	34.4327	.965122	272.887
73	327.103	42.8136	.903808	370.820
74	349.722	71.6345	.842808	422.199
75	357.516	80.6706	.812317	438.999
76	373.299	87.6844	.939266	461.923
77	385.632	110.105	25.0650	520.802
78	431.992	305.490	39.1418	776.623
79	584.027	540.255	49.9397	1174.22
80	615.313	642.444	57.1133	1314.87
81	640.095	653.646	59.9387	1353.68
82	745.712	790.549	67.2026	1603.46
83	820.561	853.951	77.0514	1751.56
84	934.026	932.010	97.9455	1963.98
85	1138.90	1219.97	120.837	2479.71
86	1247.67	1376.73	152.605	2777.01
87	1350.00	1508.00	185.000	3043.00
88	1471.28	1637.34	230.271	3338.89
89	1786.05	2023.77	328.960	4138.78

YEAR	341B	341M	341T	341
68	420.050	1048.44	10.0812	1478.57
69	498.080	1201.73	13.8292	1713.64
70	531.744	1173.58	16.4821	1721.80
71	603.623	1197.63	20.1581	1821.41
72	669.739	1231.47	25.6171	1926.83
73	969.542	2296.41	71.8559	3337.81
74	1072.25	2389.77	73.8747	3535.90
75	1192.83	2384.41	75.8317	3653.07
76	1388.77	2536.00	102.124	4026.89
77	1639.65	3152.16	133.280	4925.09
78	1911.91	3627.53	205.326	5744.76
79	2395.93	4784.16	255.670	7435.75
80	2774.64	6271.25	279.577	9325.47
81	3001.88	6871.58	323.222	10196.7
82	3489.41	8291.32	347.814	12128.5
83	4004.89	9210.41	336.944	13552.2
84	4450.22	10168.0	400.251	15018.5
85	5232.73	12238.2	473.154	17944.1
86	6196.89	14414.2	553.172	21164.3
87	7487.00	18126.0	816.000	26429.0
88	8374.08	18635.1	937.118	27946.3
89	10237.9	21394.2	1128.07	32760.2

YEAR	342B	342M	342T	342
68	891.003	624.503	19.6132	1535.12
69	967.960	941.883	30.1260	1939.97
70	1006.20	1203.04	34.8996	2244.13
71	1136.93	1470.91	36.2882	2644.13
72	1158.78	1839.06	68.8337	3066.67
73	1277.01	2062.80	71.2318	3411.04
74	1386.16	2341.49	68.1517	3795.80
75	2281.45	2672.66	74.2461	5028.36
76	2311.56	3093.95	94.4443	5499.95
77	2442.26	3451.44	103.292	5996.99
78	2510.01	4362.58	188.189	7060.77
79	2939.75	5578.82	314.183	8832.75
80	2922.67	5759.51	330.489	9012.66
81	2954.80	5814.74	332.215	9101.75
82	3033.44	6771.56	390.478	10195.5
83	3094.07	7499.85	413.061	11007.0
84	3810.13	8603.45	476.101	12889.7
85	4165.71	9202.83	504.360	13872.9
86	4161.82	9601.52	548.474	14311.8
87	4039.00	10713.0	738.000	15490.0
88	4096.54	10866.6	690.976	15654.1
89	4110.25	11222.4	732.631	16085.3

YEAR	351B	351M	351T	351
68	1612.43	3494.60	51.3618	5158.39
69	1955.83	3684.51	69.3887	5709.73
70	2010.94	3568.90	69.5298	5649.37
71	2163.69	3659.50	80.3260	5903.51
72	2212.83	4650.33	83.2908	6946.45
73	2485.45	5666.39	120.637	8272.47
74	3075.29	6634.61	157.692	9867.59
75	3324.76	7516.59	202.166	11043.5
76	3728.26	7565.09	229.574	11522.9
77	4659.41	7778.21	310.248	12747.9
78	5479.23	11712.4	402.021	17593.7
79	6762.23	15961.7	626.806	23350.8
80	8117.67	35804.3	675.448	44597.4
81	9903.05	46320.3	784.331	57007.6
82	10318.2	49941.7	794.830	61054.8
83	11092.8	50518.2	830.152	62441.1
84	11796.0	52101.2	902.024	64799.2
85	12234.8	52455.4	954.996	65645.2
86	13124.5	58526.0	1041.14	72691.7
87	14793.0	61504.0	1233.00	77530.0
88	16654.5	61364.8	1350.64	79270.0
89	20890.0	65275.8	1353.95	87519.7

YEAR	352B	352M	352T	352
68	308.855	183.593	14.4433	506.891
69	446.097	322.275	26.9850	795.357
70	548.078	398.699	39.1709	985.948
71	651.815	495.389	34.7976	1182.00
72	766.563	593.412	51.8415	1411.82
73	970.157	885.907	89.6770	1945.74
74	1137.69	1123.55	106.110	2367.35
75	1566.83	1695.10	130.097	3392.03
76	1939.36	2321.24	179.317	4439.92
77	2412.02	2892.00	209.916	5513.93
78	3081.91	3438.84	259.871	6780.62
79	3702.48	4258.30	318.029	8278.81
80	4191.01	5466.52	349.115	10006.6
81	4948.29	6346.53	399.540	11694.4
82	5655.22	6548.32	447.231	12550.8
83	7142.32	7489.90	511.623	15143.8
84	8621.20	8816.88	586.538	17924.6
85	10233.9	9764.95	643.871	20642.7
86	12083.2	11110.7	769.249	23963.1
87	14486.0	16419.0	912.000	31817.0
88	15944.9	19484.5	994.672	36424.1
89	17403.2	23460.8	1122.25	41986.2

YEAR	353B	353M	353T	353
68	729.770	613.291	87.5170	1430.58
69	861.338	1119.38	96.1047	2076.82
70	928.059	1250.01	123.832	2301.90
71	1215.43	2123.82	148.500	3487.75
72	1708.46	3488.63	140.159	5337.25
73	2178.73	5840.94	161.566	8181.24
74	2159.85	5338.00	158.051	7655.91
75	2153.42	5547.75	191.565	7892.73
76	2172.19	4964.70	186.132	7323.03
77	2172.33	4993.64	262.048	7428.01
78	2441.07	5063.53	275.059	7779.66
79	2938.35	5209.22	296.388	8443.96
80	5619.92	7393.45	387.403	13400.8
81	7605.85	9208.24	409.443	17224.5
82	8258.77	8372.26	461.699	17092.7
83	10008.2	7654.48	502.779	18165.4
84	10288.2	7041.46	486.032	17815.7
85	12196.3	10487.0	488.948	23172.3
86	12328.2	11776.2	459.742	24564.1
87	12818.0	11565.0	681.000	25064.0
88	12779.2	12725.8	714.220	26219.2
89	14992.2	19587.6	1024.61	35604.5

YEAR	354B	354M	354T	354
68	197.140	235.407	22.0263	454.574
69	235.714	264.426	31.0527	531.192
70	315.717	274.774	52.7202	643.211
71	427.358	303.355	76.9309	807.644
72	463.910	322.487	86.2693	872.666
73	522.218	363.063	143.003	1028.28
74	557.493	431.318	184.041	1172.85
75	622.361	489.123	193.801	1305.28
76	732.728	616.373	226.157	1575.26
77	780.653	699.624	266.720	1747.00
78	774.140	771.930	317.045	1863.12
79	793.107	959.729	405.260	2158.10
80	790.866	1062.57	450.611	2304.05
81	797.824	1204.16	547.960	2549.94
82	800.529	1296.02	552.312	2648.86
83	1004.57	1568.42	520.240	3093.23
84	995.855	1638.16	543.412	3177.43
85	1007.81	2049.25	591.936	3649.00
86	1020.59	2464.76	614.403	4099.75
87	1029.00	2644.00	732.000	4405.00
88	1030.70	2530.53	735.102	4296.33
89	1042.89	2627.21	748.896	4418.99

YEAR	355B	355M	355T	355
68	303.436	437.535	7.26311	748.234
69	497.483	1164.78	13.6630	1675.93
70	513.675	1131.76	13.5205	1658.96
71	571.877	1186.86	14.5709	1773.31
72	595.699	1362.52	16.5032	1974.72
73	744.961	1788.30	20.8179	2554.08
74	922.160	2017.20	27.0991	2966.45
75	975.639	2325.19	37.6989	3338.53
76	1071.00	2567.48	45.6711	3684.15
77	1240.62	3005.35	88.2980	4334.27
78	1411.14	3793.34	103.233	5307.71
79	1859.51	6141.68	125.058	8126.25
80	2021.57	6404.19	134.722	8560.48
81	2279.61	6560.14	145.634	8985.38
82	2565.38	6944.82	146.605	9656.80
83	2709.81	6862.66	223.365	9795.83
84	2849.38	7077.01	256.983	10183.4
85	3169.93	7913.36	265.897	11349.2
86	3548.18	8754.80	287.893	12590.9
87	4277.00	10500.0	335.000	15112.0
88	5350.09	13104.9	423.828	18878.8
89	7033.67	16826.0	533.023	24392.7

YEAR	356B	356M	356T	356
68	66.3782	98.5357	3.60417	168.518
69	99.7847	133.364	4.16065	237.309
70	115.256	163.323	4.61170	283.190
71	129.614	198.727	6.44173	334.782
72	146.309	229.186	7.07455	382.570
73	244.250	356.946	12.4792	613.675
74	906.990	1844.24	57.2808	2808.51
75	960.051	1768.11	55.4235	2783.58
76	1100.57	1885.36	69.7418	3055.67
77	1212.12	1970.51	83.3000	3265.93
78	1387.35	2374.05	113.694	3875.10
79	1614.24	3200.57	176.448	4991.26
80	1723.72	3445.60	200.567	5369.89
81	1968.04	3772.80	293.462	6034.31
82	2055.79	3815.11	294.004	6164.90
83	2507.82	4495.04	390.662	7393.53
84	3122.37	5990.34	424.949	9537.66
85	3477.80	6829.66	479.416	10786.9
86	4158.43	8125.62	571.333	12855.4
87	4829.00	9273.00	698.000	14800.0
88	6084.97	12295.0	847.441	19227.4
89	7371.81	15587.4	1052.46	24011.7

YEAR	361B	361M	361T	361
68	46.9643	13.1779	.324800	60.4670
69	66.7499	79.6897	.755420	147.195
70	82.9483	85.1479	1.17183	169.268
71	102.246	78.6065	1.27783	182.130
72	125.213	82.0342	1.59326	208.840
73	164.900	128.247	5.11719	298.264
74	175.221	124.057	6.19564	305.473
75	220.950	171.372	9.04037	401.363
76	298.496	251.482	11.3641	561.342
77	348.687	323.575	13.3280	685.590
78	427.659	417.863	16.2545	861.776
79	603.373	580.222	22.3146	1205.91
80	674.405	630.683	24.3019	1329.39
81	706.911	655.541	29.7171	1392.17
82	776.233	697.896	32.3317	1506.46
83	830.154	698.811	34.9671	1563.93
84	1039.90	930.807	68.4685	2039.17
85	1177.15	1064.48	73.5800	2315.20
86	1294.21	1185.14	83.1693	2562.51
87	1425.00	1383.00	98.0000	2906.00
88	1456.83	1395.09	105.616	2957.53
89	1537.30	1405.78	124.903	3067.97

YEAR	362B	362M	362T	362
68	72.8292	40.2295	2.66085	115.720
69	153.894	111.165	4.32589	269.384
70	310.356	259.855	6.72191	576.933
71	389.754	381.739	9.96157	781.455
72	403.562	351.971	10.1827	765.716
73	463.131	413.262	13.3650	889.758
74	526.997	486.391	15.8249	1029.21
75	619.552	627.564	18.3861	1265.50
76	671.077	713.398	24.3435	1408.82
77	775.676	853.674	36.7180	1666.07
78	816.297	1017.40	45.3337	1879.03
79	973.262	1273.79	61.3378	2308.39
80	1041.29	1452.61	67.9224	2561.82
81	1170.04	1830.43	69.2996	3069.77
82	1174.48	1782.75	67.5375	3024.77
83	1415.30	2446.18	128.119	3989.60
84	1431.08	2602.91	127.087	4161.08
85	1737.32	3789.08	206.804	5733.20
86	1916.93	4250.61	204.032	6371.57
87	1958.00	4256.00	194.000	6408.00
88	2051.01	5122.29	195.801	7369.10
89	2073.56	5047.11	199.433	7320.10

YEAR	369B	369M	369T	369
68	1685.75	1797.69	144.325	3627.77
69	2204.56	2364.04	220.234	4788.83
70	2272.93	2253.26	196.029	4722.22
71	2669.34	2172.40	273.129	5114.86
72	2847.32	2661.37	276.283	5784.97
73	2956.48	2651.73	319.179	5927.38
74	3348.78	3000.70	394.550	6744.03
75	4000.24	3750.19	456.308	8206.73
76	4829.50	4634.63	623.708	10087.8
77	5563.81	5987.55	962.200	12513.6
78	6766.76	9187.20	2566.82	18520.8
79	9842.93	17752.4	3429.46	31024.7
80	12983.3	28357.6	4053.19	45394.1
81	14860.8	32964.9	5090.64	52916.3
82	16135.4	36321.3	5513.79	57970.5
83	28328.2	37403.0	6334.47	72065.8
84	30869.1	41256.5	8234.21	80359.8
85	35054.8	51083.7	9479.07	95617.6
86	37873.2	58942.5	10678.0	107494.
87	40061.0	63292.0	12033.0	115386.
88	39835.8	58395.3	11570.7	109802.
89	40248.2	55069.9	12349.4	107667.

YEAR	371B	371M	371T	371
68	586.929	758.474	32.0299	1377.43
69	728.502	822.101	47.1551	1597.76
70	895.130	953.065	51.6383	1899.83
71	1860.70	1328.08	64.1530	3252.94
72	3129.10	3539.46	90.9091	6759.47
73	6332.39	7535.84	143.679	14011.9
74	6935.26	7499.43	181.207	14615.9
75	7489.55	8197.87	324.851	16012.3
76	9355.23	12440.1	363.302	22158.7
77	11521.3	14811.3	418.320	26750.9
78	12778.0	19598.6	739.465	33116.0
79	16739.5	38799.2	1393.40	56932.1
80	17857.9	42513.2	1354.48	61725.6
81	19448.1	50861.5	1662.01	71971.6
82	25567.1	67156.0	1721.27	94444.4
83	26614.9	65747.1	1648.82	94010.8
84	26934.9	62703.0	1827.97	91465.9
85	27266.1	58233.9	1661.98	87162.0
86	28354.5	59960.8	1884.63	90200.0
87	36521.0	83459.0	2109.00	122089.
88	40733.6	92615.9	2061.79	135411.
89	45848.8	104323.	2334.47	152507.

YEAR	372B	372M	372T	372
68	130.283	154.908	2.96933	288.161
69	555.974	981.254	13.9585	1551.19
70	604.564	973.268	13.8814	1591.71
71	616.112	1088.23	15.1284	1719.47
72	677.180	1183.09	14.7397	1875.01
73	940.374	1746.33	18.0314	2704.73
74	1014.44	2085.48	22.4653	3122.39
75	1117.70	2336.66	25.5799	3479.95
76	1167.68	2395.97	29.1705	3592.82
77	1833.75	3561.53	58.3100	5453.58
78	2106.49	4694.39	77.1590	6878.04
79	2259.52	5384.51	108.225	7752.26
80	3207.62	10750.4	165.836	14123.9
81	3481.90	11686.4	190.378	15358.7
82	3640.18	12890.0	258.030	16788.2
83	3803.68	12358.8	284.160	16446.7
84	3864.48	11941.5	306.781	16112.7
85	4127.15	12228.9	385.721	16741.8
86	4482.32	12885.0	403.808	17771.2
87	4717.00	13712.0	425.000	18854.0
88	5470.58	15518.9	492.154	21481.6
89	5717.50	15464.4	553.522	21735.4

YEAR	381B	381M	381T	381
68	342.089	279.454	9.44722	630.989
69	564.205	386.832	19.5358	970.573
70	665.627	532.168	29.6760	1227.47
71	747.779	635.045	65.7625	1448.59
72	864.361	826.681	71.0166	1762.06
73	1161.80	1317.22	95.9804	2575.00
74	1613.23	1779.56	111.212	3504.01
75	1937.38	2285.86	131.162	4354.41
76	2127.96	2705.11	165.501	4998.57
77	2747.43	3672.96	240.097	6660.49
78	3572.61	4948.53	306.786	8827.93
79	5900.92	8565.77	521.568	14988.3
80	6230.81	8859.61	537.252	15627.7
81	6927.70	9411.46	599.231	16938.4
82	7184.44	12842.0	632.050	20658.4
83	8381.96	13688.6	761.895	22832.5
84	9552.88	14645.2	969.215	25167.3
85	10770.6	15525.5	1050.32	27346.5
86	11644.2	16713.7	1148.29	29506.1
87	12864.0	18780.0	1434.00	33078.0
88	14990.2	21035.5	1646.45	37672.1
89	16636.6	24373.6	1983.78	42993.9

YEAR	382B	382M	382T	382
68	540.430	348.709	7.66992	896.808
69	621.974	405.735	13.7602	1041.47
70	698.371	440.279	19.2850	1157.93
71	787.876	558.849	22.2977	1369.02
72	852.027	679.358	28.2468	1559.63
73	1249.84	1165.62	53.3947	2468.85
74	1493.55	1322.69	66.0199	2882.26
75	2158.13	2031.53	122.327	4311.98
76	2266.56	3767.62	395.869	6430.05
77	3740.93	6366.81	429.190	10536.9
78	6251.59	11114.1	665.608	18031.3
79	9941.65	22443.1	911.466	33296.2
80	10766.8	23879.6	968.920	35615.3
81	15010.0	29607.1	1079.39	45696.5
82	15864.8	33443.3	1095.58	50403.6
83	17262.4	36374.5	1363.72	55000.6
84	19990.4	39501.1	1457.47	60948.9
85	21914.6	43342.5	1743.98	67001.1
86	24840.8	52209.3	1820.48	78870.6
87	28924.0	61419.0	2237.00	92580.0
88	30328.6	59009.7	2293.42	91631.7
89	32924.5	57687.4	2592.71	93204.6

YEAR	383B	383M	383T	383
68	268.094	268.305	12.3744	548.773
69	342.952	462.410	12.1032	817.465
70	390.004	604.928	12.2553	1007.19
71	468.730	754.289	13.3482	1236.37
72	557.494	1065.29	13.4389	1636.23
73	919.649	1985.90	19.4979	2925.05
74	1240.56	2818.12	44.6111	4103.28
75	3612.25	4431.77	142.146	8186.17
76	4051.54	5998.43	170.031	10220.0
77	4566.74	7393.58	166.600	12126.9
78	6188.96	10909.3	285.925	17384.2
79	8858.92	14739.1	382.056	23980.1
80	10475.3	17936.9	436.563	28848.8
81	12918.7	19956.4	512.231	33387.4
82	13889.9	23000.4	592.988	37483.2
83	15831.6	26233.6	1532.00	43597.3
84	19959.5	39263.7	1612.68	60835.9
85	23726.3	47458.2	1621.56	72806.1
86	29144.5	65595.8	1770.87	96511.2
87	37604.0	83883.0	2122.00	123609.
88	45586.1	102080.	2355.06	150022.
89	55769.1	122399.	2770.01	180938.

YEAR	384B	384M	384T	384
08	1315.34	651.105	60.3792	2026.83
69	1429.89	709.968	72.4014	2212.26
70	1495.15	814.664	75.4289	2385.25
71	1930.73	1018.22	106.139	3055.08
72	2038.25	1217.58	133.886	3389.71
73	3409.22	2146.21	237.408	5792.84
74	4102.62	3448.87	251.815	7803.30
75	4466.21	4618.20	313.558	9397.97
76	5286.63	8147.53	433.369	13867.5
77	5814.90	9614.30	522.692	15951.9
78	7394.67	11928.2	1574.76	20897.6
79	9158.19	14724.0	2236.46	26118.7
80	11891.0	18640.0	2036.12	32567.2
81	14895.2	21244.5	1997.19	38136.9
82	18911.6	24760.5	2112.44	45784.5
83	21892.1	24495.4	2645.80	49033.4
84	25781.2	27640.5	2823.26	56245.0
85	27476.9	35687.0	2916.70	66080.7
86	32711.2	50571.1	3083.52	86365.8
87	34822.0	62231.0	2954.00	100007.
88	36603.5	68326.3	2664.18	107594.
89	38334.5	75739.9	2741.32	116816.

YEAR	385B	385M	385T	385
68	44.9362	36.4278	.599220	81.9632
69	66.7533	39.1928	1.20968	107.156
70	74.7366	41.0880	2.25703	118.082
71	91.0839	43.1482	2.85612	137.087
72	99.9841	44.8140	3.04411	147.842
73	122.495	52.8039	4.63191	179.931
74	153.237	63.6827	4.97261	221.892
75	212.286	86.4828	8.61473	307.384
76	261.942	278.062	11.9179	551.922
77	393.062	329.250	20.0040	742.316
78	476.163	529.101	29.8811	1035.14
79	755.378	1121.32	59.4967	1936.20
80	1018.05	1255.65	59.8796	2333.58
81	1088.79	1438.88	123.154	2650.82
82	1130.81	1548.57	117.376	2796.76
83	1273.60	1659.44	169.563	3102.60
84	1438.36	1920.55	172.649	3531.55
85	1615.97	2138.86	174.336	3929.17
86	2020.60	2561.47	200.678	4782.75
87	2201.00	3154.00	226.000	5581.00
88	2398.83	3933.61	255.907	6588.34
89	2541.61	4478.00	335.675	7355.28

YEAR	390B	390M	390T	390
68	207.816	88.9408	3.61083	300.368
69	265.161	117.678	8.14386	390.983
70	429.526	195.477	10.6848	635.688
71	537.373	206.890	10.7646	755.028
72	691.106	371.113	20.5923	1082.81
73	810.796	468.383	26.5802	1305.76
74	874.369	502.237	28.5198	1405.13
75	962.426	573.320	35.2149	1570.96
76	1172.09	809.873	62.6965	2044.66
77	1345.18	1020.25	98.3530	2463.78
78	1700.00	1371.49	123.303	3194.79
79	2125.55	1744.22	157.408	4027.17
80	2249.25	1804.94	169.295	4223.49
81	2475.66	2050.35	210.876	4736.88
82	2726.84	2335.85	244.531	5307.22
83	3094.11	2541.05	329.350	5964.52
84	3569.49	3257.44	399.338	7226.26
85	3812.77	3786.11	440.921	8039.81
86	4538.43	4441.43	566.519	9546.38
87	5324.00	5321.00	718.000	11363.0
88	5917.82	5911.26	783.592	12612.7
89	6400.03	6757.71	904.824	14062.6

Appendix L   Capital-output ratio

YEAR	0	1	2	3
68	1.76619	.248397	.613474	1.77840
69	1.76981	.308208	.672559	1.66620
70	1.82507	.389630	.599522	1.44981
71	1.85392	.462071	.645671	1.44833
72	1.96326	.521163	.714433	1.55926
73	1.99834	.539102	.668919	1.76396
74	2.10424	.682683	.722330	1.77526
75	2.20113	.690331	.697686	1.88008
76	2.21280	.669888	.827117	1.83550
77	2.25558	.719037	.888865	1.89324
78	2.48006	1.08228	1.10214	2.04651
79	2.82043	1.37880	1.40042	2.64578
80	3.37388	1.94564	1.67424	3.49689
81	3.49227	1.77813	1.89001	3.62182
82	3.58665	1.77161	2.39593	3.77973
83	3.54130	1.72033	2.53389	3.53140
84	3.57307	1.91584	2.75703	3.28401
85	3.65859	1.97878	2.97529	3.34630
86	3.62096	2.15122	3.02073	3.21744
87	3.60109	2.52669	3.18123	3.16866
88	3.53658	2.69770	3.41076	2.96592
89	3.72312	3.62421	4.00761	3.11444

YEAR	4	5	6	7
68	6.68062	.294909	.545516	7.97005
69	6.44647	.289439	.654308	6.36089
70	6.24424	.337256	.732126	5.31770
71	6.21794	.419058	.727663	4.81339
72	6.42460	.522875	.798698	4.70357
73	6.36207	.473503	.834531	4.32192
74	6.14542	.487856	.888096	4.73480
75	6.10491	.577036	.962919	4.71478
76	5.51967	.723963	.990006	4.88228
77	6.33346	.808575	1.08684	4.53251
78	6.04150	.731533	1.17926	4.26861
79	7.12827	.786675	1.23936	4.04599
80	7.32880	.892859	1.40135	4.29915
81	7.47395	1.03078	1.41417	4.55118
82	8.16468	.964838	1.48834	4.68380
83	7.41227	.861893	1.46904	4.88770
84	6.64663	.899409	1.48610	4.83906
85	6.47371	.934088	1.50079	5.10701
86	5.56220	.947313	1.46297	5.10616
87	5.16169	.919513	1.45973	4.72913
88	4.93839	.917854	1.51404	4.60532
89	4.81434	.874200	1.67620	4.50164

YEAR	0	1	2	3
68	.862178	.149433	.270096	1.01546
69	.876239	.190039	.291906	1.00725
70	.902850	.238895	.253641	.875957
71	.923059	.280637	.274805	.890957
72	.985640	.309723	.303652	.964591
73	1.01630	.311523	.285863	1.07770
74	1.08433	.408176	.313244	1.07831
75	1.13272	.394260	.301338	1.12742
76	1.14169	.369858	.364417	1.08268
77	1.19328	.389890	.402989	1.10680
78	1.31005	.524974	.502595	1.12524
79	1.46967	.620332	.633844	1.33651
80	1.75100	.824203	.744297	1.73930
81	1.77870	.711479	.831183	1.69396
82	1.80780	.650700	1.04490	1.69263
83	1.76751	.632728	1.09298	1.49289
84	1.78139	.688322	1.18020	1.37037
85	1.81597	.693011	1.28462	1.37610
86	1.79401	.751538	1.26917	1.33482
87	1.78467	.873699	1.31321	1.34614
88	1.78144	.937516	1.38349	1.34231
89	1.89780	1.31520	1.61370	1.48728

YEAR	4	5	6	7
68	6.29220	.175585	.322011	4.47824
69	5.62701	.175675	.371341	3.48886
70	5.12642	.204052	.403280	2.83529
71	4.86200	.253000	.390980	2.55016
72	4.82727	.316089	.421472	2.55854
73	4.61444	.281920	.432820	2.49289
74	4.30046	.287997	.452236	2.88127
75	4.16434	.345619	.483625	2.91552
76	3.67021	.444542	.492065	3.15333
77	4.19838	.506571	.536524	2.97289
78	3.91649	.427703	.583234	2.61380
79	4.56606	.434196	.610713	2.33696
80	4.62389	.468547	.687740	2.36509
81	4.66093	.518433	.694699	2.40597
82	5.30235	.467806	.739704	2.39253
83	4.53377	.403451	.728401	2.43832
84	4.01183	.409461	.735606	2.35860
85	3.85630	.413737	.740259	2.43699
86	3.25846	.407726	.723581	2.38787
87	2.95822	.391704	.709591	2.18639
88	2.78063	.384332	.438842	2.08855
89	2.69115	.361821	.816862	2.00441

YEAR	0	1	2	3
69	1.79646	.877858	-3.53122	1.28583
70	2.49891	-5.42620	.159347	.648467
71	2.16419	2.87707	2.22997	1.44002
72	4.00577	2.94603	-2.93025	2.39407
73	2.25730	.784590	.422679	2.47692
74	3.38359	2.88965	1.60043	1.84496
75	3.56019	.888381	.525672	2.75564
76	2.30332	.460344	-46.0140	1.64671
77	2.68025	2.48477	1.37543	2.27685
78	4.79175	-2.60786	5.34366	2.77510
79	7.30487	5.64491	-5.43125	8.40943
80	-22.2301	-1.02774	-3.69069	-110.3080
81	5.25476	.604715	29.7707	4.88627
82	4.87954	.818019	-2.43629	6.13595
83	3.15622	1.88311	4.99570	1.91832
84	3.91043	-11.1721	9.77130	1.85703
85	4.89249	3.65505	8.77175	4.22184
86	3.31739	5.88719	3.57277	2.51297
87	3.43600	-3.02751	-9.65887	2.90860
88	2.97468	4.84255	-33.9008	1.45567
89	6.75411	-78.7009	-4.25288	7.09840

YEAR	4	5	6	7
69	5.66154	.274892	1.76425	.220185
70	5.19015	1.29275	1.40362	-.173551
71	6.09958	-4.38402	.705485	.935426
72	7.62808	-12.7138	1.42983	3.59288
73	6.01223	.278272	1.11838	2.81832
74	4.73992	.605114	1.69443	10.0060
75	5.81386	1.58985	2.16103	4.55024
76	2.90201	1.93739	1.19805	5.84059
77	17.5481	1.09568	3.42025	2.83408
78	5.15096	.463478	2.89916	2.77900
79	20.3398	1.64566	2.55337	2.73286
80	8.55130	-5.21227	-2.13852	9.94463
81	8.43295	-1.70539	1.58104	9.58431
82	20.4542	.608997	2.44543	6.93816
83	4.75713	.376774	1.26032	7.20169
84	3.55589	1.57222	1.69980	4.44733
85	5.18787	1.72082	1.67887	10.6706
86	1.96379	1.24332	1.23505	5.09748
87	1.90323	.700779	1.43801	1.81819
88	2.67046	.900405	2.00533	3.55249
89	3.65849	.602365	7.20655	3.55606

YEAR	0	1	2	3
69	.979629	.576781	-1.25981	.979419
70	1.22737	-3.25079	.023003	.389748
71	1.14036	1.67220	1.00297	.971809
72	2.15468	1.50332	-1.22317	1.52259
73	1.24271	.336146	.189621	1.47165
74	1.90611	1.89382	.763400	1.08206
75	1.81151	.033931	.218237	1.53759
76	1.25069	.119745	-22.4637	.893232
77	1.66067	1.10954	.706938	1.26710
78	2.51256	-.847614	2.48351	1.21287
79	3.57270	1.99230	-2.37222	3.36850
80	-11.2640	-.245208	-1.41973	-52.1194
81	2.19106	-.078185	12.0583	1.23498
82	2.20650	-.166703	-.996380	1.67291
83	1.42536	.400414	1.95104	.195411
84	1.92878	-3.03333	3.92164	.663694
85	2.31495	.817886	3.50677	1.45659
86	1.61681	2.01956	1.32447	1.10912
87	1.70711	-.093377	-2.20978	1.40650
88	1.75326	1.73790	-10.0406	1.31383
89	3.78843	-32.2444	-1.57250	5.37588

YEAR	4	5	6	7
69	3.39713	.175915	.874622	-.286734
70	2.51718	.771083	.678882	-.606073
71	3.67213	-2.62105	.329862	.357642
72	4.62500	-7.72777	.692808	2.64324
73	3.42351	.146808	.522471	2.23330
74	2.26363	.337644	.744503	7.84220
75	3.18619	1.00002	.986255	3.19700
76	1.46014	1.26153	.556888	.451392
77	11.4770	.717780	1.60787	2.09658
78	3.05665	.153293	1.45246	.587169
79	12.4627	.535351	1.21154	.704023
80	4.97645	-1.52493	-.995454	2.99230
81	4.90561	-.464093	.785277	2.22238
82	11.6010	.194620	1.32042	2.16416
83	2.78183	.100185	.605167	2.95791
84	1.90488	.517247	.825904	1.71657
85	2.69973	.510734	.795632	4.06464
86	.898327	.286380	.623081	1.88611
87	.515547	.265635	.615849	.630771
88	.976971	.306782	1.00345	1.25663
89	1.85733	.221646	3.47766	1.23704

References

1. Cost of Capital and Effective Tax Rate

Auerbach, A.J. (1979), "Wealth Maximization and the Cost of Capital," *Quarterly Journal of Economics*, Vol. 93: 3, pp.433–46.

Auerbach, A.J., and D.W. Jorgenson (1980), "Inflation-Period Depreciation of Assets," *Harvard Business Review*, Vol. 58, No. 5, September/October, pp.113–18.

Auerbach, A.J. (1984), "Taxes, Firm Financial Policy and the Cost of Capital: An Empirical Analysis," *Journal of Public Economics*, Vol. 23, February/March, pp.27–57.

Feldstein, M.S., L. Dicks-Mireaux, and J.Poterba (1983), "The Effective Tax Rate and the Pretax Rate of Return," *Journal of Public Economics*, Vol. 21, No. 2, July, pp.129–158.

Fullerton, D. (1984), "Which Effective Tax Rate?", *National Tax Journal*, Vol. 37, No. 1, March, pp.23–41.

Hall, R.E., and D.W. Jorgenson (1967), "Tax Policy and Investment Behavior," *American Economic Review*, Vol. 57: 3, pp.391–344.

Harberger, A.C. (1962), "The Incidence of the Corporate Income Tax," *Journal of Political Economy*, Vol. 70, No. 3, June, pp.215–40.

Hulten, C.R., and F.C. Wykoff (1981), *The Measurement of Economic Depreciation in Hulton, C.R. ed., Depreciation, Inflation and Taxation of Income from Capital*, Washington, Urban Institute Press, pp.81–132.

Ito, T., and A.O. Kreuger (1992), *The Political Economy of Tax Reform*, Chicago, University of Chicago Press.

Jorgenson, D.W. (1963), "Capital Theory and Investment Behavior," *American Economic Review*, Vol. 53, No. 2, May, pp.336-78.

Jorgenson, D.W., and M.A. Sullivan (1981), *Inflation and Corporate Recovery, in Hulton*, C.R. ed., *Depreciation, Inflation and Taxation of Income from Capital*, Washington, Urban Institute Press, pp.171-237.

Jorgenson, D.W., and K.Y. Yun (1991), *Tax Reform and the Cost of Capital*, New York, Oxford University Press.

Jorgenson, D.W. (1992), *Tax Reform and the Cost of Capital: An International Comparison*, Harvard Institute of Economic Research, Discussion Paper No. 1621, Harvard University.

Kim, Jun Y. (1991), *Cost of Capital and Effective Tax Rate in Korea*, Korea Development Institute.

King, M.A., and D. Fullerton (1984), *The Taxation of Income from Capital*, Chicago, University of Chicago Press.

Kwak, T.W. (1985), *Depreciation System and Taxation on Capital Income*, Korea Development Institute. Organization for Economic Cooperation and Development(1991), Taxing Profits in a Global Economy: Domestic and International Issues, Paris, OECD.

Poterba, J.M., and L.H. Summers (1983), "Dividend Taxes, Investment, and 'Q'," *Journal of Public Economics*, Vol. 22, No. 2, November, pp.135-67.

Poterba, J.M. (1991), "International Comparison of the Cost of Capital: A Survey of Method," Federal Reserve Bank of New York, *Quarterly Bulletin*, Winter, pp.20-32.

Sinn, H.W. (1991), "Taxation and the Cost of Capital: The 'Old' View, the 'New' view," in D. Bradford, ed., *Tax Policy and the Economy*, Vol. 5, Cambridge, MIT Press, pp.25-54.

Slemrod, J. (1991), editor, *Do Taxes Matter?*, Cambridge, MIT Press.

Stiglitz, J.E. (1973), "Taxation, Corporate Financial Policy and the Cost of Capital," *Journal of Public Economics* 2(1), pp.1-34.

Summers, L.H. (1981), "Taxation and Corporate Investment: A q-Theory Approach," *Brookings Paper on Economic Activity*, 16, pp.67–127.

Tajika, E., and Y. Yui (1988), "Cost of Capital and Effective Tax Rate: A Comparison of U.S. and Japanese Manufacturing Industries," *Hitotsubashi Journal of Economics*, Vol. 29, No. 2, December, pp.181–202

2. Estimates of Capital Stock

The Bank of Korea (1968, 1977, 1987), *National Income Account*, 1968–1990. *Economic Planning Board*, National Wealth Survey of Korea.

Goldsmith, R.W. (1975), "A Synthetic Estimate of the National Wealth of Japan, 1885–1973," *The Review of Income and Wealth*, Series 21, No. 2.

Han, K.C. (1970), *Estimates of Korean Capital and Inventory Coefficients in 1968*, Yonsei University. .

Harberger, A.C. (1978), "Perspectives on Capital and Technology in Less-Developed Countries" in *Contemporary Economic Analysis*, edited by M.J. Artis and A.R. Nobay, London, Longman.

Hulten, C.R. and C.F. Wykof (1982), "The Measurement of Economic Depreciation," *Depreciation, Inflation and Taxation of Income from Capital*, Washington D.C., Urban Institute Press.

Hulten, C.R. (1990), "The Measurement of Capital," in Ernst R. Berndt and Jack Triplett, editors, *Fifty Years of Measurement in Economics*, Chicago, University of Chicago Press, pp.119–152.

Jorgenson, D.W., "The Economic Theory of Replacement and Depreciation," in Willy Sellekaerts, editor, *Econometrics and Economic Theory*, New York, MacMillian, pp.189–221.

Jorgenson, D.W. and R. Landau (1989), editors, *Technology and Capital Formation*, Cambridge, MIT Press.

Kendrick, J.W. (1976), *The Formation and Stock of Total Capital*, New York, Columbia University Press.

Kim, Jun Y. and D.H. Koo (1992), "Capital Stock, Cost of Capital, and Investment Behavior in Korea," *Korean Economic Review*.

Nishimizu, M. (1974), *Total Factor Productivity Analysis: A Disaggregated Study of the Post War Japanese Economy*, Doctoral Dissertation, the Johns Hopkins University.

Pyo, H.K. (1988), "Estimates of Capital Stock and Capital/Output Coefficient by Industries," *International Economic Journal*.

Usher, D., editor (1980), *The Measurement of Capital*, Chicago, University of Chicago Press.

Von Furstenberg, G.M., editor (1980), *Capital, Efficiency, and Growth*, Cambridge, Ballinger Publishing Company.

Ward, M. (1976), *The Measurement of Capital*, Paris: OECD.

3. Capital Formation and A Q Model of Investment

Abel, A.B. (1982), "Dynamic Effects of Permanent and Temporary Tax Policies in A q Model of Investment," *Journal of Monetary Economics* *9*, pp.353–73.

Ciccolo, J.H., Jr. (1975), "Four Essays on Monetary Policy," Unpublished Doctoral Dissertation, Yale University.

Gould, J.P. (1968), "Adjustment Cost in the Theory of Investment of the Firm," *Review of Economic Studies*, pp.47–55.

Hall, R.E., and D.W. Jorgenson (1967), "Tax Policy and Investment Behavior," *American Economic Review*, pp.391–414.

Hayashi, F. (1982), "Tobin's Marginal Q and Average Q: A NeoClassical Interpretation," *Econometrica*, pp.213–24.

Jorgenson, D.W. (1963), "Capital Theory and Investment Behavior," *American Economic Review*, pp.336–78.

Kim, Jun Y. (1992), *Cost of Capital and Effective Tax Rate in Korea*, Korea Development Institute.

King, M.A., and D. Fullerton (1984), *The Taxation of Income from Capital*, Chicago, University of Chicago Press.

Poterba, J.M., and L.H. Summers (1983), "Dividend Taxes, Investment, and 'Q'," *Journal of Public Economics*, pp.135–67.

Summers, L.H. (1981), "Taxation and Corporate Investment: A q-Theory Approach," *Brookings Paper on Economic Activity*, 16, pp.67–127.

Tobin, J. (1969), "A General Equilibrium Approach to Monetary Theory," *Journal of Money, Credit and Banking 1*, pp.15–29.

Von Furstenberg, G.M. (1977), "Corporate Investment: Does Market Valuation Matter in the Aggregate?" *Brookings Papers on Economic Activity*, pp.347–97.

Index